Praise for *Donna's Deceptions*

LM Bertolami has written a marvelous debut novel full of twists and turns. *Donna's Deceptions* gives us a protagonist whose modesty, humility, and seeming gullibility belie her true character as a woman of purpose who sees much more than is immediately apparent. The close reader will locate clues early on that lead to an understanding of the complexity of Donna's interests, ambitions—and deceptions. I can't wait for the sequel. —***Elyse Greenfield, Chair. The Lotos Club Literary Committee***

In this warm and delicious book, we will feel the bond of friendship sitting with Tina, Loretta and Donna and Donna's delicious homemade lasagna. We laugh and enjoy their wicked (say it with a Boston Italian straight edged razor accent) refusal to be victims. HOW REFRESHING!! I await Bertolami's next invitation to feel the authentic warmth from a time when people were the opposite of psychologically and socially isolated. I will suggest this to my patients who need to feel a bond with others...—***S. Packer-Rosenthal, PsyD, LCSW, LPCC, LMFT, PPSC***

Witty, naive and captivating is how I can best describe the relationship between all the characters in Donna's Deceptions. And how beautifully and intriguing the author (LM Bertolami) intertwines everyone's lives and describes their disheartening agendas. I often found myself smacking Geoffrey in the head for his unprofessional and unethical behavior. A cute read that keeps you amused 'til the very end. It also teaches us valuable lessons: always clarify the terms of engagement before going into business with anyone. —***Ana María Rodriguez***

Donna's Deceptions is a captivating read that keeps you hooked from start to finish. With a relatable and likable protagonist in Donna, the story takes unexpected turns as she navigates complex relationships and unfamiliar territory. Bertolami's vivid, descriptive writing brings both the world around Donna and her emotional journey to life, making the book impossible to put down. It's a thrilling story full of intrigue that will keep you guessing throughout. —***Melissa Hsiao***

Donna's Deceptions is a marvelous debut novel capturing the passion of many different characters It's Alluring and Intriguing in a very special way. The fantasy to go off someplace far away and live on coffee and make believe, is magical. An analogy that is brilliantly written in an important way to society. Many lessons to be learned here. I adored this book. —***Wendy Hendelman, Sculptor***

DONNA spends her lonely nights writing a novel until an embarrassing situation forces popular author GEOFFREY to charm Donna into writing with him. Donna quickly accepts without clarifying the terms. Geoffrey never lets Donna read their story ID/XX (Identity Doublecross) all the way through, and as he tapers off their collaboration, his girlfriend SANDRA helps him finish. Donna suspects that he will cut her out unless she can prove her contribution to the book.

One morning Donna distracts Geoffrey so that her friend LORETTA can download a copy of ID/XX. Donna reads no further than the first page and sees that Geoffrey took sole authorship. It takes two weeks before Donna has the stomach to read the rest, and she recognizes passages lifted from other books. Before she can warn Geoffrey, she is accused of plagiarism – a possible ruse to prevent her from claiming that she coauthored the story or accusing Geoffrey of plagiarizing her work.

Geoffrey’s trusted friend, TOM, exposes the truth. Donna and he develop a friendship until she questions whether Tom is Geoffrey’s go-between or spy.

After one last awkward interaction with Geoffrey, Donna knows exactly what she wants and has the courage to stand up for herself.

DONNA'S DECEPTIONS

LM BERTOLAMI

Moonshine Cove Publishing, LLC

Bowling Green, Virginia U.S.A.

First Moonshine Cove Edition Nov 2024

ISBN: 9781952439889

Library of Congress LCCN: 2024921923

Cover supplied by the author, interior design by Moonshine Cove staff.

For Charles

About the Author

L M Bertolami is a native Bostonian, who has moved around so many times that she doesn't know anymore what place she can call home. The Boston she remembers has changed so much that it's almost unrecognizable to her, so she wrote about the Boston she knew. In doing so, she realized that the city was still in her blood.

The idea of *Donna's Deceptions* came to her in that split second between being asleep and awake, and that image of a dark-haired woman blossomed into a story about how an impulsive act of forgiveness caused the protagonist to encounter pride, prejudice, and plagiarism as she navigated a sea of deception. With that flash of a dream, LMB heard or rather knew that the woman's name was Donna DiGeronamo, and that betrayal caused Donna to frame for plagiarism a man who had scorned her. As LMB began writing, she learned that she couldn't empathize with a protagonist she disliked, so she thought it through and came up with a character the reader can root for and a story that is more satisfying.

L M Bertolami is writing a sequel, *Anselm's Answers*, which is a mystery set in a university.

http://donnasdeceptions.com

Preface

One of my relatives used to say, "If you don't look like something, you get treated like nothing." That expression is an offshoot of the adage, "You never get a second chance to make a first impression." Wallflowers from the Out Crowds often learn these lessons early but benefit if they develop empathy and compassion from them.

In *Donna's Deceptions,* lonely Donna meets a stranger during an embarrassing act of dishonesty, but the man uses his good looks and charm to gain control of the situation. From that point on, they develop a collaboration, which pulls Donna into further deceptions and self-delusion, until she learns, albeit somewhat late, to stand up for herself.

Donna's Deceptions is for people who like to read comforting stories about average people who prevail after their quiet lives get upended by betrayal, false accusation, and deception.

DONNA'S DECEPTIONS

CHAPTER ONE
DECEIT AND DELIGHT AT DONNA'S DOOR

Late spring 2004

Three sizes of clothing lined her closet: Diet or Die, Don't Inhale, and Dream on Little Dreamer. She yanked on the DI slacks she had worn the other day after a triumphant weight loss of two pounds, brushed her dark hair into a twist, and fished through her jewelry box for a pair of one and one-half inch hoops – the largest she owned – because anything bigger screamed Ella Zingarella, who'd do it in the back seat of anything with four wheels.

Her butter-leather pumps tapped down three flights of stairs, past the second-floor apartment of her nasty landlords Angie and Primo Infanto, past the first-floor apartment of Tina Farina, a constantly cooking, arthritic widow, and then carried Donna Di Geronamo out the door.

Several houses down, her best friend Loretta Amalfitano burst out the door of a corner bile-green three-decker and yawned.

Loretta was the middle child in a family of four girls and one prince. She loved old Sophia Loren movies, so she dyed her curly hair auburn and blended her lipstick to match the peachy pink her idol wore. Although Loretta needed cosmetics the way an old barn needs sandblasting and three coats of paint, her artistic skill and dramatic appearance made her a popular makeup artist (for women who like to look "striking") and a top seller of the Lily Floret Beauty line.

The two friends navigated the familiar East Boston sidewalks, and Loretta yawned two more times before she spoke. "My sister Gina's seeing a shrink."

"I'm sorry to hear that." Donna figured the demure Gina needed an escape from Loretta's lunatic family.

"No, not that way—I mean she's dating one. But I think he needs one himself. You can't have a conversation with the guy without feeling like you're being psychoanalyzed." Loretta slowed down to take her sunglasses out of her tan hobo handbag. "Whoa, I see England. I see France. I see Donna's underpants."

"What?" Donna slapped her left hand over her behind and fingered a large split on the seam of her pants. "Oh, shoot! What time is it? You go ahead so you won't be late. I'm going to have to change."

Donna trotted home and arrived breathless. She slipped her key ring over two fingers and panted up the stairs until the landing of the second floor, where she literally ran smack into her robe-clad landlady, Angie Infanto. Angie stumbled backwards, but Donna managed to grab her before she fell against the stained-glass window of purple grapes hanging from an amber and bottle green vine. "I'm so sorry. I'm running late." Donna's face flushed with a combination of embarrassment and anxiety.

Angie held her hand to her chest and caught her breath. "What are you doing here? I thought you left already. You never come home. If you left the stove on or somethin', you could've called me. Did you forget something? You're usually so organized."

"No. I split my pants."

Donna climbed the third flight of stairs with Angie on her heels and frantically chattering louder than necessary. "Don't you carry a sewing kit in your purse?"

"No, and if I did, where would I stitch up my pants? On the T platform?"

"Why don't you leave a small sewing kit in your locker at work for emergencies? You work in a clothing department – you could even wear a pair of slacks from there."

"I can't wait until I get to work and ride the train with my butt sticking out."

"You might get a date out of it."

"As if I don't meet enough pervs." Before Angie could utter another annoying word, Donna said, "I'm late." She inserted her key into the lock and stopped. "What?" The door was already unlocked. She slowly pushed it open. "I must be losing it. First, I put on a pair of split pants and then this."

Angie poked her head inside the doorway. "I'll come inside to make sure no one broke in." Her flip-flop slippers slapped against the bottom of her heels as she pushed her way into Donna's apartment. She peered into each room, and just as her eyes fell on the rear door of the kitchen, Donna came up behind her.

"I'm ready to leave," Donna said with a note of urgency in her voice. She glanced in the direction that Angie was staring. "I don't believe it! This door is unlocked too! I keep the chain on all the time." With an exasperated sigh, Donna re-hooked the chain. "I'm late. I gotta go." Donna headed for the front door. "Angie," she said, looking back, "I'm leaving." *Hint. Hint.*

"You want me to leave too?" Angie asked.

"Well, yes," Donna said. "Sheesh," she thought, "you'd never know this is my apartment sometimes." The Infantos insisted on having keys to Tina's and Donna's apartments for "repairs and the like." Donna just figured it was a power thing, but it always made her a bit uneasy because Primo was kind of sleazy. Whenever she was home, she kept the chains on both doors. One time Donna and Loretta searched the floors of her apartment and the attic above for peepholes.

Despite the setback, Donna made it to work on time thanks to a bus and train that pulled in just as she arrived at their stops. The lucky timing helped her to relax and arrive with dry armpits at Floegel's Department Store.

After opening the register in the ladies' career wear department, Donna went to the back room to get some things she had on hold for a customer and made her first sale of the day. "Thank you, Mr. Ambrose," she smiled as she handed the man, with the shadowy face of a poet, his purchase of black pull-on pants, a floral blouse, and a pink zippered top.

Seconds later Ella Zingarella approached the counter and said, "Hi, Donna. On Saturday I had a blouse put on hold for me." Donna retrieved the blouse from the back room. The high cut black silk was a bit modest for "any fella Zingarella."

Ella caught up to Tom Ambrose, who was slowly making his way to the escalator. She said something to Tom, who turned to smile in Donna's direction. Donna quickly looked down at the cash register to hide her discomfort from getting caught staring at them.

On the way home, Donna told Loretta about the unlocked doors. "Nothing was taken that I can tell, although I didn't look very hard. Must have been either Primo or Angie, who else?"

"They both creep me out," Loretta said. "Primo and Angie are a couple of earth pigs. She dresses like someone thirty years younger with that saggy ass in spandex, and he looks like a dissipated loan shark, which I wouldn't doubt he is. I don't think he's ever done an honest day's work since he had a paper route at age twelve, and that's assuming he even had one then."

"And they're such loud-mouths. I think Tina gets the worst of the noise because she's below them."

"She should sound-proof her ceiling. Those two act like they own the neighborhood because they've got connections and have lived here a long time, and then there's that nephew of theirs who's such a puke. They think he's God's gift because he's sold a lot of lousy books."

"Really? What's his name?" asked Donna, somewhat surprised that she never heard Angie brag about him, not that they ever had any friendly chit-chats about their family trees.

"George, but he changed it to Jeffrey with a g-e-o, a totally made-up name, something pretentious like Geoffrey Imperioli. I don't know."

"Geoffrey Imperato?" asked Donna wondering if the best-selling author could really be related to her landlords.

"Yeah, that's him. My sister Connie read his last book and thought it stunk to high heaven."

"If you mean *Won Too Many*," Donna said, "it stunk to at least number eight on the best seller list, even higher locally."

"Yeah. I think he wrote one too many. Three too many's more like it. The photo of him on the back cover probably sells more books than his crummy stories. If you'll notice, they always put a different picture on each book to help sales, I'm sure. They also run tons of ads."

"Somebody's doing something right because they sell very well."

"But look at his stinko stories. He keeps recycling the same ideas, juggling them between action and sex scenes for distraction" Loretta scoffed. "Speaking of writing, how's your book coming?"

"I haven't done anything for a couple of days, but I'm enjoying it because I love books."

"Don't give up," Loretta said. "I thought what you did on this story so far was great. A couple of weeks ago, Tina was praising your writing to Angie. She even said that you were better than her nephew – that had Angie spitting nails for a while. I'm surprised Tina wasn't evicted."

***

The rickety ride on the Blue Line, despite the jostling and the heat, was less irritating than driving in Boston's congested traffic and paying ransom prices for non-existent parking spaces in the city. The time of day and, to some extent, the time of year determined the amount of crowding on the trains; yet the druggies, pervs, and pickpockets were unfazed by any season or time, except perhaps the phases of the moon. This evening's heat was just as good an excuse to blame for bringing out the creeps. Loretta had to elbow a guy who didn't know what to do with his hands. "Next time I'll aim a little lower with my foot," she shouted at the perv, who got off at the next station followed by two other slimers who slithered away.

When Donna arrived home, she knocked on Tina's door to hand her a box of assorted chocolates. "Come in," Tina said. "Today I made sauce with meatballs, *bracciole*, and sausage. You can use it tonight or freeze it."

Donna entered Tina's first floor apartment, which, because of the front and back entrance halls, was the smallest of the three in the house. Donna's apartment was the middle sized one because out her back door there was a stairway to the attic. Tina's flat had a 1950's retro charm with a black and white checked kitchen floor, and an old-as-Methuselah stove that still worked, a living room boomerang coffee table, and a sofa and chairs with turquoise and hot pink upholstery. A wooden Pinocchio, a Shirley Temple doll, and even a Howdy Doody smiled out from a glass case.

After a glass of iced tea, Donna went up to her apartment, ate a *bracciole* and put the rest of Tina's food in the refrigerator. She then got to work on her manuscript. For the next hour Donna read, thought, and wrote. When she awoke the next morning, her only desire was to get back to her writing, which infused her with an enthusiasm she hadn't felt for anything that wasn't edible, chocolate or otherwise. Her unspoken fantasy was to take off for someplace far away and live on coffee and make-believe.

For the next two nights Donna worked on her book. Friday night she had dinner at the Amalfitano's, who lived downstairs from their daughters Loretta and Gina on the second floor, and Connie and her husband on the third.

Spumoni – the kind wrapped in paper – followed a dinner of antipasto and ravioli. As they made espresso and broke out the chocolates Donna brought, brother Vinnie stormed in with only a grunt to his mother.

"Vinnie honey, if I knew you were coming, I'd have held up supper," said Mrs. Amalfitano with a slap to her thigh. Many a night the family had eaten over-cooked, dried out suppers after waiting for Prince Vince to grace them with his charmless presence.

"I told you this morning I had things to do. I just stopped in to use the john."

Connie looked out the window. "Who's that sitting in your car?"

"George Infanto, or Geoff, as he likes to be called now. I ran into him the other day. He spends a lot of time in Eastie lately. We're headed out."

"Vinnie dear, didn't you go to school with him?" Mrs. Amalfitano asked.

"He was a year ahead of me. I knew him from when he lived up the street as a kid. He's living downtown now, but his aunt and uncle still live where Buick…” Vinnie caught himself as he was about to say “Buick Butt,” one of his secret names for Donna. That’s okay. Donna had a few names for him, too.

“Donna,” Loretta said, “he’s the author I was telling you about, Geoffrey Imperato.” Loretta stood by the window. “Let’s have a peek and see just what a hunk he really is.”

Donna went to the other side of the window. “I can’t get a good look at his face, but he’d better stick his arm back inside the car before someone rips off that watch he’s wearing.”

“Vinnie, why not invite him in for dessert?” Loretta asked the prince as he exited the chamber. “We’d like a closer look.”

“Don’t get your hopes up ladies,” Vinnie said. “I doubt he’d have any interest in the Dateless Duo. He likes babes.”

“You’re such a prize package yourself,” Loretta shot back while still gawking out the window. “I don’t get this guy. He left Eastie years ago with big ideas, and now that he’s made it, he’s around here like horse manure.”

“It’s where he grew up. He’s got a right to come here and see everybody,” Vinnie said.

Connie said, “Tell Mr. Importanto that his books are getting stale and boring as Gina’s boyfriend. I almost had to cattle-prod myself into finishing the last one.”

“I’ll do that. He’d appreciate an expert opinion from such a brilliant mind.” Vinnie slammed the door on his way out.

“See, you made your brother leave angry,” said Mrs. Amalfitano.

“He was born angry,” Loretta said. “He doesn’t have a hair across his ass, he’s got a rope.”

Donna walked home shortly after dinner. She felt safer getting inside her apartment before too late because the usual creepers came out after dark. Last winter, some guy, whose identity was never discovered, would jump out of alleys while wearing nothing but galoshes and a ski mask. Loretta naturally thought it was Primo, but of course, she had no proof.

***

A two-day sale brought in the crowds. On the second day the dressing rooms had so much activity that Donna spent most of the afternoon carrying out and re-hanging clothes. "You'd think some of these people could at least put them back on the hanger instead of leaving them in a rumpled pile," she thought through a weary smile. At first, she carried a few garments at a time, daintily holding them by the hanger. By the end of the day, she was throwing them over her aching shoulder.

From the airconditioned cool of the store, Donna and Loretta stepped out into the humidity and heat of the city. The crowded train ride was another sensory delight. They had to stand and hold the hand straps. Donna spent most of the ride with her nose inches from some guy's sweaty armpit. Although Loretta sold and often wore perfume, she became almost nauseated from the rank malodor formed by multiple combined scents. On the walk home from the station, the two friends grunted rather than spoke.

The three flights of stairs seemed like thirty. Donna's apartment was cooler than the outdoors, a fact she unfortunately learned when she opened a window and heat poured in.

Donna pulled down the spread on her bed and dropped face down onto her pillow. "Phew." She rolled over to her side to breathe better then pulled off a hair that was stuck to her cheek. The hair was longer and appeared lighter than her own. "I've got to stop taking my work home with me," she said as she flicked it onto the floor and lay on her back.

Another attempt at sleep had Donna flipping her pillow over to the other side. She heard a soft thud on the floor, so she looked down and noticed something shiny. It was a gold and emerald earring, and it was not hers. Reasoning replaced a slightly creepy, puzzled feeling. "Must be Loretta's, or Angie's, or a customer's from the busy sale," she thought. However improbably, the earring might have caught on a sweater that a customer had pulled over her head, and then transferred to Donna's top when she loaded up the clothing from the dressing room. "I'll bring it to Lost and Found," she thought as she tossed it into a drawer. "I must have walked around for hours with that thing on me. Funny that no one said anything."

***

She ate lunch at 12:00 the next day and had the runs an hour later. A co-worker helped a green-faced Donna into a cab. "Don't worry, Donna. It's quiet and there are enough of us to cover the floor."

The cab dropped Donna off just in time. With keys in hand, she bounded up the stairs. As she passed the second-floor landing, Angie Infanto swung open her door and yelled, "Donna, wait! Wait! *Stop!*"

Ignoring her, Donna opened her door, slammed it shut behind herself in Angie's face, and put on the chain. *All I need is for her to follow me to the bathroom while I'm emptying my gut,* she thought.

Angie banged on the door and shrieked to near hysteria, "Donna! Open up! Come out!" She rushed downstairs, almost falling twice, then grabbed a set of keys and flew, breathless, back up to Donna's door. Before she could insert her copy of Donna's key into the lock, she leaned against the wall and clutched her chest. "I think I'm having a heart attack! Don't you care?" After a few fumbles with the key, Angie opened Donna's door, but only as far as the chain would allow. In a hoarse voice she called out, "Donna, come out. I insist, come out right now! Damn it! Let me in! This is my house. I own it."

With her stomach still doing somersaults, Donna exited the bathroom after a two-flusher then came to the door and slammed it shut. "What do you want? I don't feel well. If you open this door one more time without my permission, I'll change the lock."

"This is my property. Let me in, you hear! I have a right," Angie panted and pounded.

"This is my apartment. I pay rent. You…you…"

Donna paused just long enough for a male voice to be heard. "Shit! I've had it! How the hell did this happen?"

Donna's belly let out a groan and a gurgle. She knew that Angie and whoever was with her were hysterical enough to shove the door open and break the chain off the wall. "I'll scream loud enough for the whole neighborhood to hear if you dare to open this door again. I mean it! It's my apartment, and you have no right to come in here uninvited. Go away!" She stretched out her arms and pressed her palms against the door. *What is going on*? With a quick tiptoe to and from the dining room, Donna propped a chair under the doorknob to brace the door against any further invasion attempts.

Outside her door the yelling changed to wails and plaintive moans. "Please, Donna, let us explain."

Donna sneaked into the kitchen to sit by the phone but stopped mid-step. Her kitchen table was littered with paper, pens, and a laptop. "What's this? What the…?" Her eyes and hands scanned the surface while her mind raced. A wave of nausea washed over her as she dug through the pile and caught sight of something: her manuscript was among the papers on the table. Donna moved the laptop's mouse to bring up the writing on the monitor screen. She read sentences that were both strange and familiar. Two sheets of paper lay to the left of the keyboard. The bottom one was from her story.

Donna's legs weakened and she fell into the chair. Her fingers danced over the papers that seemed to be placed in some deliberate order. She read what she feared she'd find. Her book, her ideas were being incorporated into someone else's!

Why would anyone do such a thing? The papers shook in her hand as she reached for the phone. No dial tone. Donna clicked the button several times before hanging up and running to the bedroom. No use, that telephone was dead too. The pages fell from her hand, and her mind was washed of all extraneous thoughts. "They're going to kill me!" Donna cupped her nose and mouth with her hands. It was the middle of the day. The neighbors had their windows open and there were people outside. She could scream out the window for help or grab her sharpest knife for defense.

Her cell phone! Why hadn't she thought of it? She ran from the bedroom to get her purse. There was a knock on the back door, which was locked and chained the way she had left it.

"Go away! I've got my cell phone and I'm calling," Donna yelled. *Wait. The Infantos have connections. Who knows if they're in with the police or even some thugs?* Certainly, a crooked politician or two were known to socialize with them. Donna brought up her cell phone's contacts and hit the first number, Loretta's. After several rings, the voice mail answered – of course, Loretta was at work and unable to take personal calls unless on break. At the beep she rattled, "This is Donna. If anything happens to me, it's Angie Infanto. She did it." She hung up and called her parents' home. "Angie Infanto is trying to…" Donna got the slightest of grips on her senses. She felt foolish saying that Angie was trying to kill her. "Mom, I'm probably overreacting. If you don't hear from me, it's Angie and Primo…uh…I'm just a little rattled. My stomach is upset, and I'll call you later."

The knocking on the door grew more persistent. The male voice called out, "Please, Miss Di Geronamo. No one is going to hurt you. My aunt just panicked. I'm sorry. Let me explain. Please."

"I'm not opening the door. I won't even stand in front of it in case you try to shoot me through it. Start talking and make it good."

"Okay, tell you what – if you like I'll slide my driver's license under the door to prove who I am," he said without actually doing so. "I'm Angie and Primo's nephew Geoffrey. Look, the first thing I want to do is apologize. Of course, I knew it was wrong to come into your apartment, but I needed somewhere quiet to work and not be bothered. Things were too hectic at my place."

"Why here? You've got some nerve! Why couldn't you find somewhere else instead of trespassing?"

"I needed a place in a hurry. As long as I was home, I had people calling me at all hours of the day and night. If I let them in, they partied. If I told them to go away, they'd bang on the outside door. You'd think they'd have outgrown that behavior by the time they reached adulthood. My neighbors complained, and one of them called the police a couple of times."

"Why couldn't you just stand up to them?" asked Donna wondering what was so difficult about getting rid of a bunch of losers.

"I finally told them the party's over, and they'd have to find another flophouse and some other sucker to bankroll their fun. By the time most of them got the message, I got stir-crazy. When I'm busy, I don't eat right. I go at it so much that I get run down. My aunt is taking care of me. She makes me lunch and snacks." He gave a weak laugh. "I guess I'm just a big baby. Can I get my stuff now?"

"One more question." Donna paused. "What were you doing copying my writing?"

A thump from Geoffrey's forehead rattled the door. He had hoped that he could clear out of there before Donna noticed what he was up to. He started to ramble, "I don't know. It was there, and I looked at it. I was so completely stressed out that I lost my head. Believe me! *Please!*" Desperation diffused through the solid hardwood door. "I'm so, so sorry. I've never done anything like this – I swear! Please… Let me explain."

"Just you."

"Okay, okay, just me."

"Tell your aunt to stay out of this and to go back downstairs. I mean it." Donna opened the door and peered out. Possibly the most gorgeous man she had ever seen stared back at her. She undid the chain. "Come in."

CHAPTER TWO
INTENTIONS AND PRETENSIONS

Donna walked over to the table. "Here, sit down. Let me get you something to drink."

"Water would be fine. Phew! I'm so sorry. I don't know what to say. This is so unbelievably embarrassing!" Geoffrey waited for Donna's reaction, which would determine the course of their discussion. Handsome, by even the strictest definition, Geoffrey Imperato was a man used to always having the advantage over anyone. Being at someone else's mercy was a new experience for him. His brain rapid-fire scanned his inventory of rescue measures and charm tactics and realized that he was short on verbal defenses – he seldom, if ever, had to use them. He sat like a condemned criminal waiting for his professional life to be zapped by the flip of a switch.

Donna took a jug out of her refrigerator and poured a glass for each of them. Awkward as the situation was, it was in her power to control. Histrionics and hysterics were counterproductive as well as out of character for Donna. She would hear him out first.

"I don't get it. Why, would someone like you need the scribblings of a novice like me?"

"You wrote some great stuff. It was like what I was writing – both psychological thrillers – mine, mistaken identity leading to trouble for the protagonist; yours, a man who deliberately allows someone to steal his identity because he's in danger." He smiled cautiously at her from across the table. "It was amazing." The burn that had flushed his cheeks and ears began to cool as he sensed that he was not dealing with a furious person.

"Did you really like it?"

"Yeah. You're pretty good."

Imagine — Geoffrey Imperato liked *her* foolish writing enough to want to plagiarize it!

"Look, I'm not calling the police so you can tell your aunt I'd like my phone reconnected. But I really don't know what to say or do in a situation like this. I mean, you did copy my –"

Geoffrey cut her off. "I've got an idea, a possible solution. Hear me out. I take it this is your first book. At least I've never heard of you."

Donna nodded.

"Well, I've had six, five of them huge best-sellers. This is my seventh, and I've made a nice piece of change. It's hard, almost impossible, for an unknown author to get a break." She gave a knowing nod, and he continued with confidence. "With my track record though, we could work together, and I could teach you everything I know. What do you say?"

"Say what?" Donna wasn't sure what she thought she had heard. "Could you please repeat what you just said?"

Geoffrey smiled and nodded for emphasis. "Can we write the book together? Like they say, don't quit your day job. Even though I've had a lot of success, each book must stand on its own. I can't make any promises."

"Well, uh, how would all this work?"

"If you don't mind having me around, I can work here during the day, and you can help in your free time when you get home or whenever you feel like it." *She's ready to bite. Reel her in.*

Geoffrey's voice and charm flooded Donna's brain. He stared at her in a way she had only seen such men look at stunningly beautiful women. No man this handsome ever focused her in his attention with such disarming and consuming flattery. Donna smiled so hard she could barely get her lips together to form any words. "It's a deal." The smile began to fade. She stood up and said, “Excuse me a minute. I have an upset stomach.” She went into her bedroom and shut the door behind herself. “It’s a deal?” she mouthed to herself as her belly rumbled. “Couldn’t I think of something more brilliant to say to him, or why didn’t I think it through before blurting out an automatic acceptance?” Yet, the opportunity to write with someone like Geoffrey Imperato was too good a deal to refuse. Realistically, what could she do? Who would believe that a famous writer, whose books were translated into several languages and sold millions worldwide, would copy an unknown? What verifiable proof did she have? There was nothing, beyond her own manuscript, that she could get her hands on. Despite Geoffrey’s dishonesty, this was a mutually beneficial agreement. She pressed a tissue over her face and returned to the kitchen.

Geoffrey stood up and rubbed the back of his neck. “This has been a crazy day. How ’bout it if we start together tomorrow? If you don’t mind, I’d like to take some time today to just put things in order.”

“Sure, I’ll stay out of your way,” Donna said. Her stomach gurgled, so she slipped across the center hall into the bathroom and turned on the faucet to drown out the intestinal explosion that was about to erupt. “I wish this stupid bathroom had a fan!” When she was through, she washed her hands and opened the window even wider to air out the odor. “Hope he didn’t hear any of that. I ’d better take something for this before I go back out there.”

A glance at her face in the mirror almost made her heave. “Sickly washed-out skin, and my hair looks like a ball of yarn a cat just chewed. Nice first impression, meeting someone when you have diarrhea and look like swill,” she thought. Donna brushed her teeth, washed off every bit of makeup, and redid her hair. She sneaked into her bedroom and slapped on some blush and lipstick, going a bit heavier on the blush to brighten her complexion.

Meanwhile, Geoffrey hastily shoved creased sheets of paper into his briefcase as though Donna just might change her mind. He looked up as she entered the room. “It’s amazing how much our stories are alike, uncanny really. One thing though, you give away too much in the first chapter. A lot of amateurs, uh, beginners do that.”

***

“I’d’ve rapped him right in the teeth,” Loretta said the next morning. “The nerve he’s got, calling you an amateur!”

“But I am. It’s a legitimate term, not necessarily pejorative. How can I get angry at the truth?”

“Hello? If he were such a pro, why did he have to steal your work? And, the truth is, they totally invaded your privacy. Don’t you feel violated? It stinks out loud like diarrhea!”

“Please don’t remind me. What a *scoom*! I was never so embarrassed. He must think I’m a total scuzz. I can’t blame him if he doesn’t show his face again.”

“If he doesn’t show his face, it should be out of shame,” said Loretta with the belief that Donna should have felt just a tad more outraged. “Donna, what part of privacy invasion don’t you understand? And if you don’t understand that, how ’bout plagiarism?”

“He was stressed out, I told you. I guess he just panicked. He’s got a name to keep up.”

“Yeah, I can give you a few names for that slime rat.”

“He *was* having a tough time writing at home,” Donna insisted. “My story just happened to be similar in subject matter to his.”

“Just happened? What a coincidence! And does that sea hag aunt of his think she’s running a hotel? She’s got no right entering your apartment without your permission. Trouble is that she and her sleaze of a husband claim they're in with every crooked politician and who knows who else."

"Is that why you can't fight city hall?"

"I'm serious. Sometimes there's no right or wrong, but who you know. When I was in fourth grade there was a pedo-perv exposing himself to kids, but no one could do anything about him because he was being protected. Then there are drug dealers no one will touch. That's the way things at a certain level work." Loretta stopped and said, "Wouldn't ya know it! Eyes three o'clock."

Donna took a quick glance to see Primo waiting on the opposite platform. "Kind of early for him – the racetrack's not open yet."

"Yeah, must be going to one of his three jobs. I'd like to show up for work whenever I felt like it and still get paid."

A train pulled in on the opposite track. Donna and Loretta watched as Primo got on. "Notice the evil glare," Donna said.

"If looks could kill!"

"If looks could kill, I'd put a mirror in front of his face. Actually, I'd just like him to be incapacitated for a while. He's got too much sense of power. Sometimes I feel as though I'm living in a prison with him as the warden and his wife as the guard borrowed from some penal colony. There's no way I could fight his nephew and not have to watch my back."

"It would do him good to feel a little vulnerable. I still think he's the one who let the air out of my aunt Millie's tires when she parked her car in front of his house overnight for a few days. Speaking of the pig, have you seen the piggess since yesterday?" Loretta asked.

"No, but I'm sure she's stopped frothing at the mouth now that Geoffrey and I came to an agreement."

"Be careful."

"Geoffrey is only her nephew, not her evil twin."

"Yeah, but he's Primo's blood relative – might have his lech genes."

They arrived at the store in enough time to hit the ladies' room. Donna said, "I'll be in lingerie today."

"Is it really going to be that hot? Sorry, that joke was stale as last year's fruitcake, which, come to think of it, is stale as – never mind."

Floegel's annual bathing suit sale created an overflow into Donna's and Loretta's departments. At lunchtime Donna called home to see if Geoffrey was there. He answered only after he heard her voice on the answering machine.

"Ay Donna, I got here at ten thirty, and I'll be going downstairs for lunch in a few minutes." His tone had the forced sincerity of a tax cheat being audited, but to Donna's ears sounded genuine and warm. Whenever the day dragged on, the thought of Geoffrey busy at work on their book gave Donna a lift. "Would I *mind* having *him* around?" she giggled to herself.

***

Geoffrey greeted her that evening with a big smile. "I'm making good headway here. It's amazing how much work I can get done now that the stress of being caught is over."

"Can I read what we've got so far?" Donna asked. Was that a frown on Geoffrey's face? Did she overstep her position by saying "we"? After all, she was the amateur and he the pro – a pro with the indignity of needing a greenhorn like herself for help.

"Uh, sorry. What did you say?" Geoffrey was reading a page he held in his left hand while tapping a pencil on his thigh with his right.

"May I have a look at what you've got so far?"

"Sure, let's see. Here," said Geoffrey handing two sets of paper to her. "Here is an outline and some notes, and this is the first chapter, a blend of yours and mine. Should keep you busy for a while," he added with a smile.

Donna sat in the living room. "Do you want me to write any comments on these?"

"Of course."

"Why am I feeling so uncomfortable in my own apartment?" Donna thought. "Dinner — I'll make pasta. Maybe we're both just hungry." Donna pulled Tina's meatballs out of the freezer, threw them into a pot with jarred tomato sauce, and put together a salad of lettuce, cherry tomatoes, red onion and olives with a local restaurant house dressing.

As they ate, she thought, *It's Friday night. He could be doing something better than sitting here with me.* That realization made her relax and ignore any perceived coldness coming from him. "Creative people often get tense when they're working. Heck, we're still strangers, and we had an awkward beginning."

They hardly spoke except when discussing the story. "I've got an idea," said Geoffrey. "Instead of having the Johnson character deliberately go out of his way to steal Andrews's identity, why not do something like our situation? Have Andrews's landlady rent out his apartment to Johnson during the day. That way Johnson has easy access to all of Andrews's information."

"Like Arthur Sullivan's first musical *Cox and Box* and, hmm, in the movie *Sunset Boulevard*, Joe Gillis and Betty Schaefer work on a screenplay where the characters do just that."

"Guess you're telling me that wasn't exactly a unique idea."

"It doesn't have to be unique to be good. Let's consider it. It might work." Donna started scribbling.

"What's wrong?" asked Geoffrey, sensing she was making corrections rather than additions.

"Just some grammatical changes – for instance, it's 'between you and me' not 'between you and I', and it's 'imply' not 'infer' if you mean to suggest not to conclude." Donna suddenly felt like her ninth grade English teacher. Was he offended or was he glad that at least she had something to contribute? It will just take time to get to know each other. "And let's see, where else." Donna flipped back a couple of pages. "I changed 'each and every' to just '*every* criminal has a gambler's belief that he can beat the system'..."

"Why, what's wrong with that? You hear it all the time."

"True, but that doesn't mean it's correct. 'Each and every' is for carnival barkers and people who like to be redundant." Now she really sounded like a fussy old schoolmarm.

Geoffrey nodded without comment.

"Sorry for being such a pest."

"No, no. That's what I want you to do. I only wish I had you for my last book. What a mess that one was!"

Donna strained to think of something complimentary to say about *Won Too Many* and had to mentally stifle the jeering remarks of Loretta and Connie. "It was ... a big seller, wasn't it?"

"It did all right, but it was a critical disaster. I'd rather write a great book that sold a hundred copies than a poor one that sold a million."

"Really?"

"Nah, I'd write any old thing if it sold well, but I know from personal experience that a terrible book deserves to be a poor seller, although it's sad when a great book does badly." Geoffrey smiled but spoke in a serious tone. "Just once though, I'd love to write something that will last beyond a couple of years in the public memory. To be like Shakespeare – well maybe that's a stretch, but perhaps like, uh, who's that guy who wrote *Moby Dick*?"

"Herman Melville?"

"Yeah, or like Hemingway. It's an ego thing. I've already made enough money from just the books alone. Sometimes I wonder, though, if I'm a joke and if I ever had any real talent."

"If you feel that way about yourself, then pity the rest of us. I'd be happy if I wrote a letter that someone treasured the rest of their life, well, a few years anyway."

They took a limoncello and biscotti break out on the back porch. "Thanks," Geoffrey said.

"For what?"

"For being so understanding and forgiving when anyone else would have destroyed me. You're too good to be true."

"You know what they say," Donna said with a grin, "'If something's too good to be true, it probably isn't.'"

"Yeah, I can tell you're probably a real witch on wheels. Anyway, if you change your mind, I'll understand. I deserve whatever I get." Geoffrey looked at Donna with an expression she took to be genuine sincerity. "Please believe that I'm very sorry and ashamed for what I did. It scares me that I could be capable of such a thing. I've never sunk so low."

Throughout the evening the taught rope between them loosened into a fluffy strand of yarn that, with each smile and giggle, looped itself into a soft chain. Donna felt a connection, if not yet a bond, begin to form thanks to her own power to forgive. Had she retaliated, Geoffrey would now have a noose choking the life out of his reputation and career, and she would have self-doubt and guilt suffocating her conscience. For two people who had just met, they worked together like long-time collaborators, each infusing the other with creativity. She might not yet be his muse, but she gave him an energy and motivation he hadn't experienced since his first success. Whether from her sense of humor or simply his sense of relief, Geoffrey, at one point, laughed harder than he had in a long, long time.

Geoffrey looked at his watch. "11:00 P.M. Do you believe it? Time really does fly when you're having fun," he said with a wide grin.

Donna smiled so hard that she felt a twinge in her cheeks.

"Thank you for being such a good sport. If you're free on Sunday, maybe we can work a couple of hours. I suppose your phone is working now," he said with a laugh that displayed straight white teeth. Donna stared at his perfect, chiseled features and tried to find a flaw – impossible that anyone could look like that naturally.

***

After work the next day, Donna's mother called without so much as a 'hello, how are you, drop dead and go to hell'. "How's your weight?" she snapped.

"Fine. I lost a couple of pounds."

"Good, finally! You were such a pretty baby. People would stop me in the street to comment. Aunt Fran was saying, just the other day, that if you lost some weight, you might get your beauty back."

Donna winced. "Aunt Fran must have been a butcher in another life because she knows where to stick the knife."

"She only said that you could be beautiful again. It's true. She was just giving you a wakeup call."

"Is that what you call it? You know Mom, sometimes when a person wants to make an uncomfortable or insulting point, they quote someone else who also said it."

The subject quickly changed. "And what was that business about Angie you were saying?"

"She and I almost duked it out, but it's blown over. You know the way she is. I gotta get going. I'll talk to you later. Bye."

Donna needed fifteen minutes after they hung up to equilibrate because such conversations with her mother usually clouded her mood. In a way, Donna admired her mother for her pessimism, which was a form of realism. This summer, however, Donna wished to escape into unrealistic optimism with Geoffrey and forget the reality that was her own existence. She poured herself a glass of iced coffee and stretched out on the chaise lounge on the rear screened-in porch.

Geoffrey had left only Donna's original copy behind, but she preferred to think a while before working on it. Her thoughts drifted back to Geoffrey. His face was clear in her memory, the way he frowned while concentrating, and the way he smiled – a smile that could melt a snowball inside a freezer. He had given her copies of his top four bestsellers: *Bolder Damn*, *The Ploy's The Thing, Lies Beneath the Stares,* and *The Empty Frame*, so she could get a feel for his writing. She examined each of his photos on the book jackets. He was much more handsome in live, three-dimensional flesh.

A cool breeze blew in through the screen. Donna held up her bare feet to cool them and took a sip of coffee. The phone rang. "I'm too comfortable. Let the answering machine get it," she thought. "Oh, but tomorrow is Sunday. Geoffrey said he might come."

Donna jumped up and ran to the phone, catching it just as the answering machine kicked in and Loretta's voice spilled out. "I know this is last minute, but Ted, the shrink Gina's dating, is having a party tonight, and he's short of women. Besides, Gina doesn't want to go into the city alone. Like to go?"

As much as Donna wanted to hear from Geoffrey, it *was* Saturday night. "Sure, why not?" A party that was short on women was as rare as it was propitious.

Gina drove the three of them to the Back Bay. "This city has nowhere to park. What time is it?" Gina glanced down at the car clock. "We've been circling forever. I should've been one of the first ones there to welcome people. We should've taken a cab."

They passed Ted's building again and found a space farther down the street. Gina put on her blinker and pulled alongside the car in front. Before she could shift to reverse, a small green sports car zipped in behind and stole her spot.

"Thanks a lot!" Loretta shouted to the tall, lean man who got out of his car.

"You're welcome," said the man with a sarcastic smile. He blew a kiss with his middle finger and strutted off.

"Let me out!" Loretta hissed. "I'll fix him. You know what – instead drive around the block once in case he's watching."

"Don't do anything to his tires. That could be dangerous," cautioned Donna.

"Oh, I'll be more creative than that." Loretta reached into her purse. "Let's see. Nail polish remover –wonder what this will do to a paint job? I never liked this lipstick – too orangey. Now what else do we have?" She held up her house key and a nail clipper with the file pointed out. "Which of these do you think is better for etching?"

Donna answered, "You don't want to wear down your key, but the file might not be sturdy enough. Got a screwdriver? Not in your purse, of course."

"I've got some wart remover, and there's a tool kit in the trunk," Gina said. "It's also got some cans of chemical stuff. Put whatever you need in the cloth shopping bag that's also back there." Such a street-tough attitude was out of character for Gina, but anger and impatience brought out the Loretta in her.

They circled the block and skulked past Ted's building as though they were under surveillance. Gina stopped a safe distance from the green sports car. "I'll flash the lights if someone comes. Make it fast. I'm double parked."

With Donna as a mid-point look-out and bag holder, Loretta made a crouching run to the sports car but was back in less than two minutes. “I heard a door slam, but I don’t think anyone saw me. I couldn’t do as much as I wanted.”

“Did you leave any message for him to think about?” Donna asked as they both threw themselves into the car.

“No, just some scratches on the side and dabs of gunk on the trunk. I wanted to write a few choice words on the windshield with my lipstick but didn’t have time.”

“I should have done that for you instead of just standing there, but I had to keep watch. Anyone could’ve looked out a window, let alone pass by.”

“It’s probably better that you didn’t write on the windshield,” Gina said. “This way, he might not notice anything until tomorrow.”

“Right,” Donna said. “He might have wanted to do a door-to-door search to find the culprits, and we’d have in our possession the smoking lipstick.”

With one last drive around the neighborhood, they found a spot. As they walked down the street, Donna touched up her lipstick, Loretta powdered her nose, and Gina combed her hair.

Before they walked through the door, Donna and Loretta could practically smell the stuffiness emanating from Ted’s second floor condo. They wound their way over to the table that served as a bar and grabbed something to drink.

Gina and Ted made the rounds together, leaving Donna and Loretta to hold up a wall. The wit and humor permeating the room were self-satisfied – no silliness or self-deprecation here. Smug pronouncements of mutually shared personal beliefs were applauded as “bold and brilliant” as if to preach to the drunken choir were daring. A woman on her fourth glass of chardonnay shouted, “Oh, he’s an idiot,” and a small crowd laughed and cheered. “He thinks school kids shouldn’t be allowed to swear in class or talk back. He reprimanded a kid who was passing around some porn. Anyone who listens to him shouldn't be allowed to reproduce."

Donna leaned forward into the noisy circle and, with a grin, yelled, "You have such clever insight and depth of thinking, don't you? You put it all so…succinctly."

"I know I do," said the woman with a quick sip of her wine. "It's true. He's a complete moron, and the rest of his pals are all just as stupid. I mean, Lisa trained under him. She can confirm that he's—"

"A total imbecile." Donna laughed and didn't care what anyone thought. This was not her crowd. She stepped back and looked about to see if there were any more geniuses in the room. "Tell me that's not who I think it is at three o'clock," said Donna as she put her glass to her lips. Loretta looked sideways to her right and nearly choked. The jerk, who had given them the finger, was chatting with a red-haired gauzy-dressed woman with an arm bracelet and tattooed shoulder. The jerk caught Loretta's stare and gave a thin smile.

"Do you think he recognizes us?" asked Donna leaning closer to Loretta.

"Don't know," answered Loretta out of the side of her mouth. "I think we got a better look at him than he got of us. That smile could be either friendly or sarcastic. How do you tell with a smarmy rat face like that?"

Before the evening ended, Donna and Loretta made small talk with a few people. Every one of them asked, "What do you do?" immediately after forgetting their names. Donna was called "Diane" and didn't bother to correct anyone.

"And what do you gals do?" asked a broad-shouldered goateed man, eyeing them up and down.

"We're saleswomen," Donna answered.

"What do you sell?"

"Loretta is in cosmetics and I'm in women's clothing."

"You certainly are, and you fill them out well," smirked the goateed shrink. "They say salespeople are very good at sizing people up. Let's test your perception. What do you make of the people in this room?" he asked with an authoritative command.

Loretta had already sized up this guy but decided to humor him. "See that redhead across the room with the flowing get-up and tattoo? I'd say that she sees herself as being a lot more attractive than she really is, and there's something, I don't know, fake and common about her. And that guy she's talking to is a total jerk, pushy and obnoxious. They deserve each other, I think."

The goateed man narrowed his eyes and gave a slight nod. "Very good. Now how about you, Diane? Let's hear your opinion."

Donna glanced at his "I'd rather be golfing" look. The man's attire was expensive, showing some wear, but nothing newer than two years. A button on his shirt, badly sewn with thread that didn't quite match, hung as though a slight tug would require another stitching. His intense, almost angry manner more than anything gave him away. "Let's take you," she said. "I'd say you're divorced, less than five years ago, but more likely within the past couple of years. Your ex-wife had a good lawyer who was persistent on her behalf, and your divorce has left you with an underlying resentment against women that you are finding hard to shake; however, you are quite vocal about supporting women."

"Ah, I don't suppose you'd tell me how you concluded all that. However, for a man my age to be divorced has about a fifty-fifty chance, no? The divorce laws would give a vulture like my ex the lion's share. You don't come out of a nasty divorce without transferring some hostility to all women. It's a natural human reaction, even for someone with my training." He cleared his throat and leaned forward. "That redhead, by the way, is my ex. Her lawyer was her cousin, and he was a pit bull."

"Was I right about that guy talking to your ex?" Loretta asked.

"Brian? Yeah, he's a first-class asshole. Just how did you two know everything?"

"Trade secret," said Donna smiling. "Seriously though, a lot of it comes from the simple experience of dealing with the public."

"I'm still impressed with how Lori here saw right through Brian. That top-heavy, over-confident personality of his usually impresses people. You can see it's doing a good job on my ex."

Donna said, "A lot of people view confidence as a sign of competence when it's often just plain conceit."

"Conceit with nothing to back it up," Loretta chimed in. "Was Brian your ex-wife's lawyer?"

"No, no, but he is an attorney – an ambulance chaser for one of those firms that runs ads on TV."

Brian, apparently aware of their attention, turned to look at them. His thin mustache stretched over a grimace, and he winked at Loretta. He had one of those even-featured faces that most people would call handsome if they saw a photo of him but would label as "just okay" or "nothing special" if they spent more than ten minutes in his animated presence.

The party was a dud as far as meeting anyone went, but at least it was a night out. Donna and the Amalfitano sisters were among the last to leave, however.

"Why did we stay so long?" Loretta asked.

"I'm dating Ted. I couldn't just walk out before the other guests left," Gina answered with an irritated roll of her eyes.

"Perhaps we were hoping that Mr. Right would materialize in the crowd," Donna yawned. "None of those stuffed shirts would be interested in us anyway. We look for love. They want business partners."

"What a bunch of pukes," Loretta said to her sister. "What do you see in that drip Ted anyway? And did you ever meet such self-important snobs in your life? How often do you have to interact with those people?"

Gina scowled and gripped the steering wheel. "Loretta, can we discuss this later? Just because we have different taste, and you like men whose major fashion accessory is a baseball cap, and who think a manicure is something you use as fertilizer, doesn't mean that anyone I like is a snob. I mean really, look at you and *your* taste! Everything you wear is either an animal print or a color from a first grader's crayon box! How you sell all the makeup you do, is beyond me. Didn't that heavy eyeliner die with Cleopatra? And to think that tonight I trusted your judgement and let you vandalize…"

"Excuse me Gina, but I thought you said we should discuss this later, and here you are getting personal, going on and on about my faults as if you're little Miss Perfect. When I said I wanted to vandalize that car did you try to stop me? As usual, you let me do all the dirty work, so save the sanctimony! Just because you're the baby in the family doesn't mean …"

"Knock it off, will you both?" Donna said. "We went out and had some laughs, even though we were laughing at, not with, those jokers. Please save it for later."

***

Donna's answering machine had only a message from Tina with an offer of fruit salad. Donna looked at the clock. At 12:20 it was too late to call anyone back.

***

Next morning Donna managed to attend the 7:30 Mass despite only five and one-half hours sleep. On the way home she picked up donuts and the Sunday newspaper. A cruller, coffee, and the crossword puzzle – what more do you need out of life? Donna lay on the chaise lounge and unstrapped her sandals. She nodded off and was blanketed by a warm breeze that was scented by wafts of aromas from her neighbor's kitchens.

Ice cream was her first thought upon awakening from a refreshing sleep. She dialed Tina. "Do you still have that fruit salad? … I've got some rainbow sherbet. How 'bout it? … O.K., I'll call Loretta."

When Loretta arrived, Donna called down, "Can you help me carry the sherbet and glasses?"

Donna put three parfait glasses and long iced tea spoons onto a tray and took the sherbet out of the freezer. "Now all we need is raspberry syrup," she said as she reached for a bottle in the cabinet, "and how about some chocolate covered mint patties on the side?" Donna opened her candy drawer. "Oh shoot, I forgot to take this to the Lost and Found." She held up the gold and emerald earring to Loretta who said she didn't recognize it. "Can't be Angie's – she'd have said something. I think this got stuck on my loose-knit top during the two-day sale. I didn't even notice it. It probably just looked like an oddly placed pin to anyone else because no one said anything." Donna lightly tossed the earring in her hand. "Hold on – I found it on my bedroom floor. Do you think…?"

"Hey, before that sherbet melts, let's get downstairs and ask Tina what she knows."

Donna and Loretta carried everything down to Tina's in silence. Once in the kitchen, they spoke softly so the Infantos couldn't hear them through the open windows.

"One time I came home from Filene's Basement with a pair of panties hanging from the buckle of my purse strap. Didn't even notice it until Maverick Station," Tina said upon hearing the story.

"If Donna had something shiny like that earring hanging off her, I didn't see it. Besides, that was before she knew Geoffrey was using her apartment," Loretta said with a tone of regret.

"You really don't think…?" Donna felt her heart sink with the voicing of the suspicion she had already heard in her mind.

Loretta shrugged. "Why don't you ask him?"

"I don't feel comfortable doing that. 'Gee Geoffrey, do you entertain any lady friends during the day when I'm gone?' He'll think I'm prying into his personal life."

"It's your apartment. You have a right to know who else has been in there. Who knows? It might be Angie's."

"If she lost it, she would have asked me, or she would have been nervy enough to just come upstairs and look for it herself."

"Donna dear," Tina said patting her on the hand. "There is a woman who comes here sometimes, well, more like often, at least once or twice a week. From what I can tell, she usually comes late morning or early afternoon. I always assumed she was visiting Angie and Primo because you, of course, weren't home. One time when I went to get my mop off the back porch, I saw her cut across the yard into the alley of the houses behind us – seemed a little odd. Since then, I noticed she always uses the back entrance."

"Could you ever hear anything?"

"Their apartment is like Grand Central Station. Who can tell? Upstairs, downstairs – too much noise for just two people, although they do yell a lot. Makes me wonder what they're up to. I think the nephew stays over sometimes, and then of course, there's the skinny blond I just mentioned."

"How long is her hair?" asked Donna, suddenly remembering the long hair that had stuck to her face.

"Oh, long, past her shoulders. She's very attractive too, from what I can make out."

Donna took a big mouthful and slapped her hand to her head.

"You okay?"

"Ice cream headache." said Donna, frozen by the obvious explanation.

"I think it boils down to this," Loretta said, "if you're personally interested in Geoffrey, then we should try to find out if she's just one of Angie and Primo's visitors or…"

"If Goldilocks has been sleeping in my bed," Donna finished. "I've only just met Geoffrey so I can't say realistically how I feel, but I don't want them using my apartment that way." What Donna couldn't say had already begun to take hold in her thoughts.

"Don't you think that if she lost the earring in your apartment, she would have looked for it before she left? You found it easily enough," Loretta said.

"Perhaps she didn't realize she lost it or where she lost it until sometime later. Then I found it before she came back here. It might not even be hers."

"It's not exactly tiny. She had to feel a little lopsided, unless…" Loretta hesitated with the dirty suspicion that the earring might have been left behind deliberately as a warning that Geoffrey was taken.

"Unless what?"

"I guess I'm saying that if you didn't feel the earring, and I didn't see it on you, then it's unlikely it belongs to a customer, unless it was tucked in some fold or other part of your clothing where it was hidden." Without Loretta telling her outright, Donna understood her intimation and let her face show the emotion she had tried to suppress.

Tina, with all the maternal concern she had shown her own daughter many times in the past, leaned forward, "Donna, do you really like him?"

"Maybe. I'm not sure, but we seem to hit it off. I don't know if I can trust him, though. It's unrealistic to even think of the possibility, so why set myself up for disappointment?"

"You never know. I never thought my husband would go for me. God bless his soul. But if you're interested, we should find out if he's even available."

"Who else could she be besides Geoffrey's girlfriend?" Donna asked.

"Who knows?" Tina said. "The place sounds like a dormitory. Maybe they're running a gambling casino, or God forbid, dealing drugs, although I don't think they would be so evil."

"Then how can we find out who she is?"

"She's usually here Monday, but she comes other days as well. You could leave the earring outside your back door and see if it disappears."

"There'd be no proof she was the one who took it. Angie thinks nothing of coming up here. In fact, she unlocks the door for Geoffrey."

"Next time he's over, you could make sure he sees the earring and watch his reaction," Tina said.

"But if he has a poker face, I'll never know. Then he might tell her to just be more careful. Though, it might force him to say something if he recognizes it."

"How many men notice a woman's jewelry anyway?" asked Loretta. "The earring could have come from somewhere we haven't thought of besides this strange woman. It could have fallen off a passenger on the crowded train. The distance home from the station isn't that far that we mightn't have seen it. And, who knows who else those slimers let in your apartment besides Geoffrey? Why should they stop with just him? You could have a marching band parade through there, and how would you know?"

"You're right."

"Tomorrow is Monday, one of her days, I think," said Tina. "I call her 'Slink' because she always looks as though she's sneaking around."

"I'm off tomorrow," Loretta said. "At 8:45 I have a hairdresser appointment, and then I'm home the rest of the day. We could both keep a lookout."

***

When the two younger women got up to leave, Tina said to Loretta, "Stop in tomorrow if you get a chance. I'll do a little housework in the morning. Then I'll sit by the window and watch TV," whispering, she added, "and for you know who."

Upstairs in Donna's apartment, Donna loaded the dirty parfait glasses from the tray into the dishwasher. A spoon fell off the tray and hit the floor with a low bounce. Donna bent to pick it up. She turned to Loretta. "I've got an idea."

***

Geoffrey never called that evening to say when he planned to come again. It occurred to Donna that she didn't even have his phone number, not that she'd call him. "What am I doing anyway? I let a man I barely know, a stranger, stay in my apartment all day. What if he goes through my closet and sees what size, er sizes, I wear."

Loretta said, "That's why I cut the tags out of my clothes. I don't even want to see the sizes. I've got my pants divided into with and without wedgies."

CHAPTER THREE
LORETTA TAKES A SWING AND A SLURP

Donna, feeling in a strange way relieved that her guard was up, left for work by herself the next morning. As she waited for the train, she called Loretta.

"Get this," Loretta said, "Ted's brother wants to go out with me. We didn't get to meet him at the party because he left early. Apparently, I caught his eye."

"Then the night wasn't a total waste."

"I didn't say yes yet – not because it's a blind date, but because he's a total obnoxious creep."

"What?"

"He's the a-hole who stole our parking space Saturday night and then gave us the finger."

"Oh no! But didn't he recognize us?"

"Guess not. Gina met him for the first time at the party, and he showed no sign of recognition. In fact, she didn't recognize him when they were introduced. She said his name was Brian and that he spent the whole time talking to a red-haired woman in a flowing green dress and clunky jewelry. He was wearing a Hawaiian shirt, and he has a thin mustache and mouse brown hair."

"Even still, do you think we just might be mistaken about him being the same guy with the car?" Donna asked.

"Nah. I remember his smarmy face when he flipped us off as well as his clothes. That woman was the only other redhead there besides me, and I saw only one other guy wearing anything resembling a Hawaiian shirt. If he shows up in the same green car, that'll be further proof."

"Then you're going out with him? What about the car?"

"What about it? If there was any permanent damage, I'll tell him if and when the time is right."

***

By the time Donna had made her fifth sale, Loretta was back from the hairdresser and sitting at her roll-top desk by the window, which overlooked the side street. After digging in an overstuffed drawer for her checkbook, stamps, and calculator, she pulled her bills out of a cubbyhole and organized them in the order of importance. "Drat! Didn't I pay that already? I need coffee." Loretta stood up just after a car door slammed outside.

Loretta looked out the window and saw a woman with long blond hair and a short skirt. The woman walked toward the rear of Loretta's house and abruptly turned into the back yard.

"What's she doing?" Loretta ran to the back porch and watched the woman for as long as she could. The woman cut across the neighbors' backyards as well, in the direction of Donna's. Loretta scrambled for the phone. "Hello, Tina. It's Loretta. I think Slink is headed your way…She parked right outside our house. At least now I can do it from here instead of there, and it will look less suspicious…No. I wasn't able to get out in time. Be on the lookout and let me know if she comes into the house. She's going by the back…Yes, I've got it right here. Bye."

Less than ten minutes later, Tina called back. "I made it to the back door and opened it a crack just in time. She came in and went upstairs, how far, I can't say. I tried to count her footsteps on the stairs, but then Primo's loud mouth drowned out everything. He was headed downstairs, so I shut my door."

"Don't suppose he was going to work?"

"Which job: the one he doesn't go to from 7:00 to 3:00 or the one he doesn't go to from 9:00 to 5:00?"

"What a bum. Can you hear anything else?" Loretta asked.

"Angie's got that booming music blasting, and I'm about ready to pound on the ceiling with my broom handle. The two of them are taking that kind of sauce lessons."

"Salsa?"

"Yeah, that's it. The Dancing Duo."

"Picture it." Loretta shook her head in mock disgust. "Let me know if you can tell where Slink is and make sure you call me when she leaves."

***

After lunch Donna called home. The phone rang until the answering machine came on. "Geoffrey, it's Donna. If you're there, please pick up the phone." The moment the words came out of her mouth, she regretted saying them. *How desperate! I hope he's not there with Slink.*

Business was brisk after lunch. Donna felt that even minus the returns, she made a good commission. One customer alone bought three suits, and another her entire wardrobe for her new job. About the time Donna was having a lull in sales, back home Loretta's phone rang.

"Loretta?" Tina whispered. "She's leaving from the back. Wait. Wait, yes, she's headed back the way she came in, across everyone's back yard in your direction."

Loretta, in flip-flops and light denim Capri pants, grabbed a broom and was out the door. "Let's hope this is where she usually parks, or at least on the day she lost the earring," she said to herself. Loretta tossed the earring under the edge of the bushes that lined the side of her yard. She peeked around the back of her house and could see Slink coming across the Bramante's yard into the Kelly's.

Loretta stepped back to the sidewalk and started sweeping softly so she could hear Slink's footsteps. Unfortunately, Slink walked softly, and she appeared at the outer edge of the

Amalfitanos' backyard so suddenly that Loretta gave a start. She tried to regain her cool and almost let go of the broom.

Now only a few feet from her car, Slink slowed down to take her keys out of her purse. Loretta had to act fast. With two rabid swipes of her broom, she whacked the earring into the side of the car. The earring bounced off and tumbled onto the sidewalk – not as planned.

Slink stopped and stared, first at the wide-eyed Loretta and then at the earring, which lay about a yard from her feet. "I don't believe it!" said Slink, bending down to pick up the earring. She stood up, holding the emerald and gold swirl in her palm, and frowned. "How did this get *here*?"

"Is it yours?" Loretta asked.

Slink looked up, a little confused. "Uh, yes. I, um, lost this last…when, let's see. How strange that it's here!"

"Where were you parked on the day you lost it?"

"Probably around the corner or on the other side of the block." Slink shot Loretta a look that was both supercilious and suspicious, but Loretta, a middle child who was used to getting the blame from both ends, put on her innocent face she learned at age five.

"Some kids might have thrown or kicked it here, or maybe a cat or a squirrel…" Loretta stopped, realizing that she was getting into the realm of the bizarre. She smirked. "Well, it's a good thing that you found it. It's very pretty. Looks expensive."

"Yes. It was custom made." Slink popped it into her purse then got in her car without saying another word.

***

Tina laughed on the phone. "A squirrel? Wait 'til Donna hears."

Loretta said, "Tina, she looked like one of these women who just stepped off a magazine page and never sweats. Her purse costs more than two month's rent for most people. And she seemed like a total snob."

"You should have tripped her with the broom."

***

After work, Donna stopped in the ladies' room to touch up her makeup, something she usually didn't do when Loretta was along, unless they were going somewhere other than straight home. With an open lipstick in her hand, she called Loretta. After hearing about the earring incident. she asked, "Was Geoffrey there?"

"Gee, I don't know. I forgot to ask Tina, but if Slink was there, then he must've been too, no?" answered Loretta, revealing her belief that Slink wasn't Angie's poker pal.

"I suppose so. At lunch I called home, and he didn't answer. It would be a relief if he hadn't come."

"Donna, I can see where this is going. Just come home, kick off your shoes, and we'll talk later. Okay?"

***

As Donna climbed the stairs to her apartment, she wondered what she would do if confronted with any more disturbing evidence. "Hello?" she called out as she opened her door. No answer. There was coffee in the coffee maker carafe, and she hadn't made any that morning. A chair was pulled away from the table, and a dirty cup and spoon were in the sink. Geoffrey had been there and left with no message, written or spoken.

Donna dialed Loretta's number. "I'm coming over. Walls have ears."

***

"He's an earth pig. What do you expect? Think about it. His aunt might have unlocked the door to your apartment, but he didn't have to go in. And, if he's using your place as the No-Tell Motel, then he's a slime mold." Loretta slung one leg over the arm of her easy chair and, with a swing of her foot, flipped her sandal and caught it with her big toe.

"I've given only him, but no one else, permission to work in my apartment. Of course, he's got a private life, but I'm entitled to my own privacy as well," said Donna staring out the side window of the living room as if she expected to see Slink's car materialize.

"This is a guy who originally came in uninvited. Why should he have any qualms about inviting someone else in?"

"None," said Donna throwing herself down on the red leather sofa. "I've given him an inch, and he's literally taken the whole place."

"Let's think this thing through," said Loretta, twirling her sandal until it flew off and landed with a graceless thump on the Berber rug. "What exactly was this guy doing in your apartment in the first place?"

"He said his home was a zoo, and that he needed a quiet place to work."

"Why your place? It's a big city. Why couldn't he go somewhere else?"

"I suppose, for some reason, even after he got rid of the barbarian horde, he was having a hard time writing at home and might have first tried to work at Angie's but couldn't concentrate. Angie and Primo probably thought nothing of sending him up to my apartment. Why then would he look any further?"

"And you and he just happened to be doing a book on the same subject? How convenient!"

"It is a strange coincidence. I often leave my writing out on my desk. He came in, and there it was – or he came in *knowing* what he'd find," said Donna with sudden realization. "Both Tina and you knew what I was writing. Didn't Tina tell Angie about it? At first, he might have looked out of curiosity, but then found something he wanted. I write regularly, and he kept coming to get my updates. I'll bet that's it!"

"That would better explain why he kept coming here instead of somewhere else. I wonder if he has other family. Sure, he does. Vinnie said he and Geoffrey dropped in on his brother on their way out one night. His parents still live in Eastie, don't they?"

"I wouldn't know. He rarely mentions them, although he talks about his brother and sister more often. The main question, though, is who is Slink? It's possible she isn't Geoffrey's girlfriend or doesn't have anything to do with Angie or Primo. There might be another explanation for why she comes here."

Loretta sucked in a breath of slight impatience. "Such as?"

"She could be his agent, assistant, or something."

"'Or something' is more like it. She cuts through back yards like a thief, and she looks like a rich *puttana* with that belt she passes off as a skirt. I don't know what to tell you. I just don't want you to get hurt. If you are seriously going to work with Geoffrey, why don't you set up a regular schedule for when you're home? During the day, he can go elsewhere."

"I can't ask him to alter his writing schedule," said Donna with a slight fear that she could lose whatever contact she had with him. "He's probably more productive by himself during the day in a quiet place."

"Why not the library or some other relative's home? How quiet can your place really be with the fishmongers downstairs, let alone the airplanes overhead? It's just creepy having some strange guy alone in your apartment all day."

"I'm not sure he's always alone." Donna recognized her growing defensiveness and strain in her voice.

"Donna, you know what I'm getting at. He may be the Infantos' nephew and hang out occasionally with my stupid brother, but he's still a stranger who broke into your apartment, for cryin' out loud. Would you tolerate this if he weren't so good looking?" Loretta softened, "Your privacy has been violated big time. You don't have to put up with anything you don't like. Speak your mind. He's the one who should be walking on eggshells."

Donna nodded. "I'm at least going to insist on getting his phone number and not let him just show up whenever he feels like it."

"That's it. Now let's have a float. How about raspberry ripple ice cream and ginger ale or cream soda? By the way, I'm going out with Brian this Thursday night. He's picking me up here."

"Maybe he's not so bad."

"Oh, I'm sure he is, but what the heck, it's a night out. He's Ted's brother so he'll have to watch himself. Won't be anything I can't handle," said Loretta as she flung open the freezer door.

The soda bubbled over the ice cream into a frothy, rising foam that Donna ate with a spoon and Loretta slurped through a straw. Small ice shards formed in the remaining ice cream that floated in a milky, pale pink pool. Loretta sighed, "The only thing better than this is strawberry shortcake."

"Or a hot fudge sundae," Donna said.

"Or chocolate!" both women chimed.

CHAPTER FOUR
BUTTERFLIES

Donna came home by herself the next evening because Loretta worked until closing. Just as well. Their previous night's conversation about Geoffrey had resumed with a brief phone call earlier that morning and would have gone on to put her in a worse mood if they were together now. A flutter of anticipation in her chest told her that he would be there after an absence of three days.

***

Geoffrey opened the door and greeted Donna with a warm smile. *Emerald earring? What emerald earring?* For years, Donna came home to an empty apartment. Tina, Loretta, and Loretta's family often would invite Donna for dinner, but for the most part, Donna spent her nights alone. Tonight, and for at least the near future, she was coming home to somebody.

"Hey, how was your day?" Geoffrey asked. "I'm making supper. I checked your schedule on the refrigerator and figured you'd be home about now."

"What a surprise!" Donna said as she walked into the kitchen and got walloped in the nose by a pungent, strange smell. A quick scan of the room told her that she could have prepared, with half the mess, whatever Geoffrey had cooked. Such a sweet gesture though was worth the half hour it would take to wash the two cutting boards, colanders, frying pans, pots, and numerous utensils that littered the cluttered counters and spattered stovetop.

"Hope you like what I cooked. This is my version of Chinese chicken salad and chili."

"Interesting combination."

They sat down at the dining room table and Geoffrey served Donna.

"Looks wonderful," she said.

"Hope you like it. I don't cook much, but I make a mean chili."

"Really?" asked Donna, genuinely interested. "What else do you like to cook?"

"I make steak, burgers, mostly things you just throw on a barbecue or in a pan on top of the stove. I don't think I've ever lit an oven."

Donna put a forkful of salad in her mouth. Her eyes widened. "M-mumf, argh." A forced swallow almost made her choke. "Oof." Donna gasped. "I'm so sorry. I don't know what to say."

"That's okay, what's wrong?"

"I think it was that green leafy type of parsley."

"You mean cilantro?"

"Is that what it was? I'm sorry for doing that."

"I'm the one who's sorry."

"Don't be. This was very sweet of you. I'll just pick it out. Is there any cilantro in the chili?"

"Uh, a little, but I don't think you can taste it."

Donna tried the chili. Tears rolled down her cheeks as she grabbed her glass of water. Cilantro wasn't the problem.

"Did I go too heavy on the chilies?" Geoffrey asked with a note of concern. "I'm sorry. I wanted to surprise you, and I surprised you in the wrong way."

"Woo!" said Donna fanning herself with her hand. "I think you're trying to kill me!" She took another gulp of water and started laughing so hard that it sprayed out her mouth. She cleared her flooded throat. "So sorry. I'll just eat around the chili pieces and hope for no more surprise spices." She had to take a deep calming breath before every sip.

After dinner she went to her bathroom to pull herself together. She looked at her reflection and smiled. They'd only just met, and she had no unrealistic expectations, but for now, he filled a void. By its sudden absence, she realized that her mid-abdomen had held a tight knot for so long that she couldn't remember when it had formed, so much a part of her natural anatomy it had become. That knot had now untied, and its tough fibers unraveled into gossamer.

They sat in the living room and just talked about their ideas for the story and the main characters. For a full fifteen minutes they discussed the protagonist: his name, age, background, appearance, personality, and character. He would not be totally sympathetic, but a bit of a cad. "You have a great understanding of people," Geoffrey said. "Part of it must come from working with the public, but I think with you most of it's innate." Donna from childhood had been shy and observant but slow to form hard opinions about others. Many people liked her, but few went out of their way to get to know her. Now Donna felt herself on the verge of a close friendship, if nothing else, with one of the few men who seemed to see something in her that transcended the usual physical qualities that most men look for. Strangely, she sensed they had a mutual spiritual connection.

At 10:30 Geoffrey got up to leave. "What time are you getting home tomorrow?" he asked with a sleepy smile.

"I'm off, but I'm busy until later in the afternoon, so I'll be home about three or four," Donna answered while trying to think of what she could eliminate to shorten her to-do list for the next day.

***

All of Donna's saved up errands were crammed into the morning so she could visit her mother.

“So, how’re you sweetheart?” asked her mother as she heaped *farfalle*, folded ribbons of sweet fried dough dusted with powdered sugar, onto a plate. “Come on, eat.”

“I will, give me time.” Donna sipped black coffee from a white porcelain diner mug and looked at the tempting mound. She held a crispy piece that snowed on the tablecloth. “If I eat this, I won’t stop.”

“Go ahead. I made them just for you. Don’t worry. They’re light.”

“They’re deep fried and covered with powdered sugar. They’re as bad as *strufoli* or *zeppole.*”

“I suppose so. So, what’s new?” Donna’s mother asked as she shoved the *farfalle* closer to her daughter. Donna wasn’t sure she should mention Geoffrey. Her mother Rita DiGeronamo would only get the wrong idea and not let go of a possible, but impossible, son-in-law.

“Same old thing — I’m working on a book.” There. If her mother were interested in hearing more, she’d tell her.

“Oh, you already told me that. You’re always writing,” her mother said with a dismissive wave of her hand. “What else? Anything *new*? How’s Loretta and her family?”

“Fine.”

“Tina?”

“Fine.”

“Before I forget, let me give you this,” said her mother as she rose and reached for a shopping bag from the almond tiled counter. “I know it isn’t your birthday just yet, but in case I don’t see you, I want you to have this in the meantime. I’ve got something else from your father and me on order for you.”

Donna unwrapped a burgundy leather shoulder bag. “Ma, you didn’t have to. This is so nice.”

“Don’t worry, I got it at an outlet. Look, it has a zipper under the flap to keep pickpockets out, and the leather is thick so they can't easily slit it with a knife. I worry about you on the subway."

"Don't. I keep my guard up. No one messes with me. Walking outside at night is sometimes worse."

"Why don't you take the bus?"

"In the time I'd have to wait for it, I'm more than halfway home. Whenever the weather's bad I take the bus, but I still must walk part way. Besides I'm usually with Loretta," Donna answered.

"How's the neighborhood?"

"Same problems with drugs and crime, like anywhere else, only Eastie doesn't have the clout to get it hushed up."

"Why don't you move to Saugus or Wakefield? We'd be nearer to each other."

"They're farther from work, and the public transportation isn't as convenient. I'd have to drive all or part of the way and then have trouble parking."

"Yes but look at all the restaurants."

"Look at me. Just what I need: more restaurants!" Donna's hand stopped mid-reach for another piece of *farfalle.*

"Why don't you have Loretta show you how to shade your face to make it look thinner?" Laying an index finger along the diagonal of her cheek, she said, "You put a dark streak here in the hollow and then some highlighter on the top of your cheekbone. Then you take a brick or rusty blush, not a pink or red that looks swollen, and sweep it over the middle, and then put more highlighter on the top."

"I'll do that sometime, like when clown faces are in style." Donna took a sip of coffee to hide her frown.

"You gotta blend it. Besides if you just lost some weight, you could use a lighter touch."

Donna pushed the platter of *farfalle* farther away from herself.

"Do you need another coffee maker? I've got four of them, and you still haven't taken that Blue Willow dish set."

"I don't have room for it, and it's not my taste."

"But you love blue," insisted her mother. "Look at your apartment – blue, blue, blue! Your living room furniture, your bedroom, half your wardrobe are all shades of blue!"

"Yes, but I don't want to eat off something that depicts two lovers jumping off a bridge because they can't be together."

"You don't see them jumping, just running over the bridge, then two birds fly away, that's all."

Nonetheless, Donna left with a trunk-load.

***

On the way home Donna stopped at a supermarket and filled the rest of her car with groceries, most of which were items Geoffrey liked. She hauled two bags and a coffeemaker up the stairs and was met at the door by Geoffrey just before 3:30.

Is there more to bring up?" he asked. Donna nodded a breathless yes. "Stay here," he said, "I'll get the rest." It took two more trips to carry everything else upstairs.

Donna opened the refrigerator to put away the frozen food first. The cold air from the freezer could not touch the warmth she felt inside. All Donna's life she was told what she couldn't do. Though an A-student from grade school through college, she was judged "lacking in confidence and leadership skills." Job interviews were nightmarish, and, after she had been asked for the tenth exhausting time what her "vision" for the company was, she destroyed her last possible chance for a corporate career by answering that she didn't hallucinate and that only psychics and drug abusers had visions. Failure taught her to rebuff herself before anyone else did. The dull ache of self-inflicted denial hurt less than rejection and disappointment from others. With little more information than a spiral-shaped gold and emerald earring, she could tell herself that she shouldn't hope for anything with Geoffrey, but this time she wouldn't – not yet if she could help it.

Geoffrey sat on the porch and Donna started to cook a chicken cacciatore dinner. While the chicken pieces, garlic, and onion browned, she opened a cookbook to a coffeecake recipe. "Geoffrey," she called out to the porch. "Do you like cinnamon and walnut coffeecake?"

"Sure. Love it."

"Good. I'll make one for you to have tomorrow. I won't have time to bake it in the morning, so I'll do it tonight in the toaster oven. We've got that coffee blend you like, and you know where everything else is." Such wonderful aromas permeated the air that Geoffrey ate half the coffeecake by the end of the evening.

Donna went to sleep that night still giggling over some of their conversation, which focused more on personal stories than on the story they were writing together. *It's good to play hooky every now and then.* "The humor and camaraderie make us more creative. We've got plenty of time to finish the book, in fact, I hope we never do. I'd love us to go on like this forever."

CHAPTER FIVE
LORETTA GOES OUT. DONNA BLOWS UP

Thursday evening Loretta arrived home from work, threw off her clothes and jumped into the shower. She applied coppery bronzer over her face to accent her greenish eyes, which she lined heavily. Three shades of lipstick were blended to a Sophia peach. A zit on her chin (probably from the excitement of ending her dry spell) got the camouflage treatment. She shimmied into a raw silk dress in a green to complement her dyed auburn mane and bronzy skin. Just as she finished brushing her locky hair, the doorbell rang.

As Loretta walked out of the house with Brian, he said, "You look *lovely*. I see you did your roots." In response to Loretta's raised eyebrows, he looked at her dress with a malicious grin. "Green to match the car."

Loretta tried to keep a straight face. "Nice. Is it new?"

"Yes. Unfortunately, the dealer's body shop can't figure out why the paint on the rear blistered the way it did," said Brian pointing to the pathetic looking trunk.

Loretta's face blushed a deeper copper. "What do they think caused it?"

"They don't know. They're perplexed. The car's less than a couple months old, and it's garaged most of the time in a secure building. I noticed it early Monday morning."

Loretta shrugged. "Could it have been a bad factory paint job?"

"Some slow oxidation or deterioration? Naw. I think someone did it purposely because there are also some scratches on the side. Those were no doubt deliberate." Brian gave Loretta a quizzical look.

"I know a guy who keys every expensive car he can," Loretta said with a slight smirk. She got in the passenger seat and had a sense that Brian slammed the door harder than necessary. After a few minutes of awkward silence, she spoke up with the belief that he would just *love* to talk about himself. "Well Brian, tell me about yourself."

"You already know I'm an attorney and that I'm Ted's brother," Brian huffed as if in response to a stupid or nosy question. "Moron!" he yelled at a car that cut him off. "What's with the idiots around here? That's the third asshole that almost plowed into me! From what Cracker Jack box do you people get your licenses? You all on crack or something?"

Brian's manner was so hostile and menacing that Loretta felt like jumping from the car into traffic just to get away from him. She forced a weak smile. "This is an old part of town. Some of the intersections are tricky."

"Boston is an old city. This part's the worst. I'd rather break down horizontally on Storrow Drive at rush hour."

Loretta looked out the window. This was her first date in months, and she was going to make the best of it. "Mind if I put on some music?"

"Yes," said Brian, still engulfed in agitation.

"'Yes' put it on or 'yes' you mind?"

Brian gripped the steering wheel. "Go 'head, do whatever you want," he snapped. As Loretta leaned forward to turn on the radio, the car accelerated and banged a U-ee. Loretta was thrown backward against the seat back. Good thing the headrest was up.

***

Given the inauspicious start to the date, the restaurant was one of the nicer places Loretta had ever been taken. As if reading her mind, Brian said, "I thought we'd slum a little tonight." He refused the first two tables they were offered and insisted on a roomy, more private booth, so they'd be "less likely to run into anyone" he knew. Loretta hid behind the large menu so she wouldn't have to look at him.

"You got that thing memorized yet?" Brian snarled.

"Not quite," Loretta answered without looking up. She pulled her shoulders back to consciously suppress the urge to squirm or slouch from discomfort. It was still early in the date, and even a grouch deserved a chance.

***

Loretta munched on a Cobb salad while Brian sucked down a half dozen oysters and ordered another six. "Playing safe with a boring salad? Not the adventurous type?" he asked.

Loretta wondered what was so adventuresome about slurping raw slime, but she politely answered, "I don't like raw shellfish."

"Ah, I see, inhibited, are we?"

Loretta snorted. "I just don't like them. The thought makes me gag."

"So, let's see, you're a guinea and a gagger?"

"You're a slime mold."

"Ooh, feisty, aren't we? How come you're so different than your sister? She's a lady."

"I could say the same thing about you and Ted. At least he's…" Loretta came up short for a complimentary comparison, so in haste, she settled for "a gentleman." She tried to imagine what sort of family could produce two such sons – one obsessive-compulsive, the other obnoxious-combative. "You've got quite a winning personality, haven't you? It must come in handy when you're shaking down insurance companies."

Brian's aura of sinister hostility expanded into seething anger, complete with the requisite bulging blood vessels, knitted eyebrows, and protruding chin. "You've got enough money for a cab, or are you going to take the T as usual?"

"You care? I'd rather walk home barefoot over guano and spit than get back in that car with you."

"About my car," Brian leaned forward with a grimace.

"What about it?"

"Come on. Loretta, cut the crap. We both recognized each other at Ted's party after I beat you douche bags out of a parking space. Tell me exactly what you bitches did to my car!"

"Nothing. Tell me that was the first time you ever pulled a fast one! I'll bet you'd have to count the people who *wouldn't* do something like that. Maybe one of your past victims got even. Who can stand a jerk like you? Look, since I have to get myself home, I think I'll just leave right now."

"Before you huff off, Loretta, just let me say one thing more. Want to know why I asked you out?"

"Why?" asked Loretta standing.

"I wanted to prove that a dog like you would be desperate enough to go out with a so-called jerk who gave you the finger. How right I was."

"You're not a so-called jerk; you're a full-blown one and a creep as well."

"Arf, arf. Woof, woof."

Loretta stormed out, her face now a tomato red. She showed up at Donna's an hour later, practically frothing at the mouth.

"Wait until Gina hears," Donna said. "What kind of pathetic loser goes to such lengths to make a point?"

"Loser! That's another name I should have called him! It's so hard to think when you're flustered." Loretta took a sip of water. "I'm not sure he asked me out just to embarrass me. I think he was trying to get me to admit that one of us vandalized his car, but I wouldn't take the bait."

"Why not? Wouldn't you want the satisfaction of telling him?"

"I didn't want to get stuck paying for a paint job or make trouble for Gina. She's agreed to deny it to Ted if he asks. Besides, I get more satisfaction standing up to him and knowing that he'll never know."

"That makes sense, especially since this is a guy who makes his living suing people. Well, at least you broke your dateless streak."

"Can I really call that a date?" asked Loretta with the hope that her unpleasant experience could at least count for something.

"Sure, why not? He asked you out for no worse a reason than a lot of men ask out women."

"That's good. Now at least I can say I haven't had a date since tonight instead of last November." Her previous date actually was last October, a miserable Halloween party that Loretta and her date, some clown dressed as a villain (or was it a villain dressed as a clown?), left five minutes after midnight, therefore qualifying in Loretta's mind as November. "Anyway, I wish it lasted at least until dessert. They had strawberry shortcake and peach pie with strawberry ice cream."

"I think I prefer warm peach pie with peach ice cream, if you can find it. It's scrumptious."

"Why do we always talk about food?" asked Loretta stuffing a Devil Dog into her mouth.

"Because our lives are so exciting."

"Speaking of excitement, how are things going with Geoffrey?"

"We worked together the past three nights. We're getting along well and have had more than a few laughs. Things were great for a while, but sometimes he's hard to figure. A couple of times he got calls on his cell phone that were probably Slink checking up on him. He'd walk out on the back porch and lower his voice, and then seem distracted or quiet the rest of the night. I'd say tonight he seemed the most off." The elated balloon that had Donna on her earlier high had slowly lost some air over the past couple days and lowered her to a level of more realistic hope.

***

Friday the store was rough. Not one, but two customers returned garments that they had worn on cruises, then found some self-induced problem like a split seam or tear to claim as a defect. As Donna fingered a cigarette burn on a stained long dress, she almost asked, "Did you roll around on the buffet table with it?" Loretta had waves of junior high and high school students, loose on summer vacation, annoy her and bother customers who were there to buy. Half of the lipstick testers were either worn to messy nubs or swiped. No fewer than three customers between them stormed off claiming they would get them fired.

On the way home a woman elbowed Donna in a race for a seat then barfed on Loretta's shoe. As the hot air absorbed the stink of vomit, a ten-minute breakdown in the tunnel enclosed them in clammy claustrophobia and, in a chain reaction, brought out the caged animal in three people, one of whom stomped on Loretta's puke-free foot and crashed into Donna's shoulder.

Donna walked through her apartment door in no mood. Geoffrey was sitting in the armchair with his feet on the coffee table and talking on his cell. His facial expression bothered her, and she suspected that Slink was the cause of his smirk. Perhaps, if he had bothered to look up and flash her one of his killer smiles, she might have shaken off her frustration.

"Hello," Donna said as she dropped her handbag and sat on the sofa, both hands on her knees. She paused a few seconds before she would look at him. "Geoffrey, can we establish some ground rules, if you don't mind? First, whenever you come here,

I'd like to know in advance. Second, you're in my apartment for hours, and yet I don't even know where you live. At the very least, I must have your phone number. If I ever get sick or for some reason don't want you here, I won't even know where to reach you."

"My aunt and uncle..."

"No, I want to call you directly. It's only fair."

"Okay. Remind me to give you my number before I leave."

Donna reached into a drawer of an end table and pulled out a blue notebook. "Here, write on this."

"O-o-o-kay." Geoffrey frowned and scribbled his number on the first page. He tossed the notebook onto the coffee table and tapped a pen on his thigh in agitation. "Okay," he finally said. "Let me set some rules of my own. First of all, we don't have to work here if you don't want to. You could come to my place on the waterfront downtown, but that would mean you'd be getting home awfully late. I'd think having me come here would be easier for you."

"That's true. I'd rather come home right after work."

Geoffrey nodded and then continued, "More importantly, I never share my ideas with anyone while I'm writing. It might sound a little paranoid, but I must protect myself and my name. I'm going to have to insist on keeping all copies of everything so there's less chance of anything falling into someone else's hands."

"Then how can I work by myself?"

"You'll work only with me. When do you have the time to work alone anyway? Besides, you'd end up going off in a different direction, and we'd waste more time trying to get back on track. I must be the one to direct the story."

"But what if I get a good idea in the middle of the night?"

"Then write it down or remember it. You won't need anything else to do that." Geoffrey made no attempt to sound beholden to her or patient.

"But if we're writing this book together, what's the difference? It's probably safer to keep everything here than for you to carry it around with you."

"Look, that's the way it's going to have to be. Let me worry about security. I keep everything, all notes, every scrap – and I don't want you to even discuss this with anyone."

"I've already told my friends Loretta and Tina."

"And who else?"

"No one."

"That's as far as it goes. Understand? Discuss this with no one. If anyone asks you what you do in your spare time, tell them you knit, roller blade, anything. Don't mention my name."

Donna thought a moment before answering. Geoffrey's offer of his place showed good faith on his part. Coming home on the train usually with Loretta made the trip safer and more enjoyable than travelling late and alone. As for his insistence on total control, possession, and secrecy, she'd just have to accept it. "All right," she finally said. "You keep everything, and I don't talk about the book. I'd like to continue working here. Besides, if you were able to work at home, you'd have done so in the first place."

Geoffrey smiled and the angry shadow lifted from his face. "Let's shake on it." He grabbed Donna's hand and kissed it. "Sorry for all the tension, but I feel better now that we understand each other."

"I'm sorry I went off like that. I had a rough day." Donna felt like a lump of jelly. All was forgiven with one affectionate gesture. It was fair enough – she'd get nowhere without him. He gave her his phone number and had offered his place. He was right that she should keep her mouth shut. As much as she trusted her friends, they could innocently say something to the wrong person and reveal the plot. So, what if he keeps everything? If Loretta or Tina insisted on reading their progress, she could honestly refuse without offense.

"It's so late. Have you had supper?" Donna asked to restore normalcy.

"I went downstairs an hour ago but go ahead. I'm just finishing an outline of some things I'd like you to work on." Geoffrey barely looked up when he spoke, but the tension was gone from his voice.

Donna made herself a turkey and roasted red pepper sandwich. She put together a plate of sliced fresh fruit and *pignoli* cookies and placed it on the coffee table. "Soda, iced tea, or coffee?"

"How about iced coffee, if it's decaf."

They sat in the comfort of an old long-married couple, who had no need to constantly fill the air with conversation or to apologize for every little disagreement. Their earlier confrontation had dissipated without analysis or residual hostility as it would in an atmosphere of unconditional love.

Donna read Geoffrey's to-do list for her: *Think of some red herrings, background sketches of some of the characters, a complete outline of the plot (what we have so far needs some work*).

Geoffrey checked his watch. "It's after ten and you've got work tomorrow." On the way out the door he gave Donna a pat on the cheek.

***

Neither Geoffrey nor Slink showed up on Monday. "Either they're together, or he's miffed about our rules discussion, or both," Donna said to Loretta.

"How 'bout none of the above?" Loretta answered. "Look at the creep I went out with the other night. At least Geoffrey called to say he'd be a no-show. You can't expect him to hang around every day like dusty drapes."

"He called and left a message that he'll be here tomorrow only because I insisted that he let me know."

"So, he's obedient."

"He's careful and clever, and I'm…gutless and gullible."

"No, just trusting, and he's probably unaware."

CHAPTER SIX
THESE LIPS DON'T LIE

The next evening Donna and Geoffrey decided to coordinate their meals. "I'll cook," Donna said, "unless it's something that has to get started before I get home."

"And it has no cilantro or hot pepper," Geoffrey said. "Maybe I'd better stick to barbecue and take-out. I'll get the wine."

"Fine, but not every night unless you need, er, want it. I'm not much of a drinker."

They sat on the porch and ate hamburgers that Geoffrey had barbecued and potato salad he had purchased from the deli.

"How much did you get done today?" Donna asked as she wiped a daub of ketchup from the corner of her mouth.

"Enough, after a later start than I had planned. My uncle needed a ride back from the mechanic's and on the way home we stopped at the supermarket. I put some stuff in your refrigerator and pantry so you're not always running to the store. How was your day?"

"Really good. At the rate I'm selling this year, I should make about fifteen percent more than last year, and that's not counting Christmas season."

"Which should start about next week."

Donna chuckled. "Oh, I think they'll wait until Halloween. Have the elves wear little witches' hats and Santa ride on a broom."

"Where do you like to celebrate the holidays?" Geoffrey asked.

"My brother and I usually visit our parents. Sometimes other relatives come over. What do you do?"

"I go to either New York or out west – California or Las Vegas, where I have some investment property. Last year I went to Portugal and Spain." Clearly "where do you celebrate the holidays?" did not mean "in whose house do you roast a turkey?"

For most of the evening they worked on the dining room table then moved into the living room for floppier seating. They sat side by side, discussing, questioning, agreeing and disagreeing.

"Why does he have to be like some superhero? Why can't he just be an ordinary guy?" Donna asked, wondering why so many main characters had to be handsome/beautiful, rich/successful, athletic/strong, smart/intelligent – in a word, perfect.

"Who'd want to read about an ugly, stupid weakling?" Geoffrey asked as if it were a given that anyone worth reading about had to be like himself. "Look, why do you think *Cinderella* has been such a popular story for generations?"

"Because Cinderella is beautiful, and her stepsisters are ugly, so the prince chooses her – the woman most little girls want to be someday. She's the belle of the ball, and he's a prince. Of course, they'd fall for each other."

"Well, sure. My point."

"I just hate stories that equate beauty with character. Fairytales like *Cinderella* and *Sleeping Beauty* do a lot of damage to young girls. 'The most bee-yoo-tee-ful girl in the land and the handsome prince lived happily ever after. Nauseating." Donna exaggerated a look of disgust.

"You talk like a hardcore feminist."

"No, I talk like a woman who must live this stupid fantasy-filled reality. The one story that didn't have the prince get goofy at the sight of the heroine was the original *Little Mermaid,* and even the ending of that one had to be changed for the animated movie."

"Donna, that proves my point – readers go for attractive protagonists who win. If you prefer *The Little Mermaid*'s original bittersweet ending, then you must like stories with pathos. Boohoo!"

"That's not what I'm getting at. Look," said Donna reaching into her TV cabinet, "here is the opera *La Cenerentola*, Rossini's version of *Cinderella* – the only one I can stomach. Her sisters are attractive, but vain and superficial, while Cinderella is kind and humble. The prince unknowingly first meets Cinderella when she's in rags, and he's somewhat attracted to her. Then he completely falls in love with her when she's all dressed up for the ball."

"See my point? He didn't really fall in love with her until she looked hot."

"Even still, the meaning of this story is that goodness wins."

"What about in real life?"

***

Over dinner the next evening they continued, without resolution, their discussion about the characters, until Geoffrey said, "Enough about them. Tell me about your friends."

"Well, you already know Tina downstairs. Then there's Loretta down the street. We've known each other since we were thirteen, and we both work at Floegel's, but in different departments. She's in cosmetics. In fact, you know her brother Vinnie – Amalfitano."

"Sure, I've known Vinnie a long time. We sometimes hang out together, especially now that I'm in the neighborhood so much. He's cool and easy to be around. Which sister is Loretta?"

"The middle one," Donna answered. "Three of the girls live in the family house. Loretta and Gina share an apartment, Connie and her husband another, and their parents are on the first floor. Amelia, the second youngest daughter, lives in Malden near her work."

"Yeah, Vinnie's folks own the green house on the corner down the street." Geoffrey, of course, already knew that. Donna nodded, remembering the night that she had dinner at Loretta's parents' and Vinnie popped in while Geoffrey waited in the car. "Invite her over." Geoffrey said with a shrug of apparent disinterest.

"When?"

"Now. I'd like to meet her."

Donna dialed Loretta's number and wondered why in the middle of dinner Geoffrey would have the impulse to meet her. "Hi, Loretta. Geoffrey and I were wondering if you'd like to come over tonight…Okay… See you in a bit." Donna hung up and sat back down. "She'll be over later."

"You know, I remember all of Vinnie's sisters growing up. Weren't they all brunettes?"

"Uh, yes," answered Donna, thinking that was a strange question.

***

Just as Donna and Geoffrey were about to start work, the doorbell rang and in walked the bronze bomber. Before Donna could introduce them, Loretta grabbed Geoffrey's hand. "Hiya, I'm Loretta, Vinnie's sister."

"Good to meet you again. I remember seeing you around years ago when Vinnie and I were kids, tearing up the neighborhood."

"And I remember you and your brother and sister. That gray paint you and Vinnie spilled on our walkway is still there." Loretta walked over to the dining room table and ran her thumbnail across the edge of a short stack of pages. "How's the book coming? Donna never tells me anything."

"Just fine," Geoffrey answered. "Donna is a big help. I've never written anything so fast. I'll finish in half the time."

“Good, good. She’s a smart girl. I couldn’t have gotten through school without her. She explained algebra better than our teacher.” Loretta sauntered over to the coffee table and stared down at the display of notebooks and printed papers. “Wow! You must be almost finished,” she said without any real way of knowing whether her assessment was true.

“How about a glass of wine?” Geoffrey asked. “It’s from one of my favorite vineyards in Napa. I think California wines are the best. Some friends and I are looking into buying a place in either Napa or Sonoma.” He poured the three of them a glass, and they sat in the living room, the women on the sofa like a couple of eighteenth-century maidens waiting to be asked to dance. Geoffrey eased himself into an armchair as though it were his throne.

“So, an Eastie kid makes good. Congratulations,” Loretta said.

“Thanks.”

“Where do you live now?”

“On the Waterfront,” Geoffrey answered after a slow sip.

“By that I assume you mean the downtown waterfront, not the East Boston waterfront by the tankers.”

“Correct.”

“I’d get out of here too if I could and go to some place quiet and less congested, with not so many people tripping over each other.”

“The airport doesn’t help, but the people here are the salt of the earth, don’t you think?”

“Some of them are more like the scum of the earth.” Loretta, realizing she was referring to Geoffrey’s aunt and uncle, immediately put her glass to her lips and took a gulp of wine. Angie and Primo were Geoffrey’s saving angels, so the remark probably passed over his head. “Mmm…good stuff.” Loretta spoke with a full mouth, and the wine dribbled down her chin.

She wiped it with the back of her hand, which she then smeared across the napkin on her lap. The insecurity that drove her usual sarcastic brand of humor began to overpower her wit and to slump her shoulders into a more passive posture.

"So, Loretta," Geoffrey said eyeing her closely, "I hear that a couple of your sisters and you live in your parents' house. Do they have your beautiful curly red hair?"

"Uh, no. Connie's hair is frosted, but I think she got a little carried away with the frosting, and she's gone more blondish now. And Gina's is a kind of chestnut, which, come to think of it, is reddish but dark brown with red highlights. Depends on the light she's in. It's also straighter and shorter than mine. Of course, mine is also from the bottle, but I've had it this color for so long I don't remember what I used to look like unless I look at an old photo of myself from high school. But even then, I had already started the process."

Geoffrey's lids lowered with a slight fatigue. "I see. You have a very nice garden. I think that's important for corner houses."

"Sure. They're on display from two sides. I'll pass the compliment on to my brother-in-law and Connie. They're the ones who take care of the yard."

"Do you ever do any yard work?" Geoffrey splashed more wine into Loretta's glass.

"Nah, not me. With these nails?" Then a light bulb went off. "Sometimes though, I like to tidy up, sweep the steps and sidewalk, and in the winter, I help shovel snow. That's one of the drawbacks of a corner house: two sidewalks." Loretta gave Donna a sideways glance.

Geoffrey turned to Donna, "I notice you've got a pretty healthy herb garden going on the back porch."

"I like to put some fresh basil into my tomato sauce," Donna answered. "I use fresh ingredients whenever I can."

Loretta spoke up, “Donna makes a wicked herb pizza crust. Have you ever had any of her bread or blueberry muffins? They’re better than anything from any bakery. What about that chicken with marjoram and oregano?”

“Uh, no,” Geoffrey answered.

“Probably because it’s too hot to use the oven. I bet if you ask her, she’ll make them for you. No wonder no one around here can lose any weight! Oh, and she makes the world’s best lasagna. I can eat the whole damn tray.”

Now we’ll just bore him to death with our culinary and horticultural skills. Donna’s mind swam. Here was a man who would be anywhere else if given a choice, and he’s sitting here with two *hausfrauen* who are ready to pull out their embroidery. Was that a yawn he just suppressed?

Loretta managed to stop the bleeding. “You two probably have a lot of work to do. Tell you what, I’ll just go sit on the porch and read a magazine. I’d go home, but Gina has Ted and a couple of other pukes over, and I don’t feel like seeing him right now after that date I had with his turd brother. I don’t want to get interrogated about whether I did a Jackson Pollock on his fancy-schmancy car. It was such a relief that you called.”

“Uh,” Geoffrey said choking back a laugh, “something tells me I don’t want to know about that.”

“You don’t. Like they say, ‘I’d have to kill you then’.”

After almost two hours of work, Geoffrey left.

“What do you think of him?” Donna whispered to Loretta.

“Handsome devil — with equal emphasis on both words. Did you pick up on the sly indirect reference to Slink?”

“In what way?”

Loretta raised her eyebrows while stating the obvious. “His questions about my red hair, my house and whether I do yard work.”

"He already knew your house because he knows Vinnie, but he did ask before you came over if all the girls in your family are brunettes."

"As most people of Italian descent are. Why would he ask those questions unless Slink told him that a redhead swept her earring out from under a bush?"

"At the edge of your yard – I'm so dense!"

"No, just infatuated. You couldn't see what he was getting at?"

"Maybe. It started to register, and I brushed it off." Donna sighed, "I'd hate to think that he wanted to meet you just to confirm you were the one who found the earring."

"And that I saw the designer diva cutting across everyone's backyards." Loretta continued, "Speaking of which, do you ever notice anything weird about *him*, not just his taste in douchey-looking women?"

"Not really, why?"

"Well, while I was stuck listening to the psycho-babbling bores that Gina had over, one of them noticed Geoffrey's book, *Lies Beneath the Stares*, on an end table. That got them talking about the way that Geoffrey treats women in his books, even the ones the main character is in love with. One called him a misogynist pig, another said he might not even realize that he must have a low opinion of women, and that got them discussing the sex scenes. I know myself that I found them a bit much and wondered about him too."

Donna gulped. "I've winced at them also and know that I'll be embarrassed if he wants to put any in our book, but I figured he's giving his readers what they must want. Just because some of his characters behave like jerks, that doesn't make him one too."

"True. It's just fiction, after all."

***

Next morning Donna met Geoffrey on the stairs as she was leaving for work. “I’ll be waiting for you,” he said.

True to his promise, Geoffrey was there with a big smile when Donna got home. “I put several bottles of wine in your pantry and a couple of whites in your refrigerator, and I ran your dishwasher,” he said. “Something smells good.”

“Tina gave me some sausage with peppers, potatoes, and onions. I brought home some Italian bread, prosciutto, provolone, and oil cured olives.”

“Actually, I meant you. Is that a new perfume?”

“Yes, by Lily Floret. Loretta sprayed some on me before we left work. It’s supposed to be a light summer scent, although I think it made someone on the train sneeze.”

They sat at the kitchen table and washed the heavy meal down with chianti and ice water. “Do you believe how much we ate?” Geoffrey asked. “This should hold me all weekend. Where’s the vomitorium? I don’t eat half as much when I’m alone.”

“I guess it’s because I’m a big eater.”

“No, you’re not,” said Geoffrey thinking that Donna might have taken his remark as an insult. “I just don’t get much home cooking – I mean aside from my aunt. Besides, you have a domestic side – a great interest in food.”

“Well, I didn’t get this way looking at it.”

An hour of intense brainstorming produced an energetic, frenetic climax to the story. “We’ve got the beginning where Johnson is murdered while he’s posing as Andrews. Then we jump almost to the ending and have Andrews reappear as himself for a showdown with the Maxim gang,” Donna said. “We then slide right to the end, but we’ll need to fill in a lot of holes in between.”

Geoffrey responded, “At least by having a good ending, we’ve got something to write towards.”

While they took a break Donna emptied her dishwasher. Something on one of the glasses caught her attention. It was a lipstick stain – a tomato red – not a shade she or any recent guests wore. Her hand shook, and she almost dropped the glass. Geoffrey was in the living room, out of view. Donna steadied the glass with her other hand and took a closer look. The lips that made the stain appeared fuller than hers or possibly Loretta's as well. Lipstick is probably the most frequently reapplied cosmetic, more so than powder. Eating and drinking, and for many women merely talking, rub off even some brands that purport to last all day. The indelible quality women desire in their lipstick is often proven on the lip of a glass or cup rather than on the lip of their mouth. Even a run through a dishwasher might remove only an immeasurable layer of color, as apparently happened in this case for the stain maintained a waxy gleam.

Donna tried to mentally calculate the glasses she used since she last ran the dishwasher. Loretta was here when? She usually wore her Sophia color anyway. The imprint on the glass was redder and darker. No wonder the bum ran the dishwasher when he usually leaves dirty dishes in the sink. Donna slipped the glass behind the others on the shelf so she could show it to Loretta later. She braced herself and put out of her mind the thought that Slink may have deliberately left the imprint after the dishes were washed. "All that salty food made me thirsty," she called out to Geoffrey. "I'll get us something else to drink."

Donna reached into the cabinet for two glasses and was tempted to give Geoffrey the lipstick-stained one to see his reaction. "The significance will be lost on him," she thought. "He'll just think I'm a slob."

To cover her anxiety, Donna became very chatty. "I was thinking, we're revealing too soon that the Andrews character is deliberately letting Johnson steal his identity. It might add an additional twist later if we at first make it seem as though Andrews is a real ID theft victim."

"Great," Geoffrey said. "That way Andrews will be a more sympathetic character until it's learned he let an innocent, well not so innocent, man be murdered."

"Also," added Donna, "After Johnson is killed, we could have Andrews get a little reckless, as though he's tempting the killers to find out he's still alive. And we might even have him assume Johnson's identity for a while, just for spite."

"Hold on a second while I get this down." Geoffrey looked up when he was ready for more.

Donna continued. "Before his faked death, Andrews should have had a girlfriend. She doesn't find out about Andrews alleged death until after Johnson is buried or cremated. That way she never sees the body to identify it as not being his."

"Okay. Go on."

"Although Andrews knows they can never be together again, he gets jealous at the thought that she may move on with her life and find someone else. He gets close enough to spy on her."

"And we should show some of their past relationship, before he supposedly dies. That way we can spice it up."

Donna smiled, more because she recalled Loretta's remark about the ubiquitous sex scenes in Geoffrey's books, and she wondered how weird writing *that* together would be. She swallowed the laugh that was ready to burst, and she picked up the speed. "Andrews, of course, needs a source of income, which he gets several ways. While he assumed Johnson's ID, he cleans out Johnson's accounts. Then he steals the identity of another dead man who was his age. He's able to live with this alias until his lies start to catch up with him and he has to move on."

"Hey, come up for air."

"Let's see. Andrews also goes after the hoard of the people who thought they killed him. And of course, he already has the stolen art. Come to think of it, I don't think the art is a good idea."

"Why not?" Geoffrey asked. Art theft had been central to the plot of his original story, which Donna had gradually dominated, page by page, until only anemic vestiges of Geoffrey's creation survived.

"Because art is too easy to trace – if you sell a Van Gogh or something, it draws attention. We need something less identifiable and easier to transport, like gold or diamonds."

"I see. You're right."

"Another thing, the girlfriend could be a married woman. That way she can't be too public about trying to find out how he, Johnson posing as Andrews, was killed. It also could explain why she never went to his wake. She becomes an unanticipated complication for Andrews."

"But, aside from his jealousy, why would we keep the girlfriend around after Andrews supposedly died, unless to have them back together in the end?"

"Because," said Donna, "she knows that Andrews had stolen some gold or diamonds which she wants and goes after. This of course, puts her in danger with Johnson's killers, who are much too dangerous for her to handle. Andrews has enough feelings for her that at some point he is forced out to protect her. I suppose even if he doesn't love her, he'd feel some obligation for having been the accidental cause of her involvement in a risky situation."

"But if she's after the loot, why would Andrews risk everything trying to protect her? Isn't that a kind of betrayal on her part?" Geoffrey asked.

"Well, she's already betrayed her husband, but not Andrews, really. After all, she, let's call her Cynthia, thinks that Andrews has been killed, so she can't betray a dead man. Andrews hopes that one day he can reveal himself to her. But of course, since she's an adulteress, she can't come out on top in the end."

Geoffrey, who had been busily taking notes, stopped. "What? Why not? Get with the real world."

"But she's not a very sympathetic character."

"Why, because she cheats on her husband? Maybe she has good reason. Donna, you're so old-fashioned."

"Then maybe she's not married."

"No. I think it's better that she is married for the reason you said earlier about why she didn't go to the wake. It makes her story more complicated," Geoffrey said. "Also, you don't know whose side she's really on."

"Her own, of course."

"Because she's unfaithful? So, what! Look, this point is slowing us down. Get with it! I mean it's just a story, and it doesn't have to reflect any personal morality." Geoffrey positioned himself to continue his note taking and made no apology for his intense manner. "Okay. Continue."

"Cynthia, thinking Andrews is dead, goes for the gold/diamonds/money. Andrews keeps tabs on her, at a distance of course, and hopes she gets the loot, so they can 'live happily ever after' together, if that's the way you want it. To get the goods though, she must get close to the killers."

"True. Risky but true."

Donna fixed Geoffrey with a stare. "Suppose that sometime in the past Andrews had given Cynthia some jewelry, earrings say, custom-made so that they are one of a kind. One day he sneaks into the house of one of the killers to look for the loot, and he finds one of Cynthia's earrings in the killer's bedroom."

Geoffrey's looked up. "And how," he said with a dry mouth, "does that help the story?"

"Since he's had no direct contact with Cynthia, he doesn't know what she's up to. Was she in the bedroom snooping? If so, he must hide the earring because it would give her away. On the other hand, Cynthia may be having an affair with the killer – the man who supposedly murdered him. So, Andrews doesn't know what to think. If he takes the earring, and she knows that she left it there, when she returns to look for it, she – and possibly the killer – will wonder how it disappeared. Whose side is she on? If she knew that Andrews was still alive, what would she do? Has she completely gone over to the killer? Was she with him all along? Is she just out for herself? It adds another complication."

"I see."

Donna continued. "The question is: does Andrews really know Cynthia? Can he trust her completely?"

"She sounds like a complicated woman," Geoffrey said. "What do you think she'll do?"

"We'll have to let her show us as we go along, although you already know what I think of her. She's immoral, unfaithful, greedy, and self-centered."

Geoffrey's expressionless face was a mask that hid layers of thought. He finished his notes, scanned them for a moment, then spoke. "Wow, that was a mouthful, but I think I got it all down. Hmm…tomorrow is Friday. You're working late tomorrow and I… I'll see you on Monday." Geoffrey packed up his things.

Donna walked Geoffrey to the door. Her mind was swimming. Had she gone too far with the custom-made earring scenario? As she reached for the doorknob, Geoffrey put his free hand over hers and set his case down. "Donna," he whispered. Then he kissed her. "I, uh, better go," he said with a hint of reluctance. Normally with less guarded women, this tactic worked.

After he left, Donna stood with her hand over her chest to hold back her gasping breath.

***

She went to the kitchen to finish loading the dirty dinner dishes into the dishwasher and then dialed Loretta's. "Loretta, did I wake you up? …Good. This might seem crazy, but can you do me a favor? … Grab your lipsticks, all of them, and come over before work tomorrow morning." She took the lipstick-stained glass from the shelf and stared at it as if the lips that were impressed on the rim would talk to her and explain everything she wanted to know.

***

At 6:18 the next morning, Loretta arrived showered and dressed, but bare faced with hair pinned back in preparation for her multi-layered make-up troweling. Although her skin was smooth, but for some embossed creases from her rumpled pillow and a few acne scars, it was uneven in color, with dark undereye circles. Her bone structure, however, was striking with the strong nose and high cheekbones one imagined were stolen from an ancient Greek or Roman statue. "Coffee, I need coffee," she said as she walked with an exaggerated stagger over to the freshly brewed pot.

Donna lined up several clean glasses. Loretta and she, with the meticulousness of research scientists, applied each of their lipsticks and imprinted them on the rims of the glasses. Loretta put on her usual blend, then each of the three colors separately, and in different combinations. Donna had seven shades of lipstick, five of them cool colors ranging from light pink to berry, coral and a pale peach.

"Now," Donna said, "let's compare them to the mystery glass."

Loretta held the mystery glass up to the light from the kitchen window. "Hmm.

Puffy. Pouty."

"And what do you think of the color comparison — compared to all of ours? Pretty red, no?"

"Tina wears red lipstick, more of a pinkish red, but she's practically lipless. This stain, even though it's been in the dishwasher, is a warmer, darker red than any of ours. You know, this looks almost freshly applied, as though it never went through a washing."

"I noticed the same thing, but I opened the dishwasher door without checking the indicator light because I already knew the dishes were clean," Donna said with a shrug. "Now I'll put these glasses in the dishwasher and see how that alters the color and size of each stain."

"If I were you, I'd compare them in both artificial and natural light. You'll see the subtle differences better."

***

The experiment only proved what Donna already knew: nothing matched the mystery stain.

***

"Cheer up," Loretta said as they walked home. "What about Angie? I think she's had lip augmentation injections from time to time. She might have had a drink in your apartment. She usually wears hot pink and fuchsia shades, but she might have that color. After all, she's *so* fashionable. Even if it was Slink, there still may be an innocent explanation for who she is."

Donna dropped off some groceries at Tina's and stopped in for a glass of lemonade. She told Tina about the lipstick on the glass. "If he's using my apartment as a secret getaway with another woman, I won't stand for it." Donna shook her head in disgusted determination. "Why don't those two skeeves use my toothbrush while they're at it?"

"Tell you what," Tina said. "I'll keep a close watch, and if you don't mind, I'll call Maura behind us and have her watch out for Slink and her car, but I won't involve you. Maura won't say anything because she can't stand Angie. She's talking about putting her house up for sale, in fact."

***

Next morning was hellishly hot and humid, so Donna headed for Shay's Beach and pulled into the first available parking space. Shays (aka Constitution Beach) was more of an inlet than an open ocean. For many years, a yacht club separated the "polluted" boat side of the beach from the other section where people swam, often dodging dead jellyfish. Children playing in the sand could only dig down about a foot and a half before they hit gray clay. The horizon was blocked by the specter of Logan Airport, which, over the years, had nibbled its way into East Boston.

With her pants rolled up, she walked barefoot along the edge of the water and tried to clear her head…Ridiculous and obsessive…Our relationship should be kept professional…Just an impulsive kiss…What could he see in someone like me anyway? Geoffrey has every right to have a girlfriend. He just has no right to have one in my apartment…On the other hand, it might be just a casual friendship that she hopes will develop into something else. …Still, I don't like competing with another woman even if their relationship isn't serious. …But what if…The hot sun beating on and the anxiety rattling inside her head slowed her walk to more of a stagger.

"Ick!" A dead jellyfish slapped against her ankle. She kicked it off like a limp tortilla. Four more steps and another one lapped her other foot. Donna jumped out of the water. *Brrr.*

Donna went back to her car and caught a glimpse of her sad eyes in the rear-view mirror. "You're becoming a whiny wimp," she told herself. "From now on you're going to be positive and strong. Get a grip on reality. There's only one reason he spends any time with you – he has no choice. Find yourself a different source of comfort and one that isn't made of chocolate."

Donna's body and spirit needed renovation, so she got to work on both. For the rest of the weekend, she refused to entertain any self-defeating, negative thoughts. Nothing fattening passed her lips, not so much as a bite of a cookie or a spoonful of ice cream.

***

After work on Monday, Donna stopped off at the local market and picked up some groceries for Tina and herself. Everything Donna bought was fresh, unprocessed and healthy.

"Come in, I've got something for you," Tina waved Donna inside. "Shut the door. Primo is on his way out," she whispered. "Believe it or not, I made gnocchi from scratch today. I haven't done that in a long time." Tina's dining room and kitchen tables were covered with tablecloths upon which lay small potato and flour pillows.

In a low voice Tina said, "As far as I know she didn't come today. He's up there, but I listened and looked out any time I heard an entrance door open. It takes me a while to get from one side of the house to another, but the only person to go in and out, other than the two beauts upstairs and him, was the UPS man."

She wouldn't have to come today if they spent the weekend together, the annoying voice of self-doubt inside her head said. Donna shut it down and spoke out with only a slightly stronger attitude. "I don't care what they do as long as they don't do it in my apartment."

"Atta girl."

Donna carried a container of gnocchi upstairs and opened her door with complete aplomb. She could handle him. But Geoffrey made one mistake – he smiled. Donna excused herself, put the gnocchi in the refrigerator, went into the bedroom and closed the door. A few deep breaths and concentration brought her back to her senses, or what was left of them.

Donna breezed into the living room. “Where are we?” she said looking down at the work spread out on the coffee table. She sat next to Geoffrey on the sofa.

“Well, I took the notes from our last meeting and” – Geoffrey hesitated, then said, “Donna, I’m sorry. I hope you weren’t offended when I kissed you the other night. I just got carried away. It won’t happen again, unless you want it to.”

Donna simply smiled down at the paper she was holding. Her heart and brain would have to give their struggle a rest until she knew whether he was sincere. He had the power to hurt her.

They worked on strengthening the plot and doing bios of the characters. Donna controlled the discussion and gently corrected Geoffrey when he suggested something he thought was a new idea: having Johnson originally take Andrews’ identity in an act of self-sacrifice because he knew that Andrews had a price on his head. “Oh, like Sydney Carton in *A Tale of Two Cities,*” Donna said.

Geoffrey chuckled and shook his head. “I guess that’s another not so original idea.”

“‘There’s nothing new under the sun’. It might be kind of late to make Johnson a nice guy, anyway. Besides, then Andrews would be even more of a creep by comparison.”

“You think he’s a creep?” Geoffrey was surprised that Donna and he saw the hero Andrews so differently.

“Look at him! He’s a thief and a manipulator, who lets someone get killed in his place. Sure, he’s a hero, but one who’s dishonest and untrustworthy.” Donna quickly thought of possible alternatives to make Andrews a more sympathetic character. “We either have to make some changes in his past behavior, but that would take a lot of rewriting, or, we can add some true, greater heroism – some redemptive act – to balance the damage he’s already done.”

"Well, let's do it," Geoffrey said. "If you see him that way, then a lot of other readers will too. I must admit, I thought he was a really cool guy."

They made the villains nastier and introduced a group of truly evil thugs so that Andrews, now justifiably a dirty street fighter, could keep the reader on his side. A few technical points about criminal behavior did not ring authentic, so Geoffrey decided he would consult a friend who had first-hand experience with such low-life creeps.

When it was time to leave, Geoffrey and Donna stood at the door and started to giggle. The giggles turned into a clumsy but warm kiss. Geoffrey let it go at that. His instincts about women were fairly accurate, and he sensed that Donna was more cautious and reluctant than most. One misstep could jeopardize their collaboration and agreement, and he knew that he would need her help and cooperation until almost the end. "See ya tomorrow," he said with the certainty of a man who had her under his control. He left with one last quick smile.

Donna pressed an ear to her door to listen to his footsteps, and when she heard the soft thud of the front door close, she ran to the window to wait for his car to back out of the driveway and to watch it drive away. She felt both foolish and happy at the same time, like a high school student having an impossible crush on her twenty-four-year-old American history teacher.

The improbability of their situation was not lost on Donna, yet flirting aside, they seemed to have a connection and affection for each other, at least. He did laugh quite a bit for someone who supposedly had been under a lot of stress, and more than one time she had caught him smiling at her, not in the devious way that someone who had pulled off a scam might, but in a manner usually associated with an expression of fondness. Was it possible that a man, who could have anything he wanted, might not need a trophy to prove himself to anyone? Her common sense and emotions debated each other for a restless two hours before she admitted to herself that she probably was in love.

CHAPTER SEVEN
A NOT SO ORDINARY DAY

Tuesday morning Loretta left for work three hours before Donna, whose schedule on her refrigerator showed her working until closing. Donna had hoped that Geoffrey would show up before she left her apartment, but as she passed the Infantos' door she could hear him talking to Primo, who answered his question about what time Angie, and he were leaving. On the train, she thought only about one thing: Geoffrey and the unlikely possibility that, despite her drawbacks, she might have a chance with him. She arrived at Floegel's, still with that one question teasing her emotions.

"What are you doing here?" asked Stacey Walsh. Just as the realization dawned another coworker said, "Happy birthday Donna!"

"I can't believe I forgot my own birthday!" Donna was so distracted by Mr. Smiley Face that she totally forgot that she had traded hours with Stacey and had today off. Nice way to start your birthday – riding the grimy subway – but spending the rest of the day with Geoffrey would make up for the wasted morning. All the way home on the nearly empty train, anticipation of a truly happy birthday grew. "How did I forget my own birthday? Easy! I had something better to look forward to," she thought, suppressing an urge to laugh. Donna stared out the window, but the flashes of subway tunnels and East Boston scenery blurred past her for she was in her own blissful excitement.

As Donna's train pulled into the station, she noticed Primo and Angie, absorbed in their own cloud of negativity, standing on the opposite platform. With any luck, they'd stay out all day and forget where they live. She quickly exited the station before her train pulled out, and then she walked home at a fast pace, stopping only to pick up a bottle of sparkling wine.

"I hope Geoffrey is upstairs already. This will be our first whole afternoon together – and on my birthday! I'll surprise him," she smiled to herself. Donna quietly opened the front door to the house and slipped off her shoes to tiptoe up the stairs. Before she got even a fourth of the way up to the second-floor landing, she froze with an exhalation caught in her throat.

A female voice said, "I didn't hear anything. Loosen up. When are Angie and Primo coming back?"

"Not for a few hours. They said it was okay to use the guest room," said a low voice that sounded like Geoffrey.

"Why not your little girlfriend's? We could use the kitchen table or desk as a start. I've got some good stuff I'd wish you'd try."

"What?" thought Donna. "Is he in fact writing with someone else? Perhaps he really does have an assistant. And what's with the 'little girlfriend'?"

"No," Geoffrey said. "Let's not, after the remark she made about the 'woman with the lost custom-made earring'."

"I told you that copper-topped pal of hers, who found my earring, must have told her about me. Who cares what those two fat-assed frumps think? Forget all that. Why don't we just start out here and see where that takes us?"

"Someone might catch us," Geoffrey said.

"Yeah, someone just might – the old bag downstairs?"

Donna gripped the railing.

Geoffrey answered, "She can't climb the stairs very well."

"Then she'll just have to listen."

By now, from the tone of their voices, it was clear that they weren't about to work on any book. The sounds coming from above her drowned out Donna's anxious gasps. She slid down onto a stair and sat with a hand over her mouth to muffle the scream that was fighting to come out. A wave of nausea passed over her as the physical and vocal activity increased above. Donna put her head between her knees. All she'd need now is to vomit and spoil their fun.

The door to the Infantos' apartment opened and slammed shut as though pounded by a padded battering-ram. The question that for weeks had floated through a cloud of wishful and magical thinking was now answered. With the lifting of the haze, the clarity of reality slapped Donna across her numb face. *Fool! What were you thinking? Did you ever seriously believe the fairy tale you had written for yourself? You were just a situation that had to be managed.*

Donna held onto the railing to steady herself, then staggered out the front door. When she put her shoes back on, a dizzying swirl forced her to sit on the top step of the porch. After fitful gulps of fresh air, Donna wiped her face with a tissue and reentered the house. She climbed the stairs defying the exhibitionists to hold their ground. Only muffled sounds emanated from within the second-floor apartment. Yes, her question was finally answered in a way that made her wonder why she had ever asked it in the first place. *Of course, she's what you suspected and feared she was! Whatever made you think otherwise? An earring in your bedroom, a lipstick stain on one of your glasses, witnesses who saw her – how thick can you get? Did you allow yourself to be duped to evade any guilt for having feelings for someone who might be taken?*

Donna entered her apartment. The door, naturally, was unlocked. "This really galls me. Any psycho could walk in here," Donna thought. "First, he invades my privacy; now he jeopardizes my security. We'd better finish this damn book fast," she muttered as she locked and chained the door. She put the sparkling wine in the refrigerator then flopped on her bed and cried silently but profusely until she almost choked from a flood of fatigue. “Oh, no you don’t!” she said as she forced herself up before getting too comfortable in her misery. It would be all too easy to sleep away the rest of her birthday in depressed exhaustion. *Better you know the truth. You’ve been saved from a lot more sadness than you’re feeling now.*

She washed her face and rinsed it with cold water. “No, no, no!” She simultaneously patted each cheek, almost slapping them on the last “no.” *“Put it off until tomorrow! Don’t you dare make this day any worse than it already is!”*

To celebrate her birthday Donna picked out summery turquoise slacks, not her usual dark bottom. She held a necklace of coral nuggets and another of yellow Venetian glass beads against the turquoise; the yellow looked more cheerful. A pair of low-heeled gold sandals would complete the outfit. She changed her clothes, reapplied her makeup, brushed out her hair and let it hang.

Before Donna left her apartment, she clicked on the light over the kitchen sink and a nightlight in the entrance so she wouldn’t come home to a dark house, even though the summer daylight would last longer than anything she’d likely do today. “Should I lock the door, or shouldn’t I? What a stupid question! As far as I’m supposed to know, he’s not even here.”

A Mona Lisa-like smile spread over her lips as she made her way downstairs. Surprise, surprise, the Infantos’ door opened and out stepped Geoffrey, looking a teensy bit rumpled and abashed. “Donna, how long have you been home?” he asked with an innocent grin.

“All day,” she wanted to say to see his reaction. She quickly calculated how long she had been inside her apartment. “Oh, about thirty, forty minutes or so.” Donna watched his frozen expression. *Close call, eh?*

"I see you're headed out," Geoffrey said. "Didn't you go to work earlier?"

"Yes, and yes. It's my birthday, so I got the day off," answered Donna fighting a sudden urge to cry. "I'll see you when you come again."

"Too bad. You look very nice. Really nice."

Nice try. "I noticed," she said, "that my door was unlocked, and you weren't inside. I'd like it to be locked if no one is there. Last week there was a break-in down the street."

"I'm sorry. I've been working in this apartment because they've gone out. My aunt unlocked it before she left, and I never got up there."

"Oh, you must have been *so absorbed* in your work," she said, looking at her watch. "I'd better go."

"What's the rush? I have to leave in a couple of hours. It's going to be a whole day until I see you again."

He's stalling me. Madame Bovary must be sneaking out of the back alleyway. Donna slung her bag over her shoulder and broke past him. "As I said, it's my birthday, and I'm going *out*. See ya," she said then, in a mischievous gesture, blew him a kiss.

Okay. Where is she? They must have heard Donna bustling around upstairs. Slink or Sandra, as Geoffrey had called her, could have left while Donna was getting ready, but probably not. *No, I'll bet she sneaked out the back when Geoffrey stopped me coming down the front stairs. Depending on where she parked, she's either still walking to her car, or she's already driven off.*"

Donna glanced up and down the street and opened her car door. The heat of an oven poured out from the light blue subcompact, but she couldn't spare a second to let it cool. "I think I'll take a little spin around the block." She turned the corner at Loretta's and then the corner of the house behind and drove slowly down the street. There was Sandra, just getting into the car Loretta had described. Pretty, thin, of course.

The silver Jaguar shot out of its parking space. If it were possible for a car to strut with its nose in the air, this one did.

"Now where do I go?" Donna asked herself, realizing that she ran out with no plans because of the distraction. In reality, her birthday was just another day and now more than half over, but it was still a reason to celebrate. Donna pulled over and dug out her cell phone. "Hello Tina. It's Donna. I was hoping you'd be home so we could drive up to Maine for lobster or something. See you later maybe." Where to go? Someplace close, but not too close. She headed alone toward Swampscott and Marblehead.

Donna found a restaurant near the water. After studying the menu, she surprised herself by ordering a salad instead of a fisherman's platter. She looked around the room.

A man sitting at a nearby table somehow reminded her of someone she knew. The unruly hair, sculpted cheekbones, aquiline nose, and sad eyes should have created a face that was too interesting to forget. Years of working with the public, however, made everyone look familiar. The man rose. "Donna? Do you know who I am?" he said with a voice she almost recognized.

"I think so, but I'm not sure from where."

"I'm Tom Ambrose. We've met at Floegel's."

Donna leaned back. "Oh Tom, I'm sorry. You know if I see someone I don't know well in a different place, I uh …"

"Don't readily recognize them," Tom smiled. "May I join you?"

"Sure."

"You seem a little down. What's wrong? Man problems?"

“Wha…Why?” Donna thought she had been doing a good job keeping her emotions in check, but she was worn out enough to unload, and Tom provided an impartial ear. “Well yes, in a way, although it’s not someone I am or could ever be involved with.”

“Then how do you mean?”

“There is this fellow, a writer, who because of a sticky situation, allowed me to help him with his next book.” The words were out of her mouth before she realized it. Tough! Besides, she didn’t specify how she was helping Geoffrey. She could be sharpening his pencils for him or changing his printer ink. Furthermore, she didn’t identify Geoffrey by name, so she wasn’t breaking any promise she made to him. “His aunt and uncle are my landlords, and while I was at work, they would let him use my apartment without my knowledge or permission. Before I found out what was going on, I’d come home and find things out of place or soiled, a strange earring in my bedroom, and doors unlocked when I was certain I had locked them.”

“Nervy of them.”

“Anyway, I’ve taken a few writing classes and was trying to write a book of my own. One day I came home unexpectedly and found that Ge – George had been writing in my kitchen and had found my story. There was a huge scene. He explained he needed a quiet place to work and meant no harm. After a while we made a kind of truce. I’m a total novice with almost no chance of getting published so he agreed to let me work with him.”

“He agreed? What a sport.”

Donna did not mention that Geoffrey had been *copying* her book. She had made him look dishonest enough without calling him a plagiarizer. Her near slip of his name made her wish she had used a pronoun or something like “Bob” to refer to him and hadn’t mentioned her book at all.

"Ge…George, continued coming to my apartment while I was at work. At night I'd come home, and we'd work together. We got along very well, I thought, but I had no realistic expectation of anything other than a professional relationship."

"Why not?"

"Tom, I have no delusions about myself, but if someone, even someone like him, shows an interest in me, I assume they're being sincere. He either led me on, or I let myself be led on. Luckily, I found out today, in fact, that he was just playing me for a fool."

"What happened?"

"This morning, I went to work, forgetting it was my birthday and that I had the day off, if you can believe it. George, of course, was not expecting me for hours, so I thought I'd surprise him."

"Something tells me you were the one who got the surprise."

Donna nodded. "I came in the front door quietly so I could sneak up the stairs. Before I could climb more than a couple of steps, I heard George and a woman on the landing or stairs above me. They were talking about the possibility of using my desk again or his uncle's spare room, so I naturally thought they were working together. She referred to me as his 'little girlfriend' and said she thought they were arousing my suspicion. Well, they started their 'work' out in the hall with a lot of heavy breathing. They, or rather she, seemed to enjoy the idea that they might get caught to the point that I thought she might have exaggerated all her moans."

"That sounds like Sandra."

"How did you…? That's what he called her!" Donna almost shrieked.

"Sandra LeRoi Young. Even though it's pronounced LeRoy′, some people call her Le′roy behind her back because she's gutsier than most men. I simply call her SLY, because that's what she is. And George must be Geoffrey Imperato."

"You know them both?" Donna's face and neck flushed.

"Sandra and I are at the same university. She's in the English department, and I have a dual appointment in medicine and computer science, though I also have another occupation. Geoffrey and I met when he once interviewed me. We kept in touch since then and became friends."

"But Tom, I only mentioned Geoffrey by his real name, George. There are so many writers in Boston. How could you possibly know that I was talking about the two of them?"

"Because of something Sandra told me when we last ran into each other."

"What did she say?"

"Oh, that she suspected Geoff was involved with a Floegel's saleswoman from East Boston named Donna. She said where you worked and—"

"Did she say I was fat?"

"She described your hair—"

"But did she call me fat?"

"She was obviously jealous."

"Then she *did* call me fat!"

"Donna, you have a nice figure."

"Yah, Rubenesque."

"Look, she's a nasty, self-centered woman. You're a threat. She sees someone else replacing her."

"Me? There was nothing going on between Geoffrey and me, just some brief silly flirting."

"Apparently she didn't think so."

"Just because we spent a lot of time together? Geoffrey had to tell her what we were doing." Donna's curiosity about the mystery woman was suddenly greater than her need to know if Sandra's suspicions had any foundation. "What's she like?"

"Self-absorbed, conceited, superficial, materialistic – you know the type. She came from some money and married more when she took a fifty-year-old fool having a mid-life crisis from his wife and kids. Now, Geoff and she are carrying on behind the back of her most recent sucker."

"Who is her husband?"

"Husband-to-be. He inherited most of what he's got but made some good investments so naturally he's just Sandra's type. He travels a lot, so Sandra has enough time to do whatever she wants. She has an excuse not to travel with Rich, her sucker, because this summer she's teaching a class or two at a community college on the North Shore."

"And I live in East Boston on the same side of the bridge and tunnel. She must come on the days she teaches. Neighbors have seen her skulking around. I even saw her today. When I left from the front of the house, she must have sneaked out the back. I drove past her as she was getting into her car."

"What did you think of her?" Tom asked with a smirk.

"She does have that up-to-the-minute fashion cookie cutter look. There was something imperious, supercilious, about her as though she could do whatever she likes and get away with it. I hope I never get her as a customer."

"At the university she's done things that should have had her drop-kicked to Cleveland. She is said to have a student sex sofa or a class credit couch. I've heard her and others have seen her in action. She, I'm sure, would argue they're consenting adults."

"If she's such a puttana, I hope everyone uses industrial-strength condoms. What about Geoffrey? Is he just another casual fling?"

Tom hesitated long enough for Donna to know his response even before he spoke. "He acts as though he's in a monogamous relationship, if you ignore the fact that she's engaged to someone else. His justification is that he knew her before Rich.

Since Sandra met Geoff – and got engaged to Rich - she supposedly toned down her activities with everyone else, so I guess she gets credit for that."

"I still don't know why she should see me as a threat. She's engaged to someone else. At some point she'd have to let go of Geoffrey."

"She wants what she wants and doesn't think ahead or about any consequences. It's a good idea to stay out of her way, if you can. Donna, if you need to call me about anything, here's my phone number," said Tom, handing Donna a business card, which had telephone numbers for his university office and a business called Factotum Inc.

Donna put the card in her purse and grabbed her pen to give Tom her number. She stopped. What did she know about him? They met here by accident, and he asked to join her at her table. That was enough.

"You know Tom, I promised Geoffrey that I wouldn't talk with anyone about our collaboration, but I was so upset and felt so used, that I couldn't help it. It all came tumbling out before I could stop myself. I feel terrible now. Please don't tell anyone. It could hurt his career. Please, I'm so sorry."

"You didn't tell me Geoff's name. I already knew who he was because Sandra had told me about you and that you were working with Geoff. Don't worry about it. You have my word. I won't tell anyone."

As Donna and Tom got up to leave the restaurant she said, "Thank you so much, Tom. I thought this day was going to be a waste, but you made it a happy one. It was such a wonderful coincidence to run into you today of all days."

"Yes, it was. We were meant to meet each other," Tom smiled and patted her on the shoulder. "I'll see you around sometime."

Donna drove home to her empty apartment in a better mood. Her mother, despite all her annoyances, had a present delivered. The priority mailer contained a small box wrapped in pinwheel-printed paper and tiny blue bows. She opened it to find a ruby ring, which she slipped, rather pushed onto her finger. "Another five pounds and it should be no problem," Donna thought with a slight dread that it may have to be cut off. She called her parents to thank them and had a pleasant conversation devoid of the usual frustration and complaining.

The day had been full of some sad realities. A note with a smiley face and "See you tomorrow" had been slipped under her door. Geoffrey had given her a full day before she had to face him.

After eating two pounds of ravioli, Donna, Loretta, and Tina worked on a jigsaw puzzle on Tina's card table and kept the conversation upbeat. Loretta told a story that Gina had heard about Ted's brother Brian. "We're off the hook – seems someone else recently keyed his car, and they left him a nice etched message, actually more of a command. Now he's all paranoid because he thinks someone, he scroodled is out to get him. He just doesn't understand how he provokes people."

Italian rum cake and asti spumante finished off the evening. Any other night a story like the sex on the stairs would have been impossible to contain, but Donna chose not to pollute the final hours of her birthday with any discussion of the skank and the skunk.

CHAPTER EIGHT
KNOWLEDGE IS POWER

Untrue to his promise, Geoffrey did not show up Wednesday. Just as well. Solitude made a better companion for tonight. His presence would only suck Donna into a vortex of loneliness and rejection. She fried a couple of eggs for supper and did a quick clean of the kitchen and bathroom. There was still another hour of natural light. One of life's simple pleasures was to read on the back porch during the warm weather months. She had spent so much time putting out her own thoughts that it was time to pour some back in. Donna picked up an old favorite, Jane Austen's *Pride and Prejudice,* and skimmed over it, having read it before. She reached for the blue notebook and pen and copied passages she wanted to remember.

"*Vanity and pride are different things, though the words are often used synonymously. A person may be proud without being vain. Pride relates more to our opinion of ourselves, vanity to what we would have others think of us."* She copied and labeled the paragraph "J.A./P&P." In the margin she wrote: "*How does this affect a person who steals someone's ID?"*

Donna flipped through the book and read the last chapter, which helped her to relive the joy of a happy ending. She peeled herself off the chaise to get another book. Slipping *Pride and Prejudice* back into its space on the shelf, she reached for *The Scarlet Letter* by Nathaniel Hawthorne. "I've never read this one through. Let's see if I can get into it. The heroine is an adulteress. It might help with understanding the Cynthia character."

The book had a long introduction, which she was tempted to skip over, but decided it was probably included for a reason. It provided some insight into Puritan life in colonial Massachusetts.

More than halfway through the introduction she spotted a paragraph that reminded her of how some criminals prey upon their victims. She liked Hawthorne's description, so she noted its page as a very loose reference for the way identity thieves go through trash to get information: "*But one idle and rainy day, it was my fortune to make a discovery of some little interest. Poking and burrowing into the heaped-up rubbish in the corner, unfolding one and another document and reading the names of vessels that had long ago foundered at sea or rotted at the wharves, and those of merchants, never heard of now on 'Change, nor very readily decipherable on their mossy tombstones."* Two pages later she read another sentence: *"But the object that most drew my attention in the mysterious package was a certain..."* She copied up to "it was my fortune," and decided the rest wasn't worth the energy to write.

She was no longer in any mood to read so she cleared off the small table, put the book back on the shelf and tossed the notebook and pen onto her nightstand. TV or music? Music: something light and breezy for a summer's eve? No. Traditional jazz was needed to blast away anxiety and frustration. Let the neighbors put up with some noise coming from her apartment for a change. By the third song Donna was relaxed enough to lower the volume.

Donna's mother called. "I heard about a great new diet you should try. I'll send it to you. You could lose three pounds a week. I know you said you lost some weight, but where? …. Did you check your bra size yet? You're bulging over the top. You should also watch that panty line – you might need a bigger size in that too…You're right there on the same floor, for cryin' out loud." Eighteen minutes of Louis Armstrong's inflation equaled ten minutes of her mother's deflation, almost a two to one ratio. From now on, she'll talk to her mother first and play music afterward.

Donna sprinkled some eye makeup remover onto a cotton pad and was just about to attack two coats of black mascara and city grime when the phone rang again. She let the answering machine take the call. "Donna, it's Geoffrey. Sorry I was a no-show today. I realize I should have called earlier, but anyway, I'll be there tomorrow. Love ya."

"Love ya?" Donna replayed the message. There was no explanation why he didn't come after he said he would or why he didn't call earlier. Probably figured "love ya" would make up for it.

Donna got ready to retire but couldn't sleep, so she rolled off the bed and grabbed a different book, *Ethan Frome*. "Let's try a man with woman problems for a change." She recalled how *Madame Bovary* was so beautifully written that she marked up almost the whole book, making it unreadable to anyone else – thus the practice of using a notebook began. Like an art student who copied the masters to learn their craft, Donna copied the memorable words of great writers, or at least made a notation of the page. Something in their style should rub off eventually. She drifted off and two hours later woke up to the realization that her nightstand light was still on. Squinting and blocking the light with one hand, she groped for the switch and turned it off. She fell back into a deep sleep and dreamt.

Hours, perhaps minutes, passed and Donna found herself standing before a long pedestal mirror with an ornate mahogany frame and foggy glass. Her hair was swept up as usual, but with tendrils hanging down the sides of her face. Mud stained her feet and the hem of her long ecru lace gown.

Donna turned and saw Geoffrey standing, hand outstretched and beckoning her to follow him. Unlike Donna's antique outfit, Geoffrey was wearing a cranberry polyester-knit leisure suit with a white belt and slip-on shoes. Several gold neck chains shone from his open collar, and a diamond pinkie ring sparkled from his left baby finger. A gold and emerald earring pierced one ear.

They descended three flights of stairs to an entrance hall with water-stained walls. Donna looked up and noticed that the ceiling was leaking as well.

Geoffrey led Donna outside to a waiting sleigh. He escorted her to the front seat and sat behind her. The sled took off through a snowstorm and increased speed as it raced up, over, and down hills like a roller coaster. As it whipped around a hairpin turn it headed down a steep slope toward a giant leafless tree.

Just before the point of impact Donna awakened in a cold sweat. Almost immediately she realized that she was calm despite the nightmare. She kept her eyes closed and recalled as much of the dream as she could. "I'll remember this," she whispered to herself.

Donna fell into a light sleep until her alarm rang. A pleasant surprise awaited her: she could fit easily into a medium skirt.

***

Loretta, wearing a white shirt-waist dress and spectator pumps, popped out of her house just at the exact moment Donna arrived out front. The customers that day were an assortment of 98% nice/no problem, 1% difficult, and 1% totally impossible.

***

As Donna and Loretta turned up their street on the way home, Donna realized that this would be the first time she'd work with Geoffrey since the sex with Sandra episode. *Knowledge is power*. "I know what a slime he is, and he doesn't know that I know. All his manipulations and 'love yas' won't work now."

With five pounds less to carry Donna bounded up the stairs. Mr. Love Ya in the flesh greeted her at the door. "I brought supper," he said, "fried clams, shrimp, onion rings, French fries and coleslaw."

Donna dumped a quarter cup of ketchup onto her plate and alternated mouthfuls of greasy crunchies with the tartar sauce and the ketchup. There goes the five-pound weight loss. Although her feelings toward Geoffrey had cooled, she was nonetheless distressed to see that she ate more than he did.

Geoffrey said, "A few minutes before you came home, I noticed that you had a notebook with some dialogue for Andrews."

"What?"

"JA- Jason Andrews. You wrote something about the difference between vanity and pride. I thought with a few changes we could use it to show how he feels that another guy is going around posing as—"

"Those notes are from *Pride and Prejudice* – J.A. is Jane Austen. Geoffrey, that notebook was on my nightstand in my bedroom. Could you please let me have some privacy and confine yourself to the rest of my apartment? I'd like at least one room to be my own space."

"I didn't know you were so sens- felt that way."

"Well, I'm sorry, but I do. I need to keep some part of my life private. As it is, this whole arrangement is a little strange." Donna would not have spoken with such acerbity if the Sandra surprise hadn't turned her sweet bliss into bitterness.

Geoffrey flushed and stammered, "S…sorry." He paused to do some quick thinking. "Tell you what. Let me go outside and come back in so we can start the night over again."

Donna threw up her hands. “Okay, okay.” She got up and cleared away the dishes. “Let’s get back on track and get to work.” She escaped to her bathroom to brush her teeth and let off steam. “The worst is, he’s clueless,” she told herself. “He must think I’m moody and bad tempered for no good reason. At least I’m too angry to cry again.” She resented him for turning her into a shrew and treating her like a chump. It took a few minutes for her to cool off, and she returned with a frosty air. “There’s one thing that confuses me. Although you’re the professional writer and who am I to say, but your working methods are all over the place.”

“That’s just the way I work. I do whatever I have the urge to do.”

“You sure do,” Donna said, double meaning intended. “As long as it all results in a book, I suppose it’s fine.” After a few minutes she added, “You know, sometimes at night and on weekends I have some extra time to work, but I can’t really because you take everything home with you.”

Geoffrey sucked in his exasperation. “I told you before, I do that deliberately. It’s difficult to write fiction with another person. If you were writing by yourself and going off in another direction, we’d really be all over the place. I have a name to protect, so I must have some control. Besides, I thought we had settled that issue already,” he said with a strained edge to his voice. “I’ll let you know beforehand when I’m coming, and I won’t invade your space, but we write this thing on my terms like we already agreed.”

Donna sighed. “Look, I’m tired of bickering. We should stay focused and not let any personal disagreement get in the way. Let’s get going. It’s already after eight thirty.”

They settled down and got a lot done. Geoffrey tentatively agreed that the main female character, Cynthia, should be a double-crosser – at least for a while. The trick, he told Donna, was to have enough twists and turns to make the story interesting, but not too many to be confusing. "We're much further ahead than I ever thought we'd be. I'll come by tomorrow and then at least all next week. In less than a month we should be getting near the point where I can work alone."

"Alone?"

"Yes. At some point I must give it totally my voice, to make it mine. It has to be compatible with my other books."

"But it's not going to be a book solely by you, but by the two of us, so it can be different than your others."

"Donna, I must be completely satisfied with what I read. My name is on the cover."

"And mine too!"

Geoffrey forced a smile. "Don't worry. I'll take care of you."

If, at the moment, her thinking had been quicker and clearer she would have demanded a contract, or at least an explanation. After the evening's earlier confrontation, Donna decided not to start a full-blown fight in a weak emotional state. Her pathetic insecurity joined forces with her almost pathologic need to please and appease. To change the subject, she asked, "Could I look over the story so far?"

"Uh, it's actually kind of late, and I should get going." Geoffrey got up and started to pack his things. He flashed Donna a smile that she now took to be phony. She, in turn, forced a smile that he would have missed if he blinked. The atmosphere felt a little tense, and Donna felt a rising agitation.

"It's awfully hot in here," she said unbuttoning the second button of her blouse and shaking out her hair. "I'll put on the fan."

As if unbuttoning her blouse to the bottom of her collarbone were some kind of come-on, Geoffrey grabbed Donna by the arm. "You're right. It is hot. We've both been tense all night."

Donna's anger cancelled out an urge to laugh. She pulled back just as Geoffrey reached for the third button. "It *is* late, and I work tomorrow. Goodnight Geoffrey." The ridiculousness of the situation brought a genuine smile to her face. Donna walked to the door with Geoffrey, gripping his laptop and case, following. He leaned forward and kissed Donna on the cheek as if to backpedal his forwardness.

"Sheesh! As if!" Donna muttered under her breath as she shut the door behind Geoffrey. She now wondered if she would even like him by the time the book was finished.

CHAPTER NINE
A PLOT OF A DIFFERENT KIND

"Not to get into a kvetch fest, Loretta, but Geoffrey is totally insincere and out for himself," said Donna, both annoyed and relieved that finally 'light dawned on Marblehead'. "You know, he's really not my type, handsome as he is. I was just lonely enough that I let myself get taken in."

"At least you didn't go out with some creep who gave you the finger and called you a dog to your face. Talk about lonely!"

Donna had never given Loretta too many details about Geoffrey and herself, but Loretta sensed that Donna had, in fact, let her emotions take over. The whole story would come out, someday perhaps, when and if Donna was ready for it to be shared. Throughout their long friendship neither ever forced the other to say or do something that was against her instincts or better judgement. As close as the two women were, they never went into the intimate minutia of their lives, whether because they felt that what was personal should remain so, or because the intuitive simpatico between them was so strong that there was no need to explain what was already understood.

"What's wrong with us anyway? Why can't we find decent men?" Donna asked.

"Look at what we do. You sell women's clothing, and I sell cosmetics. The few male customers we get are buying gifts for their women. Isn't there some club or something we can join? Should we take more classes?"

"Those writing classes are what got me into this mess. I should have taken welding or martial arts."

Loretta shook her curly auburn mop. “All I know is that this butt will never touch a bar stool again.”

“Who needs to meet more jerks? I’m spending almost every weeknight with one.”

“Think how many women would envy you,” Loretta said. “They’d take him any way they could.”

“They can have him. I’ve had my fill of his charm and false flattery. The worst is, Loretta, that I think he’s going to claim the entire book as his.”

“But you’ve been writing it with him forever. Of course you’re co-author!”

“Sure, but I still haven’t so much as read it all the way through. He keeps every scrap of paper, and when he leaves, he puts the disk in his case. I have no real understanding of how much of the book is my work, although the day we met my manuscript was at least half to two-thirds written, and his first chapter was derivative of mine. Although I had much more than he had, and my story became the template we used, we’ve made so many changes throughout that it may not be recognizable.”

“Now you don’t actually believe he’d try to cheat you?” Loretta asked then reconsidered her question. “Then again, he’s not exactly a Boy Scout, is he? You need a safety net, some security.”

“First, I’d at least like to read the whole book. How else can I know my input?”

“Insist on it.”

“I could, but I don’t want to be confrontational again. It would just give him an excuse to get angry and cut me out completely. He has already said that our work together should end in less than a month. That means he’s going to finish it himself.”

“Oh, come on! He can’t cut you out and get away with it. Be confrontational! You could reduce him to writing instruction manuals for potholders. What's the matter with you? At the very least, you've got to have some evidence that you've contributed to the book."

Donna thought for a few seconds. "Anything I keep in my apartment he could find. Unfortunately, I've dictated a lot to him and have had very little of that in my handwriting."

"What about your original manuscript that was practically finished?" asked Loretta, thinking she had the obvious, simple solution.

Donna blushed. "I still have some of my original notes and other bits and pieces on my computer as well as a few ideas that came to me when I was alone, but we either changed or didn't use most of those things. The handwritten part, which was most of it – he has. I think more clearly when I'm writing by hand. Part of our agreement is that he keeps everything for security."

"Even your original handwritten manuscript?"

Donna lost her voice and could only shrug.

Loretta gasped, "What were you thinking? Why didn't you hide a copy for yourself at your parents' house or with Tina or me?"

"You don't have to tell me how I've got *pasta fagioli* for brains. He caught me off guard. I can't believe I was so stupid, even though something told me at the time —"

"Don't be so hard on yourself for being so trusting. That's just the way you are. We'll figure something out." Loretta checked her watch. "We've got five more minutes of lunch left."
The afternoon passed with only a handful of sales for Donna. A free gift promotion kept Loretta hopping. Before they got off work, heavy rain pounded the city for an hour then dropped to a light summer shower for the evening commute.

***

Donna entered her apartment to the smell of Chinese food. "Geoffrey?" she called out.

He walked out of the kitchen and placed a vase of flowers on the dining room table. "You look very pretty," he said. "I thought we'd have Chinese tonight."

Just like old folks.

"Wow, what beautiful flowers!" For a moment, Donna thought he'd be perfect, until a flood of memories washed away her brief joy.

"Well, you're beautiful."

Donna would have half believed her welcome home as a sincere, thoughtful expression if he weren't such a rat turd. Empty compliments and implied promises, she now saw, were his weapons of manipulation and control. She felt a chill from the dampness on her body and the coolness from within. "Thank you," she mumbled then excused herself so she could freshen up and take off her wet skirt. In a hurry she grabbed a long jersey dress that hadn't fit in two years and pulled it on without any tugging, then combed out her wet hair and returned to the dining room.

"I see you've picked up some books from the library," Geoffrey said, "Raymond Chandler, Dashiell Hammett, and *The Count of Monte Cristo*."

"Yes, I like to read. It helps to fill the well, as they say. *The Count of Monte Cristo*, of course, is about a man who assumes a different identity after being betrayed. I copy parts that I think are interesting or well written to help me learn. Silly, I suppose, but I've found it's easier to learn and think by writing things out."

"Great. We can get some ideas. There are no new plots, you know, just clever recycling. Lots of writers borrow something from someone else, even if they don't realize it."

"That's okay if you don't 'borrow' too much," Donna said then realized that Geoffrey could have interpreted that remark as an insult for he had stolen more than borrowed her original story.

“Let’s eat before the food gets cold. It was delivered about a minute before you got home. I waited for you, but then decided to go ahead and order without you.”

“The rain slowed the evening commute. We got wetter waiting for the bus than if we had simply walked home,” Donna said as she draped a towel around her neck.

“Well, glad you’re home and didn’t melt. I got a little of everything: beef, chicken, shrimp, vegetables, and rice.”

“Oh good – fortune cookies. I’ll make some tea. Let’s eat in the kitchen so we don’t get any stickiness all over the place. Chopsticks?”

“And a fork and knife.” Geoffrey watched Donna artfully twirl the chopsticks. "You have very graceful hands. That’s a ruby on your ring,” Geoffrey stated as a matter of fact rather than a question.

“Yes, my birthstone.”

“For what month?”

“July.”

“Something tells me I missed your birthday,” Geoffrey said with an apologetic tone.

“There’s no reason you should have known beforehand, but actually, it was this past Tuesday,” Donna said watching his face for any hint of recollection. “That was the day I ran into you on the stairs as I was going out.” Donna recalled that she had mentioned her birthday then, but of course Geoffrey was too preoccupied that day to remember.

“Did you do anything special?”

“I had lunch with a friend, then later a small celebration with Tina and Loretta.”

“Oh, I was under the impression you were going out alone.”

"I met him at the restaurant." Never mind that the "him" was a mutual acquaintance she met at the restaurant by accident. "More tea?"

"Sure. What is it about Chinese food that I can eat so much of it beyond the point of fullness?" Geoffrey asked.

"It's just so good." For once, Donna noted, Geoffrey was eating more than she. "It's a nice break from all the Italian food I eat, as much as I like that too."

"My mother is Irish, so I'm an Ir-It, but I had a lot of Aunt Angie's cooking. Do you like Indian food?"

"Love it."

"Good, I'll pick some up on Monday. You're a very good cook. Did your mother teach you?"

"A little – when I still lived at home. Tina taught me how to make things like *pizza dolce* and *cannoli*. Sometimes I watch cooking shows and I've taken a couple of classes. A few times I did food demonstrations in Floegel's housewares department."

"It all shows. It seems that most women today would rather eat out or take out."

"I wouldn't say that, at least not every day. Maybe the women you know are that way," said Donna knowing that she was referring to Sandra without Geoffrey knowing it.

"True. I don't know too many people like you. Cooking is only part of it. So much about you is different, as though you were born in the wrong era, much like someone else I know. Except for the few heated discussions we've had, which were justifiable, there hasn't been any disagreement between us. It's been easy."

Donna gulped. "For me too. I'm glad you see it that way, especially after I jumped on you for reading my notebook, and for any other times as well. It's been a lot of fun."

"Don't mention that talk we had. I could tell when you walked in that something was bothering you."

"It's been a strange week, for sure." Donna looked around the room as if searching for another topic of discussion. She mentioned the book and hoped that Geoffrey would take the hint that she wanted to read it through.

"It's coming along really well," he said. "At the rate it's going we should be in a good place in about two weeks."

"Then you'll finish it on your own?"

"Whoa, I just got a hot chili," Geoffrey said in a distracting change of subject.

Donna's brain fidgeted. Was there something besides a hot pepper sticking in Geoffrey's throat? Should she repeat her question with the assumption that he wasn't being evasive and would cough up the answer? Given Geoffrey's compliments on how easy it was with her, especially after the hard time she had given him, she would do what she needed to, without confrontation, and let him have a final chance.

"Well, here's the reason for not wanting to cook – no dirty pots and pans to wash," Donna said abruptly. "Just a quick rinse of the dishes, and everything goes into the dishwasher."

Compatible, congenial emotions always created productive nights for the two, Donna noticed, and tonight they wrote more than they had on three of their most tense evenings combined.

Her disappointment in Geoffrey was suppressed, rather than changed. She'd pushed her feelings back to the early days of their first interaction, when she viewed him as she saw him now, as simply someone who would not change her life in any meaningful way. Somewhere in her weary head she knew that her pain should erupt and engulf her in sadness, but she shoved it right back down as soon as it bubbled to the surface. Her fountain of tears had overflowed lately, and it was time to dry up.

They worked until after eleven. Geoffrey had monopolized his laptop as usual, with Donna giving mostly verbal suggestions interspersed with hand-written notes. Her usefulness for the night petered out as her ideas piled up faster than Geoffrey could assimilate them. At one point Donna took a book into the living room and read.

"Man, it's almost 11:30," Geoffrey said rising. He packed up everything, slipped the disk into his briefcase, gave Donna a peck on the cheek, and was gone.

"It's amazing how one person can be deceived by another," Donna thought with a belief that she was too gullible and may have been an accomplice in her own deception. She did not let this concern keep her awake tonight as it might have if she had any hope that either Geoffrey or she would change any time soon.

***

The next night Donna came home with the kind of feeling one has going to a job for which they have been underpaid and know will end soon without any show of appreciation for their hard work. Yes, it had been fun, especially in the beginning, and she had learned a lot from him – about writing and reality. He had taught her how to put a good idea into a form that made a reader want to turn the page and keep reading while at the same time hoping that the book would never end. From him she also learned a lot about herself that she wasn't sure she wanted to know. It did her no good to see herself as a weak, naïve fool, unless she had the ability to change.

"Man, are we on a roll," Geoffrey said. "I don't know what's the fastest anyone ever wrote a book like this, but I'll bet we're setting some kind of record for something." Donna could have replied that they didn't exactly start with a blank page. Her own book had, at least, provided the framework in some now mangled or recognizable form. Having never done any creative work, beyond school projects, with anyone, there was no way for her to tell in what ways this collaboration was normal or unusual.

At any hour of the day, a twinge of anxiety would send Donna into an uneasy sense of regret and worry that she had handed, without guarantee of credit or compensation, her long-labored creation to a man she hardly knew. If she had only insisted from the beginning, when he would have willingly agreed, that she be given a contract or some proof of ownership, she would have no reason for self-reproach. Now any attempt to rectify her initial mistake would require actions that were ugly and out of character, and most likely fruitless. Sure, she could scream to the world that he had plagiarized her book and had cheated her. The embarrassment for Geoffrey might only give Donna slight satisfaction, but anything she could now get by force was repugnant to her. She made her mistake and would have to accept part of the blame.

***

Nurses, restaurant workers, and store clerks all share the inconvenience of having to sometimes work on nights and weekends when other people are free. The irregular schedule, however, kept medical, dental, and beautician appointments, utility servicing and other errands from wasting vacation time. A weekend of work at Floegel's, like this one, meant freedom and flexibility during the weekdays. More often than not, Donna and Loretta had the same hours, which gave them a schoolgirl feeling of playing hooky together.

"Time is ticking away," Donna said. "We'd better figure this out. He's had plenty of time to do the right thing."

"What do you think he meant when he said he'd 'take care of you'?" Loretta asked. "With that uncle of his, you never know. Your body could be found floating in the Charles or feeding lobsters at the bottom of the ocean– just kidding. He's a dirt bag, but he's not that bad – I hope."

"It's not Primo I'm worried about. All this summer I let a man, a stranger really, into my life and now I'm second-guessing my judgment."

"Like closing the barn door after the cattle have left."

"More like shutting my back door after my creation was taken."

"You could really make a lot of trouble for him, you know, if you have the stomach for it."

"I don't want trouble. I just want fairness."

"Once the book is published," Loretta said, "it'll be an embarrassing headache to do anything."

Donna shook her head. "I don't know. If I can just read the stupid thing, I can plan what, if anything, I should do next. It would give me something to present to him as an argument that the book is just as much mine as his."

"But he knows how much you worked with him."

"But will he readily admit that I contributed much that he used? I have a just claim if I can show my influence all over it."

"If he's always got the story with him, then it's within your reach, and you should somehow get your mitts on it. Does he ever use your bathroom? You could make a copy then."

"Too unpredictable and I could get caught too easily. Besides, he's got the bladder of a camel. There isn't much time. Will you help?"

"Of course," Loretta said. "Let's get scheming."

Donna checked her schedule with Loretta. They both had Thursday off – perfect. They devised a plot so simple that Donna feared they must have overlooked some obvious complication. Loretta assured her that as long as Geoffrey was present that day, their plan easily could be adapted to any likely changes or obstacles. Their scheme had a strong element of deceit, if not outright dishonesty, but Donna kept reminding herself that she had done everything short of tearful begging.

"Don't you dare feel guilty," Loretta told her. "The S.O.B. is making you do it. He's lucky that's all you do."

"Guilt is one of the weaker emotions I'm feeling. I think I'm just trying to justify my actions."

"You can't steal something that's yours. He's the one who needs to justify his behavior."

***

After work Donna sat on the porch reading and taking notes until dark, then she moved into the living room. When she started to drift off, she placed the notebook on the coffee table and dragged herself to bed. In the minutes before she fell fast asleep, she had some quiet time to think. "We're just friends. Forget anything else, but what about the book? I've never read the story through. I have no written contract, no real proof of my contribution, no guarantee of anything. I'll have to protect myself." Her dreams that night were light in spirit, and one actually made her laugh out loud in her sleep. If only she could carry that humor into her daily life.

CHAPTER TEN
INSULTS AND ASSAULTS

On Monday Donna worked until closing and did not see Geoffrey. She neither knew nor cared if Geoffrey showed up as long as Sandra kept her bony butt out of her apartment. When Donna arrived home, she went straight to Tina's apartment for a late dinner of Greek salad and eggplant parmesan.

"Of course you can count on me," Tina said. "Just give me time to move my keester."

On the way up the stairs Donna had the misfortune of running into Angie. "Lucky girl," Angie said with a sarcastic tone. "You get to spend so much time with my handsome nephew. Just don't get your hopes up."

Donna smelled alcohol on Angie's breath. "Our relationship is professional and platonic."

"It would have to be. He has to beat 'em off with a stick. In fact, a stick is something you should fetch. Of course, when he does marry, it will be to someone who's somebody."

Donna could feel her face burn, and to suppress an impulse to grab Angie by the throat, she said with steely calm, "Well, I suppose with his taste in women, he would end up with *some body* – fifteen percent silicone and zero percent fat. I'm merely helping him to write a book."

"*Help*? A best-selling author needs help from *you*? The millions he's sold! Every single one a huge hit!" Angie's painted eyebrows shot up only so far as the Botox would allow. "Do you have any idea what an absolute *genius* he is?"

"Angie, you know perfectly well what was going on the day I came home unexpectedly and found that the genius was copying *my* book."

"Your book? Ha! You couldn't write a grocery shopping list! As for copying, no such thing ever happened! As I recall, you invited him in. How could you resist?"

Donna almost lost her balance at the sudden rewrite of history. Of course, if things ever got nasty, Angie could be counted on to lie for her nephew. "Angie, it's late. I'm tired, and I really don't want to get into a foolish argument. Think whatever you like. Imagine, with all the gorgeous women around, Geoffrey spends almost every weeknight with me."

"But not the weekends or the weekdays – today in fact," Angie yelled as Donna walked up the stairs to her apartment. Donna was certain that Geoffrey was nowhere in the whole house because his aunt would never have spoken so boldly, no matter how sloshed she was.

Donna locked and chained her door behind herself then looked around to find any evidence that someone had been in her apartment. The navy sailor outfit she had decided not to wear this morning was on her bed exactly as she had left it, as was the pair of anchor earrings she didn't have time to put away. *They were either very careful to put everything back or…*

She washed down her kitchen and dining room tables, after noticing some telltale powder on one of them, then entered the living room. Wait. The throw pillows on the sofa were in a different arrangement than normal and, on closer inspection, there were two long blond hairs. As she backed away from the sofa, she noticed a water ring and several crumbs on the end table.

"At least he kept his promise and stayed out of my room," she thought with disgust. "I'll see about fumigation tomorrow."

Donna went to bed with an even stronger determination than she had before.

***

The next morning a commotion rumbled downstairs. The yelling and screaming bellowing up from the Infantos' apartment were more intense and urgent than usual.

"Hurry the hell up. We'll miss the plane," Primo hollered.

"Where the hell are my gold sandals? Help me find them, will you? How do you expect me to look glamorous?" Angie fired back.

"They're on your feet!"

"Hallelujah! Couldn't come at a better time," Donna almost shouted out. "Wonder how long the mafioso and the medusa will be gone? It must be difficult to get the same vacation days from three different jobs." Although Donna started work at noon, she didn't mind being woken by such great news. She rolled over with a big smile on her face.

Angie yelled one last but sweeter request. "Geoff honey, are you ready to take us to the airport?" Minutes later, the Infantos' windows followed by the back door slammed shut.

"Ah, peace at last!" Donna had another two hours of blissful sleep before waking up refreshed. While she was applying her makeup, she heard the downstairs shower. Either she had been dreaming earlier this morning, or Geoffrey must have returned from the airport.

Donna brushed her hair back off her face and let it hang loosely. Yesterday's rejected sailor suit would do for today. When she was putting on her shoes, her brother called with a belated birthday wish. She glanced at the clock. "Art hon, gotta go. Thanks for calling."

As Donna raced past the Infantos' apartment Geoffrey called after her, "My aunt and uncle left for vacation, and I can work in here until you get home."

"Sure, wherever you're comfortable. I work until closing so I won't be home until late."

***

Donna's rule for closing nights was: "Never wear anything you can't run in, especially when you're travelling alone." Pants, low heels, and a crossbody bag she could clutch to her side comprised her night uniform. Close calls were rare, especially to an alert, street-smart person like Donna, but tonight was a first for her – she had to run both to and from the T. After leaving work she first tore down Cambridge Street when a couple of knife-wielding dirt bags thought her ring and gold chain would look better on them. A loud "NO!" bellowed up from her diaphragm, just at the perfect split second of distraction, and gave Donna a flying head start. She tucked the chain inside her top and almost twisted her ankle while rushing down the stairs to Government Center Station, where she collided with a toll booth. To the rest of the passengers on the half-empty train, Donna must have appeared shivering and shell-shocked.

On the walk home after exiting Orient Heights station she darted across the street when a car drove too close and too slowly for something with racing stripes.

"Get her!" one of the creeps yelled, prompting the driver to almost clip Donna's heels. Something hard whizzed through the air and through an open window of the car. One of the creeps shrieked.

The car did a quick screeching U-turn and sped off. A shadowed form of a figure, that Donna might have taken to be Tom Ambrose, if Tom would have had any possible reason to be in Eastie, appeared then disappeared into the darkness. Donna clutched her chest as if to slow her racing heart. She gulped and rushed home with the sense that someone was following her.

Geoffrey was watching TV in the Infantos' den when Donna pounded on the door.

“What’s wrong?” he asked. “Are you okay?”

“I was almost mugged twice tonight. I came home by myself. Loretta opened.”

“What happened? Are you hurt?”

“The first was an attempted robbery at knifepoint in the city, and the second I don’t even want to think. A couple of blocks from here a car with two or three men followed me and then…and then just before…someone scared them off.”

“Should I call the police?”

“I already did on my cell and was able to give a brief description of the creeps in the city, but as for the others in the car, I didn’t get a good look at them. I can’t even say what kind of car it was except that it had racing stripes. They said they’d look out for it.” Donna fought back tears. The sad reality of modern life hit her with all its desperate anxiety.

“Gee, you’re really shaking. I’ll make you some tea. Like some brandy in it?” He put on the kettle and set out a cup, then guided her over to a chair. “Have a seat. You look as though you’re about to collapse.”

“It was so ugly and evil. The two creeps in the city were bad enough. At least one of them had a knife, but they were too out of it to chase me. I ran all the way to Government Center Station. My heart was still pounding when I got off the train. I was in such a hurry to get home that I didn’t wait for the bus. How stupid of me!” Donna started to cry as much from her own inability to protect herself as from the double fright she had suffered.

Geoffrey bent over to touch her shoulder, but his hand shifted to answer his cell phone. He stepped back and whispered, “Hello…Oh, hi… Uh, it’s probably not a good idea tonight. I’m still at Primo’s. I decided to stay here while they’re in Florida.”

A loud “*What do you mean*?” shrieked in Geoffrey’s ear, and he withdrew into the bedroom.

The kettle whistled, and Donna got up to turn off the stove. “I’ll take care of myself,” she muttered then left. At the moment, she could hardly tell which experience of the night was worse.

Anger dried her stream of tears as a warm shower did its best to wash off the touch of the creeps with the knife along with the rest of the miserable day. “The important thing is that I’m alive and well.” She crawled into bed and said a prayer of thanks.

***

Once again as Donna was descending the stairs the next morning, the door of the Infantos’ apartment swung open. Geoffrey, looking scruffy, stepped halfway out the doorway. “’Morning. I’m sorry about last night. I called on the phone and knocked on the door, but you didn’t answer.”

“I was in the shower.”

“Well, I’m sorry. I should’ve been more helpful, and I should have kept trying until I reached you.”

“No problem,” muttered Donna, looking away. *There are a lot of things you should have done.* “It’s my problem, not yours.”

“No, it’s mine too,” he mumbled. Had she bothered to look him in the face, she might have noticed an expression of regret or shame, and he may have felt encouraged to explain his behavior. “What time will you be home?”

“Six-thirty, seven,” Donna answered.

“I can work in here, although it’s not as comfortable as your place.”

“I can unlock my door for you, if you like.”

“Don’t. There’s a copy of your keys here that I can use. That way your apartment will be locked when it’s empty.” As Geoffrey spoke, Donna thought she heard a faint sound coming from within. Was it just the wind or an outside noise coming in through an open window? Or was someone else in there? A look of suspicion must have flashed across Donna’s face because Geoffrey's jaw dropped. After a moment of awkward silence, Geoffrey smiled, leaned forward and whispered, "I'll miss you."

In a quick-thinking attempt to lure out any hidden fox, Donna kissed him on the cheek and left a lipstick print. She said, louder than necessary, "Oh Geoffrey, I can't wait! I'll miss you too!" On the way out the door she retouched her lipstick and smiled to herself. "Hope the fox, if she's there, has good ears."

***

At 6:45 PM Donna returned with salad ingredients and salmon. She rapped on the Infantos' door. Geoffrey came upstairs ten minutes later with a bottle of pinot grigio as Donna was mashing potatoes and preparing a spinach salad.

Over dinner Donna brought up the co-authorship of the book. "Geoffrey, I don't want to sound petty and distrustful, but it occurred to me that all this time we've been working without a contract."

"A contract is something that comes from the publisher."

"But I guess I'm a little confused about our relationship, I mean our working relationship."

"Don't be."

What did that mean? Donna was unsure how to continue. "What are you saying? With all my input I haven't even read the manuscript all the way through yet."

"You will."

"When?"

"At the appropriate time. Donna, you know the expression 'too many cooks spoil the pot'? This is awkward for me too. I've never let anyone in so close to my working process." A note of exasperation rose in his voice.

"But I've been writing it with you, almost from day one. I should be allowed…should have the freedom to read any part or all of it whenever I want, not just bits and pieces whenever you dole them out to me. It's not as though I don't trust…" Donna interrupted her disingenuous remark and backed right down. It was her own stupid, naive fault. She should have pressed the issue at the beginning when they first started working together and her bargaining power was greater. An argument at night after a long day of work put her at an emotional disadvantage. She consoled herself with the thought that there was still time for a resolution.

Geoffrey became very quiet and appeared to fold in at the chest. He had done wrong and was forced to look inside himself for some difficult answers for his behavior. The questions, which Donna could not hear, and he could not confront, reflected and bounced through his conscience as though in a hall of mirrors. There was nowhere his inner eye could look without facing censure. His self-preservation was costing him his self-respect.

As Donna took care of the dishes, Geoffrey set up his laptop. He called her over. "Here, read this part. It's in its finished state."

Donna sat down and read the third chapter. It was written like Geoffrey's other books – masculine, what some might call "gritty," but she could detect her influence. This must be what Geoffrey meant by protecting his name. He had to maintain quality, both in the sense of standard and compatibility with his other books. She felt a pang of guilt but not enough to betray her sense of self-preservation.

"It's very good," she said rising from the chair. "More wine?"

"Sure. I'm not driving anywhere tonight," he said. A sad smile tried to convey his feelings of regret, gratitude – and something else he couldn't express. Somewhere in Donna, it all just grazed the mark.

For a while Donna sat with the warm feeling that must come from the comfort and security of a loving relationship. The feeling soon sank with the one hundred-ten-pound weight of Sandra LeRoi Young – Sandra doing who knows what throughout Donna's apartment. And there sat her fading comfort in the form of a cad named Geoffrey Imperato. "Why," she thought, "if I had to be in this situation, couldn't it have been with a nicer person? But a nicer person wouldn't have done what he did in the first place. What a disappointment! My whole summer wasted on him! I'll bet if one of those thugs had slit my throat, he'd feel well rid of me. He could even tell himself that he wrote the whole book, as if I never existed." Geoffrey sat oblivious to the heat of anger seeping out of Donna. In an attempt to mentally cool off, she said, "It's too hot in here. Let's sit out back. We'll get more of a cross breeze."

Donna and Geoffrey put up their feet and listened to the summer sounds of crickets and cruising teenagers. An Oldie streamed from a passing car, and the aroma of pizza wafted from the neighboring porch.

"Ginger ale," Donna said.

"What about it?"

"Most people associate ginger ale with either mixed drinks or being sick, but to me it's warm midsummer nights." The childhood recollection took Donna out of the present and restored her sense of calm. "When I was little, we would watch TV and drink ginger ale on nights like this."

"Let's watch something together. I need a break. I've been working since early this morning, both here and downstairs, and I'm ready to drop."

After discussing whether to watch a comedy, drama, or mystery, they decided on *Sunset Boulevard,* which offered some of all three.

"I must have seen this movie ten times at least," Donna said.

"I'd never seen it before, but I can see what all the fuss was about. Thanks for suggesting it. It's classic and campy." Then he joked, "I should take some warning from it."

"Huh?"

"It's about a writer being destroyed by a deranged woman."

"Who thinks she can write."

"I'll be careful not to turn my back on you."

"But I'm not the Norma Desmond character," Donna said as she threw an ice cube at him. Geoffrey in turn dropped one down the back of her shirt. It was so darn hot that Donna let the ice slide into a melt on her skin. "We didn't get as much done as we should have," Donna said.

"No, but we needed the break. I've been up since before six, and I got a lot of time in without the distraction of other people in the house. I think the wine and the humidity got us both a little irritable earlier. And you're probably still a little tense from last night."

How sweet that you remembered I was almost a statistic! Donna took a sip then held her glass to her cheek. "I'm off tomorrow so we can make up for the time we lost tonight, but Friday I'll be home a couple of hours later than usual."

Geoffrey did some mental calculating before he spoke. "We've got all day tomorrow, so I'll take you to lunch to break up the day."

Donna also had to do a little quick thinking. "That'll work." She glanced at her watch. By this time tomorrow night it would be over. Three months ago, she could not sit in this man's presence and feel what she felt now – nothing.

"I guess I'd better get downstairs now," Geoffrey said with some hesitation.

"I'm sleepy myself. See you what time tomorrow?"

“We could start early, eight, eight-thirty or so. That’ll give us about five hours until lunch. I don’t like going to restaurants before one. They’re usually too crowded.”

Their work together would soon end with a simple celebration shadowed by deceit and disappointment. A touch of melancholy lifted before either realized that it was mutual.

Geoffrey grabbed his laptop and briefcase and headed toward the back door. He turned, stepped closer to her and said, “Donna, since I’m staying here tonight, what do you say? …”

“I say goodnight, Geoffrey,” Donna answered with the conceit of a woman who was certain that she was about to be propositioned. With a forgiving smile she opened the door to let Geoffrey out. He shook his head and chuckled.

Donna ran to her phone and called Loretta. “Hello, Loretta,” she whispered. “Sorry to call you so late, but I think I have the time narrowed down for tomorrow. We may not need Tina at all because we’re going out to lunch. You could do it then.”

“But what if he takes the disk with him and turns off his laptop? If I have to reboot, I won’t know —”

“You’re right. It’s got to be an emergency to get him to run out in a hurry. There’s one other hitch, though. He’s staying downstairs and will be up here at eight in the morning.”

“Oh great. That means I need to get there by when?”

“Let’s see. If you can sneak up the back without being noticed, I’ll try to keep him toward the front of the apartment.”

“Yeah, but your kitchen is in the back. It might be hard to confine him without it seeming like something’s up. I don’t know. I’ll be quiet as possible. Just make sure you set out two large empty jars and some toilet paper and hand sanitizer on the attic stairs just in case, and a thermos of iced coffee and some biscotti or something. Make sure it’s nothing sticky. I hate sticky hands with nowhere to wash.”

"How about some hand wipes and a disposable toothbrush?" Donna said with a touch of sarcasm.

"That would be great. You know what, forget the coffee. I'll make my own. That'll help save time. Got any muffins or fruit? I've just got melon – more mess."

"I've got bananas and peaches. The peaches are hard so they're not juicy."

"Just a banana then — I can't stand peach fuzz unless it's just washed."

"This is going to be a little touchy with Geoffrey downstairs. I'll set everything out either when I think he's asleep or in the shower. I'll let Tina know when to begin. Now, let's go over the plan once more."

"Okay," Loretta said, "let me get something here to write…Okay, I'm ready."

"Now plan A: You simply copy his disk into my laptop, which you then take home with you when you're through. You use my computer only if you have a problem with the laptop. I don't want any evidence in my apartment. The disk should be in either his laptop or briefcase, which I hope and pray he leaves open or unlocked. Shoot! I don't remember where he put the disk before he left tonight – of all times not to notice!"

"Don't worry. I'll find it. Besides, there's always plan B: I use a blank disk to copy it from his hard drive – that is of course if the story is saved on it."

"Must be, but you never know with his paranoia about someone stealing *his* work."

"I've got another idea. How about a plan C? If he's got the story printed out, we won't have to worry about getting it from the disk or laptop. I could copy it while you're both at lunch."

"Uh, it's long and if it gets messed up – but it's worth a try, though I don't even know how much he carries around with him. I think he leaves a lot downstairs at Primo's." Donna said. "And

Loretta, remember if you have to use plan B, remove all evidence that you've done it."

"That's right. I open the window for the hard drive then for the A drive and I…?"

"Oh shoot! Recheck with Connie and pray for plan A."

***

Tired as she was, Donna's body rested, but her mind raced. Tomorrow was her chance. Although she saw Geoffrey as a complete disappointment and had been stung by his disregard, she still felt a strange bond of friendship from the many good hours they had spent together. They shared humor and a kind of *simpatico*, but not trust. Was it even possible to have a friendship without trust? Not if the distrust was justified and serious. Ironically, now she was the one who was the sneak, for sure. Poor Geoffrey had offered her a partnership, albeit with one arm tied behind his back, and today she was preparing to duct tape the other one.

Donna got up to open a window wider. Geoffrey's voice whispered from below, "Hey Donna, how ya doin' up there? Want some company?"

She pretended she didn't hear him and fell asleep while Geoffrey was still rumbling around downstairs. For the second time since they met, Donna had a dream about him:

They were laughing together on Donna's back porch when an autumn chill filtered through the screens and made Donna shiver. Geoffrey grabbed a wool granny square Afghan to cover her. He twirled it in the air, and it turned into a silk shawl as Sandra appeared and yanked it from his hands. Geoffrey and Sandra looked at each other as though they were oblivious to Donna's presence. Sandra took a step closer to Geoffrey and, with a forceful lunge, pushed him through the screen. He slid down the side of the house and grabbed onto the gutter of the second-floor porch and hung on. Donna snatched the silk shawl and dropped one end of it out the broken screen for Geoffrey to grab. She braced her legs against the lower wall of the porch as Geoffrey and she hoisted him up until they were face to face. With a scream that Donna felt rather than heard, Sandra shoved Geoffrey and Donna back over the edge.

The nightmare was merely a lucid dream that Donna changed without waking. At the end of her dream, she floated down the stairs to Tina's, and Geoffrey opened the door for her and invited her in. "Thank you for trying to help me," he said. "I know you tried, even though I don't deserve it."

The rest of the night she slept soundly for someone who had good reason to struggle with anxiety. She did get up once at about 3:00 to use the bathroom – an indication that she may have been nervous or merely had drunk too much ginger ale. She walked out into the kitchen and slowly passed through the dining room into the living room, all the while trying to recall where Geoffrey put the disk before he left. Several times she visualized him at their past moments of mutual contentment and joy and wondered whether she would have been better off to never have known that happiness if it all had to end this way. *We did have fun, and I learned a lot. Could have been worse.*

She went back to bed and realized that Loretta, Tina, and she never discussed what they would do if they were caught. Over and over, she rehearsed the plan and repeatedly told herself that it was simple and almost foolproof. It was the *almost* part that had her worried, but since she had been such a fool in all this, how much worse could her situation be if it all backfired? Besides, once she confronted him with proof of her input, she'd have to explain how she got it anyway. "Stop thinking!" she half-shouted and fell back to sleep.

CHAPTER ELEVEN
DOUBLE XX

Donna woke up at 6:40 AM, tiptoed into the kitchen, and got an empty pickle jar from the recycling bin under the sink. The opening of a pepperocini jar was too small so a glass vase would have to be sacrificed. She sneaked out her back door and up the stairs to the attic where she placed the vessels on the top step. Into a paper bag she dropped a banana, a small box of raisins, a few biscotti, a handful of hard candies, a chunk of foil covered cheddar cheese, a small packet of crackers, and a bunch of hand wipes. "In case she needs something to read," Donna thought as she gathered a few magazines and a flashlight. "That and perhaps a roll of toilet paper, a couple of bottles of water, and a pillow should make a comfortable roost for Loretta." With three stealthy trips up and down the attic stairs, everything was in place.

There was still no sound of running water coming from the second-floor apartment, so Donna sneaked down the back stairs and unlocked the rear door to the house for Loretta. Under Tina's door she slid a note that said, "Read then destroy: We signal each other with one ring. Plan for 9:30." As Donna was about to ascend the stairs, Loretta appeared with a thermos, a cosmetic bag, and a folding mirror – all the essentials – in a large tote bag.

Donna and Loretta climbed deliberately in step up to the third floor. "Made it," Loretta whispered as they reached Donna's back door. "Good thing he didn't open his door as we were passing. I pulled a Sandra and took a circuitous route to get here in case he was looking out the window."

"Good thinking. Got your cell phone?"

"All charged, ringer off, vibration on, and ready for action. And I've got an extra blank disk for just in case."

"Remember to listen for the signal," said Donna, "and whisper if you have any phone calls – better to text instead. My laptop is on my desk, and my computer in the spare bedroom is also on. I'd better get going."

Loretta crept up to her post and snickered at the sight of the display. Meanwhile Donna went inside to get ready. After her shower, she combed out her wet hair and used large clips to secure it in a twist. She did a light makeup that she could easily touch up later, then blew-dry her hair. A powder blue light knit would do for lunch, but more casual, active clothes would be needed for this morning's task. The second-floor water pipes squeaked, indicating Geoffrey must be taking a shower. Donna took this opportunity to go down to Tina's. It took Tina about twenty seconds to make it to the door. Today, however, her arthritis would come in handy.

"Did you get my note?" Donna asked, "and destroy it so he doesn't find it?"

"Yes, you call me, and then I call you at 9:30 or whenever you're ready. Just give me a minute to get out there after I signal. Remember, one ring."

"I put the ringer of my house telephone on loud so Loretta will be sure to hear it, and she knows to listen carefully for the doorbell. She's already in position. I'm wondering if we shouldn't have scheduled it for earlier. It's a long time to keep Loretta up there, but he's got to have his laptop set up, and he could be late."

"It all has to look natural. Don't worry. It'll be fun."

Donna went back upstairs in time to get the coffee going. "If I make a big breakfast, we may run over 9:30," she thought. "We probably should have planned it for ten." A knock on the door cut short Donna's worrying. Geoffrey walked in with the smell of after-shave and freshly shampooed hair. Donna pointed to the dining room and said, "Why don't you get set up while I make us some breakfast? Let's see, we've got eggs, frozen breakfast sausages, bagels, lox, wheat bread, oatmeal, cereal, bananas, peaches, coffee, and tea."

"A bagel, banana, and coffee would be fine. I'm still full from that wonderful dinner you made last night," Geoffrey said as he walked into the dining room and laid out his things on the table.

While Donna set up breakfast in the kitchen, she kept a wary eye on Geoffrey. *The disk, the disk, where is it – in his briefcase, laptop case? Did he remove it last night before he left?* Donna froze at the impression of a stiff, flat form in the breast pocket of Geoffrey's shirt. *Oh no! If he doesn't take the disk out of his pocket in time, what'll I do? I'll have to spill something on him to get him to take off his shirt.*

Donna walked over to the coffeepot. *All I need to do is scald him and we'll spend the morning in the emergency room. Water won't do. I need something that will stain or be uncomfortable and sticky.* She opened the refrigerator. There was a quart of skim milk and shoot, no orange juice. She flung open the freezer and pulled out a can of frozen orange juice which, through her nervous shaking, managed to drop on the floor and split open.

"What are you doing?" Geoffrey called out.

"I thought we'd have some orange juice. I'm out of fresh but I just smashed a frozen can on the floor," answered Donna as she picked up the sloppy mess and threw it in the sink.

"Don't go to so much trouble. A little coffee is fine."

Donna bent down to wipe the floor and did some quick thinking. What if she shook a can of ginger ale and opened it near Geoffrey? Too unpredictable – no telling where it would squirt and she'd have to waste more time cleaning, and it might wet the disk in his pocket. Could she somehow smear jelly or cream cheese on him? She could stall no longer. She'd think of something yet. They sat down for breakfast.

"What's on your mind?" Geoffrey asked. "You seem very distracted."

"I was just thinking."

"Obviously."

"Sorry." Donna tried to look attentive but soon drifted into a blank stare. There was one obvious way she could get his shirt off, but she wasn't about to start something she had no intention of finishing.

"Did you sleep well?" Donna asked trying to make small talk.

"Eventually. You kept me awake."

Donna raised an eyebrow. The window had been open. What did he hear? "Was I snoring or something?" Donna asked.

"No, no," Geoffrey chuckled then turned serious. "Just thinking about you kept me up. I know I haven't treated you well. I, uh, said and did some things that made everything between us worse instead of better, perhaps irreparably. I don't know how you can stand being in the same room with me. You must know that I'm very sorry for everything."

Donna took a gulp of coffee and stood up a little too abruptly. Geoffrey, getting the hint, rose and carried his dishes to the sink. "I'll take care of them," Donna said. "You go and get set up."

"I pretty much already am."

Donna glanced into the dining room. The laptop was set up but not on, and the briefcase was open. Okay girl, make a decision. A piece of bagel slathered with cream cheese was sitting on a dish. Instead of letting the bagel chunk slide into the garbage, she grabbed it so that her palm got smeared with cream cheese. For no explainable reason, Donna spun around and grabbed Geoffrey's arm in a clumsy pratfall. She wiped her hand on his sleeve as she descended to the floor.

“Are you okay?” Geoffrey said as he bent down to help her up.

“Yes. I’m so sorry…your shirt. Let me wash it for you.”

“That’s all right. I’ll just wipe it off and change before lunch.”

“No, no. It might set a stain.”

“All right.” Geoffrey unbuttoned his shirt with one hand while reaching into his pocket for what turned out to be not a computer disk, but a thin square package wrapped in dark pink paper. He handed the shirt to Donna who checked the laundry label, then ran the sleeve under water and rubbed some liquid soap into the cream cheese smear.

Donna reached under the sink and pulled out a plastic dishpan. “I use this for my knits and delicates. I’ll have your shirt washed and ironed in no time.”

“You don’t have to. Don’t worry about it.”

Donna noticed that Geoffrey was wearing a wife-beater undershirt. *Where’s the tattoo of the naked lady?* “No problem. I’m glad to do it.” Donna filled the tub then plunged the shirt into the warm soapy water. She gently kneaded the shirt, pressed it against the bottom of the tub, and dumped out the suds. As she filled the dish tub with fresh water she glanced at the time. It was already after nine. Out of the corner of her eye she noticed that Geoffrey was staring at her. The countdown to 9:30 and his gawking made her nervous, but she kept on rinsing out the shirt. With one final wring, she drained out the water. “I’ll hang this in the shower. The air from the open window will dry it,” she called back to Geoffrey as she carried the dishpan into the bathroom, then quickly returned so she could observe Geoffrey’s movements.

“I might as well turn on the laptop,” Geoffrey said quietly.

Once the laptop was on, Donna signaled Tina with one ring to let her know that everything was set to go, and then she slipped her cell phone into her pocket. She squeezed a too large glob of hand cream onto her hands and rubbed it up to her elbows. The time was 9:28. It occurred to her that Loretta, Tina, and she had not synchronized their clocks. It really shouldn't matter though, as long as they get their signals straight.

The telephone rang – once. One minute passed, then two. Just as Donna was about to have a headache, the doorbell rang. She hit the buzzer and said, "Hello. Hello? Is anybody there?" There was no answer. "I'll be right back, Geoffrey. I'll go see who it is."

"Would you like me to go?"

"No, no, no. You just continue what you're doing. I'm on my way." She raced out the door and down the front stairs. By the time she reached the first floor, Tina was coming through the front entrance door. "Okay Tina, let me help you down. How will you be most comfortable?"

"Oof." Tina whispered, "When do I start yelling for help?"

"As soon as I get back upstairs – I don't want him down here too soon. There needs to be enough time to signal Loretta." Donna ran back up to her apartment and burst through the front door with a feigned sense of urgency.

"Geoffrey, my first-floor neighbor Tina has fallen and she's dead weight!"

"Should we call an ambulance? What if she broke any bones?"

Donna responded, "This has happened before. She's fine, I'm sure. I know how to handle her, but I could use some help."

Donna followed Geoffrey downstairs. She reached into her pocket for her cell phone and tapped Loretta's number.

"I've fallen and I can't get up! Please help me," Tina called as if she were really in distress.

"Are you hurt?" Donna asked, suppressing a smile and knowing perfectly well that Tina wasn't.

"No. I went down easy. Oo fa! These damn legs of mine! It's just hard to get back up because I'm so stiff."

"What if you broke your hip?" Geoffrey said.

"No. I didn't exactly fall, but just slid down on my fat ass as I was trying to uh, uh, uh –"

"Tie your shoe?" Donna volunteered then gave a quick glance at Tina's feet only to realize that she was wearing slip-ons.

"Yeah, that's it – tie my shoes."

"Just take it easy," Geoffrey said. "We'll help you." Geoffrey reached under Tina's armpits.

"Give me a minute to catch my breath," she grunted looking at Donna as if to get a cue. Geoffrey let go of Tina and sat on a stair to wait until she was ready. Meanwhile, upstairs, Loretta sneaked into the apartment in search of the disk.

"You're such a wonderful fella to help me, and Donna, you're one in a million, the sweetest girl in the world," Tina panted. "I'm so lucky to have you as a neighbor. Imagine if you weren't here. I'd have to wait for one of those two beauts up – uh, uh, I could rot here before anyone'd find me." She paused several seconds. "I'm ready. I'll try to push up as much as I can." Despite her promise to help, Tina at first allowed herself to be dead weight and would moan and gasp as though any pressure on her legs caused discomfort. When her rescue became too much of a struggle in the confined space, she cooperated and helped Donna and Geoffrey to get her to her feet. Tina leaned on Geoffrey while Donna opened the door, and the three of them entered Tina's apartment.

"If you can get me to that armchair and bring my walker over to me, I'd appreciate it," Tina said.

When at last Tina was seated Donna said to Geoffrey, "Watch her a second while I get her some water." Donna went into Tina's kitchen and called her own apartment, with one ring of the phone. “I hope you’re finished, Loretta,” she whispered to herself. She carried a glass of water back to Tina who was gushing about Donna.

“I don’t know what I’d do without her. It’s so hard being alone and arthritic the way I am, but I always know that Donna is there for me. She’s an angel. You never hear a mean word come out of her mouth. Have you ever seen such a beautiful face? Like a Raphael painting.”

“Yes, she’s very special.”

“And beautiful,” Tina said to tweak Geoffrey to agree.

“Yes, very.”

Donna’s hand shook so much that water splashed from the glass. A forced compliment could not be trusted and, even if sincere, in this case would serve as a form of control, anyway. Tina reached for the glass of water and invited Donna and Geoffrey to stay for coffee. “I made crullers this morning, with and without raisins. They’re still warm.”

“No wonder I can’t lose any weight,” Donna said.

“You look like you lost quite a few pounds. Besides, you’ve got a beautiful shape, not like these sticks with bones poking out all over the place, like a sack of wire hangers or a scrawny turkey carcass. Then they go and put these huge melon breasts on their chests. Who are they kidding?” Tina took a sip of water and said, “Donna, you know where everything is in the kitchen. Geoffrey, would you be a dear and go help her carry everything? We’ll eat in here.”

Geoffrey reluctantly followed Donna into the kitchen. He wanted to get back to work but found the situation awkward. Might as well humor her. The day was still young. He leaned against the counter by the sink and nibbled a piece of cruller. Donna stepped into the pantry, dialed Loretta’s cell phone and let it ring until Loretta answered. “Hello, Loretta. Tina made some crullers this morning, and I'm in her kitchen making coffee. Are you free to join us?"

"Yes, I finished my morning chores." Loretta lowered her voice. "Is anyone within earshot?'

"Uh huh – yes."

"I was very productive. I got everything done from A to B. Now I'm just strolling home through the backyards. If anything failed, I'll come back if you like."

"Geoffrey, come here and talk to me," Tina called from the living room. "I have a question to ask you." Geoffrey politely obeyed. "Now Geoffrey, do you have a girlfriend?"

Donna almost dropped her cell. "Ah Loretta, so what are you doing on your day off? Are you coming over? What time do you go in tomorrow?" Donna asked any random question she could think of to avoid going into the living room with Tina and Geoffrey. She did, however, listen in between her own words to hear Geoffrey's response.

"Not really. I'm not engaged or anything. In fact, I'm not tied to anyone. Never have been," he answered.

"Confirmed bachelor, are you?"

"No. It's just not easy, no matter how many people you meet."

"Broken a lot of hearts, then?" Tina asked.

"I don't think so. Someone must really love you before you can break their heart."

"Don't tell me you're the one who gets heartbroken!"

"No. I never cared enough."

"You just haven't met the right girl." Tina paused and giggled, "Or have you?"

Any answer that Geoffrey may have given was inaudible, and his facial expression out of Donna's line of vision.

After the burn faded from Donna's cheeks, she joined them in the living room, and they finished their coffee with no more embarrassing remarks from Tina who was, after all, just trying to help. Tina saved her nosiest observation for when Geoffrey returned to Donna's to work, and Donna stayed to clean up the dishes. "Donna," Tina said as Geoffrey headed upstairs, "I noticed he wasn't wearing a shirt. Did our little plan interrupt something?"

"Are you kidding? I'm not exactly his type."

"Don't be so sure. That's not the impression I get. You should have seen him blush when I was talking to him about his love life, especially when I hinted about you."

"Well sure!" Donna had to control herself from saying, *duh*! "It didn't mean that it had anything to do with me."

"I don't know. He seems very comfortable with you."

"He's probably relaxed with most people. I don't think he ever had to work to get anyone's approval. He just has to walk into a room and, before he even opens his mouth, everyone is won over."

"It's more than that. Haven't you noticed the way he looks at you?" Tina asked. "I still think he likes you."

"Why shouldn't he *like* me? I've never done anything but help him to write his next big seller and not retaliate against him or his aunt. If he looks at me, it's probably in disbelief." Donna paused to shake free the Geoffrey obsession that seemed to cling to the back of her neck like a hungry koala to a eucalyptus tree. "Tina, thanks for being such a good friend. Loretta might come over, but I'd better get back upstairs. This is probably one of the last days we'll work together, and there's a lot to get done."

***

Geoffrey was so absorbed when Donna returned that he barely looked up from his laptop. "I can't figure – what the...? Ah, here it is," Geoffrey said with relief. Donna didn't dare ask what was wrong but was grateful that Geoffrey fixed whatever Loretta had bungled. When Geoffrey looked as though the problem was forgotten, Donna looked over his shoulder.

"Geoffrey, I think that Cynthia should really stick it to Andrews."

"Why?"

"It's what she would do."

Although Geoffrey knew this, he was reluctant to see the inevitable direction the characters were going. "They should end up together, otherwise he'll end up alone or we'll have to create another love interest for him."

"Why? Lots of people – most people – are alone at least sometime in their lives. Maybe that's what he deserves. Besides, why are you so protective of *her*?" Donna asked. "She's totally out for herself. Of course she would betray him. Can't you see where it's all leading?"

Geoffrey leaned back in his chair and rubbed the back of his neck. "I don't know. Andrews should come out on top. Why do women have to be so complicated?"

"Are women complicated or are men just simple? So many men care only about superficial …" Donna stopped short of finishing the sentence. She was starting to get personal, and she wasn't sure that Geoffrey didn't notice. "Besides, Andrews can still come out on top, even with Cynthia's betrayal. The two are not mutually exclusive. A read through the story might make the choice obvious," Donna said with the hope that Geoffrey would offer her a legitimate chance to read the story before she did it on the sly.

"We'll see," Geoffrey said. "We've gone back and forth over this before. In the meantime, why don't you go over this section. The conversation seems a little stilted for slick characters like these."

Donna obediently complied, and the two worked in relative silence until Geoffrey looked at his watch. "We should be leaving for the restaurant soon. I'd better go put on a shirt."

Donna went to her bathroom, brushed her teeth, and changed her clothes. Had this lunch seemed like more than an obligatory act of appreciation, she would have chosen a nicer outfit or painted her nails at least. Instead, she stuck with her original choice of a blue favorite she hadn't worn in two years. An eighteen-inch silver chain with a dragon fly pendant was teamed with a long strand of pink pearls. She flicked on a bit of mascara and powdered her T-zone. Two shades of pink lipstick competed for selection and agreed upon a compromise ala Loretta. The rosier shade glided on first with the paler pearly pink sliding over it. Although Geoffrey supposedly only had to change his shirt, Donna was ready before he was.

They left East Boston with the airport encroachment and oil tanks behind them and headed north. Congestion from two rotaries strangled the highway through Revere and loosened only slightly in Saugus. "There are so many restaurants on Route One, but we're going to one that's tucked away and a little quieter. Today might be the last chance to take you anywhere," Geoffrey said as though they would never see each other again. They chatted about random subjects the rest of the ride until they came to the restaurant, which was indeed out of the way. It was dark and busy with private booths and lots of space between tables.

As they sat to wait for their table, Donna noticed several people looking at them. She was certain that at least two women looked back and forth between Geoffrey and herself, as if asking, "What does he see in her?"

Geoffrey's cell phone rang, and he was suddenly absorbed in a conversation with someone Donna suspected was Sandra. Without so much as an "excuse me," Geoffrey got up and went outside to finish the call. No wonder he took her to an out of the way place. Even he didn't want to be seen with her! One of the women, who Donna imagined had gawked at her in disbelief, smirked when Geoffrey left. *"Even you know what he's up to,* Donna thought as she found herself staring daggers at the woman who she believed was mocking her. The woman shot Donna a startled look when the hostess called Geoffrey's name. Donna stood and signaled to the hostess then went outside to get Geoffrey.

In a voice loud enough for the person on the other end of Geoffrey's cell to hear, Donna called, "Geoffrey, our table is ready."

In a soft tone Geoffrey said, "Gotta go," into his cell. He gave Donna a quick glance as he held the restaurant door open for her but would not look her in the face until after they sat down and were handed their menus. Donna looked around to see who was staring at them now: no one. *Get a grip, Donna.*

Donna ate half a roll and ordered a salad.

"Is that all you're going to have? Aren't you hungry?" asked Geoffrey who had ordered a salad and a steak. Donna had to suppress the urge to yell, "Why? Do you think I'm such a big eater that I should wolf down half a cow?" Instead, she just smiled and nodded. No sense giving herself *agita* over an imagined insult, when there are enough deliberate ones darting about.

"Geoff, my man," a voice called from several feet away. A tanned, designer-casual man – a player – with $3,000 sunglasses hanging from his shirt pocket, and a wristwatch from a stratosphere Donna couldn't recognize, approached their table.

"Blake!" said Geoffrey, somewhat startled. "What's up?"

Something tells me Geoffrey won't introduce us. Let's see if I'm right. Donna looked up at Blake who gave her the once-over.

“Well,” said Blake, who seemed to speak for the benefit of everyone in the restaurant, “the Beacon Hill property started a hot bidding war. It’s already 250K above asking, and there are two buyers who are determined to get it. We really could have priced it higher. And I think if we throw another two or three mill into the winery, we can really make it a class operation.”

Geoffrey answered, “Let me think about it.”

“Sure, no rush. My accountant’s crunching the numbers still, so we’ve got time to decide.” Blake glanced down at Donna again and tossed a “see ya” to Geoffrey before returning to his table where a clone of himself and a Sandra-type woman waited. If people are judged by the company they keep, then Blake the boor and Sandra the slut offered poor testimony for Geoffrey. Donna congratulated herself for not being his type. Geoffrey had once hinted that although his book royalties notched up his tax bracket, his investments really ratcheted up his wealth to a level where his money now worked for him. Still, something drove him to write. Perhaps it was a need to create – the only thing the two of them shared.

“So, Donna, what are your plans?” Geoffrey abruptly asked after a twenty-second silence.

“My plans? For what? Tomorrow? Life?” She realized that she was just making a pleasant conversation more difficult. “I don’t know. Please excuse me. I don’t mean to be flip.”

“I’m sorry. I was just trying to break the ice. We spend so much time together and talk so easily during our breaks, but sitting with you outside your apartment almost seems—”

“Strange?”

“Awkward, like a first date.”

“Let’s talk about the weather then.”

“Okay,” Geoffrey said. “It sure is hot!”

“But it’s the humidity, not the heat.”

"They're predicting rain this weekend, just in time for my vacation."

So that's exactly when he's going to make the break. Donna asked, "Where are you going?"

"The Cape for about a week or so until I finish up, then off to either New York for a business deal unrelated to the book or to somewhere hopefully cooler than here."

"Where?" Donna asked, suspecting that if he wanted to tell her, he would have.

"To northern California, probably." He leaned forward and whispered, "That winery is getting a little too complicated. I've got to get out there and take another look before I commit to anything."

"Are you going with anyone?" Donna asked with an air of genuine disinterest.

"Uh, yes, at least for part of the time."

Donna was curious about which part and with whom he meant, however she had already used up her nosy question card, so she decided to move on. She clearly was not part of the picture in his future and was fine with it, or so she told herself. Was Geoffrey a friend? Yes, in that she had some pleasant times with him; no, in that she could not trust him. For now, however at this time and place, she was sitting in a cozy restaurant with a man who could fill the gap of loneliness, if only for an hour or so. Donna let loose the knot of anxiety in her chest and became more animated. "We've gotten off the subject."

"What were we talking about?" Geoffrey asked.

"The weather. People often think that talking about the weather is useless, but it's actually very important – both the weather and discussing it. Talking about the weather is an icebreaker and a space-filler for social interaction. Also, most living creatures are very affected by and dependent on the weather."

"I never thought of it that way."

"It's true. My mother was born at home during a blizzard. Her mother became ill, and her father was stuck in the house for almost two days before he could get help. She was so happy that I was born in the summer so she could get to the hospital."

"Well, it's summer now, so when is or was your birthday?"

"A few weeks ago," said Donna remembering that she had already told him twice.

Geoffrey mentally counted. "It's now about mid-August, so that would have been July. What day?"

"Don't remind me."

"Why?"

"It's really not important," Donna answered dismissively.

"So is the ruby ring you're wearing your birthstone?" Geoffrey asked then slapped his shirt pocket in the realization that he did not have the pink wrapped package. He thought a moment to recall where he had left it.

He must be bored out of his skull, Donna instinctively switched to a subject of more interest to Geoffrey: himself. She asked him everything from his favorite color (red), favorite pig out food (pizza), if he ever had a weight problem (no), and other slightly inane questions, then moved on to a more serious discussion about his writing. No sense talking about Donna's life. He probably wouldn't remember anything she said.

Geoffrey talked on and on about how he got his start and where he got his ideas. The discussion topics flowed from Geoffrey's career to easy small talk about what they wanted out of life. He made no direct mention of Sandra or any other specific girlfriend, for that matter,

"You're the least ambitious woman I know," Geoffrey said. In response to Donna's raised eyebrows, he added, "No, no. Don't misunderstand me. I meant it as a compliment. Many women I meet are so aggressive that they have absolutely no charm, no appeal."

Why are his compliments always so backhanded or forced? Donna erased the negative thought and said, "James Barrie, who wrote *Peter Pan,* said something like, 'If a woman has charm, she doesn't need anything else; if she doesn't have charm, it doesn't matter what else she has.'"

"Yes. That's true."

"It's an old-fashioned idea, and I'm not sure that it is true, but I think the same can be said for men as well. Actually, I think a person needs more than charm."

"Like what?" Geoffrey asked.

"Charm can be deceptive – some of the worst people are charming. Kindness and decency are more important."

"And you've got them all, Donna. I wish…" Geoffrey shook his head in regrettable confusion. "I wish things could be different."

Donna wasn't sure what he meant or what she should say. Should "things" between the two of them or "things" in human nature or the world be different?

"Let's leave," Geoffrey said abruptly. He signaled the waitress, handed her several bills then whisked Donna out the door. "Let's head up to Maine."

"Maine?"

"Or New Hampshire – near water."

"There's always Revere or Nahant Beach. They're closer."

"And crowded, even though the summer peak is winding down. Are you in a hurry to get back?"

"I thought we had to finish up."

"There's time for that. There's not much time for us."

Donna, totally confused, looked out the car window. What's with this guy? He runs hot and cold, attentive and dismissive, intimate and distant, all in the matter of days, if not hours. She would go along for the ride – literally - but would sit tight emotionally.

They found a nearby lake and walked along the edge of the water.

"I'm used to being around forceful, aggressive people, who put a price tag on everything. No one has time for anyone or anything unless they can profit from it. They have a way of pulling you into their manic misery and making you believe you must be just like them. Sometimes I don't know who my friends are," Geoffrey said.

"That's just the way a lot of people behave. I suppose to be successful a person should be a little driven, but that's no excuse for not being decent."

"It's been so different with you. You're more than decent – and kind." Geoffrey squinted at the distant ripples of the water. "There's a sadness in you that is calming, strange."

"I've made friends with my feelings a long time ago. If something can't be changed, it's less overwhelming if you just accept it."

"You just accept whatever happens?"

"After a while I do." Donna shrugged with the resignation that fit like old flannel, worn, but too comfortable to take off. "There's only so much effort one person can put out."

"You're probably putting your effort in the wrong direction."

"Maybe, but I'm happy if I can lay my head on my pillow at night and not worry or obsess over some problem or crisis. I accept boredom and resignation over turmoil and stress. Life is what it is. It could be worse."

"That's the problem. It could be worse, and I always try to fight it. The pace sometimes gets too fast. It's hard to let myself slip. I'm not an addict or an alcoholic, no way, but…"

"What?"

Geoffrey shrugged. "I don't mean to imply that I'm way into all that stuff, but I didn't come to my aunt and uncle's just to work, as you know. I had to put some space between some of my acquaintances and myself. I'm no angel, but I just don't have much attraction for anything other than good wine, and it's hard being around people who need more than that. They suck the energy out of you."

"Some friends – but you chose them!"

"It's true that misery likes company, and the company I kept had no interest in my welfare, just their own good time."

Donna felt empathy tinged with disgust. How tough could this man's life be? Self-indulgence and hubris are his biggest problems. Nonetheless, one struggling soul recognizes another. They drove home in relative silence, yet Donna felt as though they had a telepathic conversation the whole way.

When they entered the apartment, Donna took a pitcher of iced tea from the refrigerator, and they sat on the porch. Donna said, "Geoffrey, before we get back to work, I'd like to discuss something that has been bothering me all along about Andrews."

"What's that?"

"He's the protagonist, but I don't like him."

"Still? Look at all the great things he did. He's a hero."

"What are his redeeming qualities other than his bravery? In fact, how brave is it to allow someone to steal your identity when you know that there are people out to kill you?"

"Donna, remember that was originally *your* idea."

"I know, but where's his conscience? You can't hurt someone and then go skipping off into the sunset. There at least should be some soul-searching and regret."

"It's kind of late for that."

"No, it isn't. You can always change—" Donna paused. "I know how we can do it. I'll write it out now."

"Go ahead, but I can't make any promises. It's got to seem like a natural evolution of his behavior."

"Fine, it will be," said Donna, pulling off her ring from her slightly sweaty finger. "Let's get to work." She took a deep breath and scribbled away. "Got it," she said.

Donna's home phone rang.

"Hello, Donna," Loretta whispered. "Can you come over or would you like me to bring the disk to you?"

"I'll be right there."

***

Loretta brought up the story on Donna's laptop and let Donna have a seat. Donna had no time or intention to read the whole book, but just craved the chance to look at it unrestrained. She got no further than the first page: *ID/XX (Identity Double Cross) by Geoffrey A. Imperato.* Donna blinked. Could this be an earlier version that Geoffrey worked on before she started co-writing with him? No. She remembered when the two of them came up with the title. She had no stomach to look any further. He had, in fact, cut her out as she feared he would but hoped he wouldn't.

Loretta looked over Donna's shoulder. "What does the middle initial stand for?"

"Aidan or Allen, I think."

"'A-hole', more like it."

"Loretta, do you mind holding onto all this? I'll be tempted to confront him with it and, even more, I'm afraid I'll break it over his head."

***

"What's wrong?" Geoffrey asked when Donna entered her apartment.

"I'm just a little tired, I guess."

"What do you say then, we have a pizza delivered for supper?"

"Okay."

"Have any beer or chianti?"

"No, but we could go out to get some and bring the pizza home. I could use some fresh air." The fact that she had just come in from the outside passed right over him.

They went to her favorite pizza parlor.

Donna's cloud lifted with the sight of Ella Zingarella sitting at the counter with a couple of friends. Big hair, halter tops, and major hoop earrings will never be out of style with the likes of Ella around. "Ay, Donna, how's it goin'?" Ella snapped her gum. She smiled approvingly at Geoffrey. "You Irene Infanto's son? Sure. Sure. 'Member the time I caught you bangin' my friend Joanie in the bathhouse. Oops, sorry Donna. I just had a couple of beers."

"No problem, Ella. We're just good friends, aren't we Geoff, er Georgie. Besides, I'm sure that was a long time ago," answered Donna giving Geoffrey a playful pinch on the cheek.

"Sure was," Ella said. "That girl's put a lot of miles in since – been married three times already – all of 'em losers. When she was nineteen her family tried to ship her off to It'ly to marry some distant *paesan* 'cause she was gettin' kinda wild, so she ran off with some guy she met at a carnival. He busted her jaw. They hadda wire it together."

"I'm sorry she's had such a rough time," Geoffrey said. "What's she doing now?"

"She's in Vegas and has a kid – doin' okay, gettin' by. We hear from 'er once in a while."

On the way home Donna thought about Ella's friend Joanie and wondered at what point had the unfortunate woman's path been set and whether she would ever have the power to redirect it.

Donna recovered enough balance to get through dinner. Geoffrey and she sat on the floor and ate off the coffee table.

They watched a cable news show and disagreed over several topics being discussed.

"Who cares about trees?" Geoffrey said. "They can grow back. It's not as though they're talking about the Amazon Rain Forest and some rare species of plant that can't be replaced."

"It's not just the trees. Animals live there."

"Tell them to move. If there's a forest fire, those animals, and not to mention houses, will be destroyed."

An athlete accused of assaulting a woman aroused the sharpest argument. "They think that just because they're famous and get paid millions that they can do whatever they like," Donna insisted.

"Look, these women put it out there. Let me tell you, I'm nowhere near as high profile as this guy, and you wouldn't believe the propositions I get. Even today at the restaurant, some woman came outside when I was on the phone and slipped me her number. You think all your sisters are like you?"

"You mean sisters like poor Joanie? You don't sound as though you have much respect for women."

"Not a lot of them. I wouldn't even call it disrespect. They are what they are – easy. I've never," said Geoffrey aiming a raised eyebrow at Donna, "well, almost never, had a woman refuse me."

"Hope you get tested, like frequently."

"I'm careful. Don't think that because I get offers that I just accept them. I'm very picky."

Donna wondered what kind of skanks he met if Sandra was one of his chosen. What a total skeeze! It angered Donna that he justified his disparagement of most women by being selective in the ones he used, as if they, by association with him, were elevated to some regal status. Suppressing an urge to grit her teeth, she looked him square in the face and said, "Geoffrey, what do you think of me?"

"You? You're not one of them. We've been together for all these weeks and – nothing."

Donna thought she detected a little contempt in the way Geoffrey said "nothing." "You think that just because you're alone with someone night after night that something is supposed to happen between you? Sorry to disappoint you, but I don't owe anyone an explanation for *my* behavior," Donna said.

"Are you –" Geoffrey halted, and Donna cut right over him.

"What do you think of me as a person?"

"You want to be appreciated for your mind?" he said with a smirky smile.

"I'm serious. What do you think of *me*?" Her voice rose in anger. Appreciation and respect were the least she wanted at this point. "Do you have any respect for me?"

Geoffrey put a lid on the smart-ass side of his personality and took a deep breath. "Sorry, I was being inconsiderate and disrespectful to all women, and then I was being sarcastic when I meant to be funny. As for you, I think you are different. You are unlike anyone I have ever known. I just don't know what to do about it."

"About what?"

"What I feel. I want you to always be my friend. I can be myself, whatever that is I don't know anymore, around you but, I just can't." He grasped for the words, but Donna wouldn't let him off the hook.

"You can't what?" she asked.

"Let it go any further."

"You mean let our relationship go any further or let me be the co-author of the book?" asked Donna, wanting him to confirm what she already knew from the disk.

After what seemed to be an interminable pause, Geoffrey answered, "Both."

At this point Donna didn't care about their personal relationship. He was a total earth pig and could go roll in the mud with the rest of them. Credit for all her work, which had only been sealed with a virtual handshake, was her only conscious concern. She should have screamed "theft" the day she discovered Geoffrey stealing her story.

Donna shook her head in self-disgust. "I'm so stupid," she said. "I deserve this. For weeks I put aside everything else for what? My whole summer wasted! Anytime I brought up the subject of a contract or firm agreement, you brushed me off, and worse, I let you!"

"Donna, I told you I'd take care of you, but I never said you would be a co-author. You just assumed it. I told you that I have a name to protect. Don't worry. I'll pay you for your time and input. I even plan to dedicate the book to you."

"Now you tell me!"

"You've got to understand, I've got five books, six really, out in my name, one worse than the other despite their huge sales. How would it look if the best thing I've written since my first hit had someone else's name on it? I'll get hammered. People will say that I've lost it and that I need the help of a total unknown."

"You should have been more up front about it, Geoffrey!"

"I thought I was. There's no guarantee that the book will even sell, but if it does, I said I'll gladly pay you. Hell, I'll pay you even if it doesn't sell. You put a lot of time in, and you should be compensated for that."

"Talk is cheap."

"If you don't believe me, I'll have my lawyer draw up a contract. He'll work out a way to give you a fair share of the royalties as well."

Now he's going to give her a contract. What a sport!

Donna wasn't sure she could believe him anymore, and worse, she knew that Geoffrey, from his behavior, believed she didn't have the power to retaliate. "Geoffrey, this is giving me a headache. I cannot even describe the way I feel. Disappointed doesn't even touch it, and yet, it's my own fault." The day they first met Geoffrey would have written a contract in his own blood, if she had demanded it then, before he knew her complacent nature. "How stupid am I? Have you ever met such a sap?"

"What?"

"Name one person who would have behaved the way I did. You know, you're lucky I'm such an idiot."

"Please Donna, just give me a chance. This whole situation was so awkward I didn't know the best way to handle it. I promise not to let you down. I just need to have only my name on the book. Please understand it's my whole career. I'm both my employer and employee. I'm totally dependent on myself."

"I depend on myself too, and I earn a fraction of what you make."

"I'm so sorry Donna. I'm such a jerk."

Yes, you are, she wanted to scream but was too tired of fighting and too ready to cry. Instead, she said, "You just never had to work for it. Growing up, you never had to develop your personality or character to please other people. In a way, I feel sorry for you."

Geoffrey leaned his elbow on the sofa cushion and ran his fingers through his hair. "You're right, Donna. You must learn something before you can know it. My parents never taught me anything of value. God knows what they thought they had in me. They pushed me in school, in sports, made me play the damn piano and trumpet, and even forced me to be a child model for some stupid clothing ads. All in the middle of everything, my father took off to go live with some woman. Then one day, he came home as though he had merely gone out for a walk. He never showed any remorse for what he did to the family.

Through all that my mother got even more ambitious with us kids."

"Gee, I didn't know any of this." Donna's anger diffused slightly.

"My parents were so screwed up that my brother, sister, and I had to live with my aunt and uncle for a while."

"You mean Angie and Primo?"

"They were more like parents to me than my own mother and father. My sister, who's older, got sent home first, then my brother. They kept me longer because I just couldn't take it. Imagine pushing a kid to a near breakdown."

"Geoffrey, I had no idea that's why you were so close to Angie and Primo. Were they living in this house at the time?"

"Yes, in fact, when the three of us were here, I slept in your bedroom, my brother in the other, and they kept my sister downstairs. If you peel the wallpaper under the left corner of your rear window down to the plaster, you'll find my initials."

"No wonder you felt so comfortable here!"

"You mean it's why I showed such poor judgement coming in here while it was your apartment. Any comfort I felt came from you. No one has ever been as genuinely sweet and sincerely nice to me and for so little reason."

"How can you say that in the middle of an argument?"

"Because it's true. There's only one other person I can trust besides you," he answered barely understanding that he was once again manipulating her. "I don't know what people want from me sometimes."

It still doesn't explain why you felt so comfortable stealing my work and not giving me credit for it, Donna thought with a wilting anger. A sudden realization turned her emotions and attitude. Although it may have been manipulation, Geoffrey had been telling her how different she was than everyone he knew, that she was the only person who never wanted anything from him or pushed him in any way. Now, despite how he saw it, she was asking that he give her something bigger than possibly anyone had ever demanded from him: his reputation. Why did she need to be named co-author? Wasn't the payment enough? "Geoffrey, I'm sorry. You're right," she said with the relief of certainty and release. "I don't know why I didn't see reality before. This is your book, and it would be wrong to deny you full public credit for it. It's not what I would have written on my own, and I wouldn't want my name associated with any sex scenes you probably included. You've offered to pay me for my help and that's fine. I don't want anything else from you. It's your career and it's nothing to me." Money talked and she listened.

True, to Donna payment meant more than credit for the book, which she might find embarrassing or not even like once she read it; however, she could barely admit to herself what she really had wanted once, because any hope for it had been taken from her on her birthday. Donna had wasted her summer and had not been honest with herself about why. The book had merely provided an excuse to keep him near. They could have spent their time copying the dictionary instead of writing *ID/XX*, and she would have felt the same.

For several minutes they sat in silence, each frozen by the uncomfortable heat of their worn emotions. She wished to run from the discomfort and discomfiture.

"Donna?"

"What?"

"It's been a long day. Can we just not end it in an argument?"

Once again, Donna reacted like a battered wife and did as she was told. She had wanted them to get back to the discussion about a contract for payment – a definite *when, where, and how*, but she couldn't rouse the strength to fight for the one crumb he held out to her. Her residual hurt now ached with the pain of emotional abuse. With her cooperation, he had led her on and showed her what a chump she was. He gave her no respect and she had little of her own left for self-defense. On some level, physical violence or rage would have been normal responses compared to Donna's passive acceptance.

As if he read her mind, Geoffrey, whether to show his sincerity or to mock her, hand-wrote a makeshift temporary contract for Donna. At the bottom it read: "*This is to be replaced by a proper legal one a.s.a.p.*" Donna gave an automatic smile of acceptance, which by now had become her programmed response to almost every disappointment.

They carried their dishes to the dishwasher. On the counter sat the thin pink package from the morning's cream cheese incident. "Your shirt – it must be dry by now."

"Forget it. Here, I meant to give you this at lunch," Geoffrey said as he handed the present to her. "That's why I brought up your birthday. It's from Crotone Italy. They make some of the world's most beautiful jewelry there. I already knew it was your birthstone."

Donna unwrapped the paper to find a black velveteen-covered square envelope. Inside was a ruby encrusted gold pin. "It's so beautiful. Thank you." Donna held the swirled form in her palm.

"It's the letter D," Geoffrey said tracing with his index finger. Donna recalled Sandra's gold and emerald earring, whose spiral shape, she suddenly realized, was the letter S – must have been a gift from Geoffrey as well. "Let me pin it on you."

"Wait a minute," said Donna as she reached into a jar of loose change. "Here's a penny – just a silly superstition that I don't really believe in, though my mother does. It's supposed to keep the friendship from breaking whenever one person gives another a pointed gift."

They sat out on the back porch drinking ginger ale and listening to Rossini overtures until the blaring horns of *William Tell* made one of the neighbors shut their windows. The music ended and within minutes Donna fell asleep. Geoffrey's cell phone rang, and Donna's sleep lightened enough that she was vaguely aware of her surroundings. "Hi, sorry I didn't call," she heard Geoffrey say. "Well, I was busy finishing up…What time should we meet? … My place of course…How long will Daddy Warbucks be away? … Good…Thank God for cell phones. Let's hope he doesn't hear the ocean in the background…Pack light. You won't need many clothes…I'm at Primo's…Her? She's asleep. We worked almost the whole day…No, really, we did… Why would I? … We went to lunch but spent the morning and afternoon working. There's not much left to do. We're, uh, I'm months ahead of schedule. I can finish at the Cape. Then I got to get to New York…No, I think it's best you stay away from the city. All we'd need is to be seen together…Yes, the city is big, but the area we stay in isn't. We'll have plenty of time together… Bye."

Geoffrey let out a big sigh then spoke as if he didn't expect Donna to hear. "Donna?" No answer. "I'm sorry, Donna. You're everything I need, but not what I want." He carried their glasses to the sink, packed up his things, and left with one nostalgic glance back at the place that had been a refuge during two trying periods of his life.

Donna curled up on the chaise. A lone tear ran down her cheek.

CHAPTER TWELVE
D FOR DECEPTION OR D FOR DISAPPOINTMENT?

The next day Donna was scheduled to work until six. Although the ruby pin would have been perfect for her outfit, she didn't wear it. Instead, she ironed and folded Geoffrey's shirt, and after one last admiring look, placed the pin in the pocket and carried it down to the Infantos' apartment.

Geoffrey opened the door. "Hi, Donna, I was just packing."

"Here's your shirt."

"Just put it in my suitcase over there."

Donna did as she was told. "Have a good time," she said leaving and not looking back.

"Hey, can you stay a while for coffee? I feel I ended things badly last night."

More than you know. Donna said, "I've got to be leaving for work."

"What time do you get home?"

"Not until later this evening. I get out at six, but I'm going out after work."

"Oh?"

"Yes. I haven't gone out much lately." Donna's lunch date and pizza excursion with Geoffrey yesterday didn't count for much.

"Are you going out with Loretta?"

"No." Donna had learned Geoffrey's game of giving clipped answers to prying questions. "When are you leaving?"

"Tonight," Geoffrey answered.

"Well then, see ya. It's been interesting and fun. Thanks for everything." Donna dashed down the stairs as Geoffrey mumbled something barely audible. All their mutual emotional output ended with a whimper. She mentally kicked herself. "Why are you thanking him?" As if to shake off the disappointment, she hurried down the street like a person unsure they were being chased. Twice she looked over her shoulder as if he might shoot another demeaning dart into her back.

***

That evening Donna and a co-worker, Ginny Alexander, went to an Italian restaurant in the North End. Ginny was a single mother who rarely got out, but her birthday was a week ago, so the women decided to celebrate.

"Happy belated birthday, Ginny!"

"Happy belated birthday, to you too, Donna. It's so good to get out."

"Who's watching Lisa?"

"My sister." Ginny pursed her lips in a mock attempt to suppress a subject that many women find uncomfortable, then let it spill out. "My brother Brad is coming for a visit next week. I think the two of you would really hit it off. Would you like to meet him? He lives in Pennsylvania, so you won't have to get serious with him or anything. Just have some fun." Donna normally hated blind dates, but could Ginny's brother be any worse than her recent experience?

"Yes, I would like to meet him. If he's half as nice as you are, I'm sure we'll have a great time together."

Ginny had her car, so she drove Donna home. When Geoffrey heard the car door shut, he looked out the window. He grabbed his suitcase, locked the door, and headed downstairs. Donna was at Tina's doorway when Geoffrey reached the first floor.

"Good evening, Geoffrey," Tina said. "Where're you off to?"

"The Cape."

"For how long?" Tina asked.

"About a week or so."

"Do you have time to come in for a bite?"

"Sure. I'm not leaving until tomorrow. I'm staying at my condo tonight so I could take care of some last-minute things and pack more clothes."

Donna wanted to say, "Gee, I thought you weren't going to need many clothes." She said, "Do you need much more than that to sit on a beach and write all week?" Before Geoffrey could open his mouth, she shut it with an abrupt, "Good night." She headed upstairs to cut short the conversation.

Tina called after her, "Donna where are you going? Come and keep us company a while."

Much as Donna wanted to get out of there, she didn't want Tina to say Lord-knows-what to Geoffrey in her absence. "Okay, it's been a long day, but I can spare a few minutes." Donna prepared some decaf coffee and set out some of Tina's home-made biscotti. Donna and Geoffrey sat at opposite ends of the sofa, facing Tina, who was perched in her easy chair and ready for the interrogation.

"So, Donna, where did you go tonight?" Tina asked.

"To a restaurant," and anticipating Tina's next question, added, "with a friend."

"Anyone I know?"

"No." Donna looked away with a slight frown.

Tina moved on to question Geoffrey. "Will Donna be joining you at any time while you're away?"

"Uh, no."

"You're going to be there all alone? Do you have any friends there?" Tina asked.

"I won't be alone. I've got a, friends."

"He undoubtedly has a girlfriend who'll be joining him, won't she Geoffrey?" said Donna looking at him.

"Yes." Geoffrey's expression was difficult to read.

"Tina. I know you've got the wrong impression because Geoffrey and I spent so much time together. The fact is he's involved with someone else. Besides, even if he wanted me to visit him at the Cape, I can't because I have work, and a fellow from Pennsylvania will be in town for just a week." So there, you never know when a friend's brother will come in handy. Donna glanced sideways at Geoffrey and noticed that he was staring open-mouthed at her – as if she gave a rat's patoot. She stood up. "It's been a long day, and Geoffrey has some 'last minute things' to take care of."

***

As Geoffrey backed out of the driveway, he looked up at Donna's living room window and saw her silhouette looking down at him. She could have been a cardboard cut-out for all the emotion she felt. Geoffrey's car carried him home to find a marinated Sandra with a dry martini waiting.

***

Donna was so busy Saturday that she hardly had time to think, and when any thought percolated into her consciousness, it was filtered through a gauze of emotional exhaustion. Ginny had set up the first date for Donna and her brother for Tuesday night. The Tuesday night date would prove to be the first of three, punctuated by family commitments.

***

After a tantrum-and-traffic-tense ride, Geoffrey and Sandra arrived at her family's summer home on Cape Cod early Saturday evening. Geoffrey had a headache from the waves of Sandra's sulky silence, whining, complaining, and angry outbursts. Her colleagues, other drivers, her ex-husband, her future husband, and Donna – especially Donna – all took turns at the center of her poison dartboard, at which she threw projectiles of vitriol and venom.

Geoffrey wheeled their suitcases to the door while Sandra angrily searched for her keys, which she momentarily thought she had lost or forgotten. "Why the hell didn't you remind me to bring them? Never mind. Here they are," she said then pushed open the door.

They were met with a nasty surprise: small rats or large mice had eaten their way into the house and had nested in two of the kitchen cabinets.

"Who the hell left food in here?" Sandra shrieked and threw her keys. "Do something!"

"It's Saturday night. What stores are open around here?" Geoffrey asked knowing that the task would fall to him.

"Who the hell knows? Just get some traps and rat poison, will you, or else we'll have to stay in a hotel. This time of year, we'll probably end up in some dump. While you're at it, pick up more wine and another bottle of vodka or we'll run out by mid-week."

"Half the trunk is filled with booze."

"Yah well, you should've filled the other half. And make sure it's the good stuff."

Geoffrey got in his car and drove around until he found variety and liquor stores that had what they needed. Sandra was too repulsed to touch anything. She dialed a neighbor. "Hello Ilsa, this is Sandra. Can I have your housekeeper tomorrow? In fact, I'll pay her extra if she can come tonight. Someone left this place a pigsty. I'm airing it out now, but I'll have to spend the night in a hotel."

Geoffrey returned and dutifully set the traps and poison. "You really need an exterminator to get rid of them completely now that they're inside the house. We're going to hear traps snapping all night."

Sandra angrily puffed on a cigarette. "I called around and found a motel, probably some shithouse, we can stay in until my neighbor's maid gets this place cleaned up. I'll call for an exterminator from there. Right now, I just want to get the hell out of here. I don't want any vermin crawling over me while I'm sleeping."

"Doesn't it make sense to have it cleaned after the extermination?"

"Whatever. I'll deal with that later. Let's just leave."

"Mind if we go for a swim first to unwind after the drive?" Geoffrey asked.

"I'm not getting in that shower afterwards. There's probably rat shit all over the place." Sandra smashed out her cigarette. "And *I said* I want to leave right now! You deaf or just thick?"

They drove to the motel and swam in the pool, which they shared with two other people. Sandra clung to Geoffrey until he broke away to do some laps. Sandra pouted and insisted they go to their room and have dinner delivered from one of the restaurants across the street. After two martinis and some pot, Sandra relaxed. "Did you buy me a present?" she asked while they were in the shower.

"Of course. It's packed. I'll get it later."

Geoffrey was so tired that he fell asleep still wrapped in his towel. Sandra wasted no time. She fished around in Geoffrey's suitcase for what she hoped to be something with diamonds. Instead, she found in the pocket of a shirt, something with rubies: Donna's pin. "Hmm. It's okay but not worth waking him up to show my appreciation." She put the pin on the night table and went to sleep.

***

The next morning in the light of day Sandra got a more clear-headed look at the pin. She jabbed Geoffrey in the side to wake him up.

"Geoffrey darling is this my gift?" she asked holding out the pin for him to see.

"Wait, where did you get that?"

"Let me guess," said Sandra holding the pin between her thumb and forefinger. "Is this D for dunce, D for dupe, or D for doormat?"

"Who said it's a D?"

"I know this artist's work, as well as you do. If this isn't the letter D, then I'm D for dumb."

"I gave that to Donna just to thank her for all her help. That's all."

"A token of thanks is a potted plant or a box of candy, which she needs like horizontal stripes. You don't buy something like this for some stupid, useless, little helper. You had to order this weeks ago. Is that how long you've been carrying on with her?"

"Sandra, you're being unreasonable. She worked hard for weeks and got nothing out of it."

"*She* worked hard? What about *me*? Who introduced you around and got you a better agent than that schlockmeister you had before? Who agreed to help you edit and proofread your manuscript so that no one else will see how lousy it is? Who gives you whatever you want, whenever and wherever you want it?"

Geoffrey was unwilling to point out that Sandra's help with the book was only recent and just shy of useless. As for the people he met through her, most of them were the same *arazzo* – woven from the same flimsy, artificial fiber as Sandra. Over time, the threads from Sandra's complicated tapestry had been slowly unraveling and tangling Geoffrey in the process until they now worked their way up to his neck and formed a tight noose. Once more, Geoffrey choked back his pride and coughed up a strangled apology. "But Sandra, I got you a present, a much nicer one. You just didn't look hard enough for it."

"Get it for me!"

Geoffrey got up and reached into the pocket of his suitcase. "Here," he said, tossing the package to her. It was, in fact, diamonds. Sandra held up her glitzy white gold and diamond pin against Donna's ruby one. "Yup – red but positively anemic by comparison. Actions speak." All was forgiven, at least for a while.

It was after her third cup of coffee that Sandra's mind began to race. "Geoffrey, what was her pin doing in your shirt pocket?"

"Donna must have put it in there when she returned the shirt to me."

"What was she doing with your shirt?"

"It was in her apartment."

"Obviously. What was it doing there?"

"She washed it for me after it got dirty."

"And you couldn't do that yourself?"

"She insisted."

"If she insisted that you take off your pants, would you have?"

Geoffrey smirked. "Probably."

Big mistake. Sandra grabbed Donna's pin and tried to scratch Geoffrey. She missed her target and grazed his thigh.

"Ouch, you crazy bitch," he yelled and put as much distance between them as the room would allow. He examined the scratch and opened his laptop. "Why do I put up with you?"

"Because up is where I keep you, sweetheart," shouted Sandra with the full belief that she was the most important part of Geoffrey's life. "Where would you be without me?"

"I'll be nowhere if I don't get this book finished. You make such a fuss over a lousy pin that took all of one phone call to order."

"It's the thought that counts, and the fact that you even thought to give her anything bugs me. She doesn't need any encouragement. Hasn't she had enough?"

"She didn't get anything but a lousy pin, which you'll notice, she gave back. Drop it!"

Sandra rolled off the bed to get a little rolled something. She lit a joint and held it in front of Geoffrey's mouth. "I brought my little medicine chest with me. Name your poison. How 'bout loosening up for a while? You're way too tense."

"Get that stuff away from me and throw out all that other crap! Can't you see what it does to you? You want us both in rehab?"

"I want us to be together, mentally and physically. You've been ignoring me, and I promised you I would have the gallies ready to go. Why did I bother to come?"

"Supposedly to help me. I could have taken Donna."

"I hate that name! What's the matter – you never did it with a fat girl? Is that the attraction?" Sandra flopped back down on the bed and scowled at her fingernails. "Shit! Chipped already. You'd think I did housework. Go get my red nail polish in my cosmetic case."

"Are you going to paint your nails or help me?"

"What do you think I've been doing for the past few weeks? I told you I would finish up and have it ready to send off. I'll make sure this book gets the attention it deserves. It'll be worth chipping my nails some more. Move over," said Sandra pushing Geoffrey off the chair. "I'll take over. Go relax a while. You're so tired from working so hard," Sandra said in a mocking tone.

"I'm going for a walk on the beach," Geoffrey said. "I'll have my cell phone in case you have any questions." He grabbed his sunglasses and left without inviting Sandra to go along for even just a little bit.

Sandra opened her suitcase and pulled out a notebook. "Okay Donna, I'll show you how the big girls do it."

Geoffrey went on some walk, over two hours, lost in thought. He opened the motel room door to the sound of a drawer slamming shut and the sight of a jittery Sandra. "Give me half an hour to get ready and we'll go to lunch," she said. Sandra touched up her makeup and slipped into a short white shift that contrasted with her smoky eye shadow, tomato red lipstick, and tan. With her freshly painted nail tips, Sandra walked like Marie Antoinette going to a hoedown.

First, they had a drink from the bar of a seafood restaurant across the street from the motel. Sandra sat sideways on the swivel stool and crossed and uncrossed her legs. In no time most of the people in view were looking at her. Geoffrey at first noticed with pride all the attention Sandra attracted until he caught the direction of the stares – women were scowling at Sandra's face and men were gawking lower. "Sandra," Geoffrey said with a cringing embarrassment, "what are you doing?"

"What do you mean? These plebs aren't used to seeing a truly beautiful woman. You should show more appreciation." She fanned herself with the coaster. "It's hot in here. I'm just melting on the seat." When they were called for their table Sandra slid down from the bar stool ahead of Geoffrey and strutted behind the hostess. A stream of titters bursting into howls followed her.

"Uh, Sandra," Geoffrey said catching up to her. "Your dress, in back –"

"Did it ride up?" Sandra said playfully while tugging at the rear hem. "It's so sticky and sultry in here that I was glued to the seat."

"No," Geoffrey whispered in her ear. "There's a red stain."

Sandra looked down in shock as a thin trickle of blood ran down her thigh. On impulse she slapped Geoffrey, the bearer of bad tidings, across the face.

It was a long walk to the door.

"Get me out of this shit hole!" Sandra yelled as she stormed into the motel room. "Pack up my stuff and have it in the car by the time I get changed – now!" Sandra grabbed a tampon and a red sundress and slammed the bathroom door behind herself.

They drove around and could not find anywhere with vacancies that met with Sandra's satisfaction. Finally in frustration Geoffrey went back to their original motel. "Look," he said, "you had chosen this place because you thought it was better than some of the others because it was more expensive. I'm sure all the people in that restaurant are gone by now and are probably staying all over town anyway. You're just as likely to run into them anywhere else we go."

"I'm not afraid of anyone."

"I know, I know." Geoffrey softened. "Most of these people will probably be gone after the weekend. If you like, I'll get some take-out."

Their original room was being cleaned, and Sandra insisted they be given a better one away from the street. After they had settled into their new room, Geoffrey went out to get scampi and linguini, and a bottle of chilled white wine for lunch. Sandra, who feared no man, nonetheless insisted on staying in that evening. "I'm achy and bloated. No more booze for me tonight." After another take out dinner Sandra opened her medicine case for menstrual relief of the opiate variety.

Next morning Geoffrey worked furiously. "Huh? What's this?" he said to the zonked-out figure on the bed, as if expecting an alert answer. "There's something in here I don't quite remember. It must be something Donna threw at me one night when I was tired."

"Wha?" Sandra said sleepily.

"Never mind, I'll just smooth it over, so it blends into the story better. Then I'll have to finish the last chapter," said Geoffrey, finally realizing that Donna was right about the Cynthia character. *Come to think of it, she was right about Andrews too.* While Sandra was still safely asleep, Geoffrey reached into his briefcase and pulled out the pages that Donna had written the last night they worked together. After reading them a second time, he began to type:

Andrews should have felt better than he did. In fact, he should have been exhilarated. However inadvertently, his "interception" of the Maxim Gang's cargo had yielded not only great wealth, but also two hostages and chemical weapons. This clever hijacking had started a chain of events that led to the extermination of three dozen vermin. The world may never know how many lives he had saved, but he knew that he had great cause to celebrate.

With his favorite wine in one hand and a corkscrew in the other, Andrews stood on the balcony and drank in the water of the Pacific. His mind danced along the pathway formed by the glints of moonlight on the waves. A brief weak smile slipped into a frown. What was wrong? Why didn't he feel like the hero he supposedly was? He shrugged as he pierced the cork with the metal worm of the corkscrew. Johnson – he had done to Johnson exactly what he was doing to this cork. He had escaped danger, but he could not escape his conscience. He was meeting himself for the first time...

***

Later that day Sandra was alert enough to do some proofreading for Geoffrey, who needed a break from Sandra, not from the book. "Make yourself scarce for a while," she told him. "Hang out at the pool, and I'll call you when I need you." It took almost two hours – a long stretch for a person as wired and undisciplined as Sandra – before she would need him. Tired of flopping around in a motel room, she called her neighbor Ilsa and learned that her house had been exterminated and scrubbed completely clean.

"We might as well stay here the night since we're already paying for the room until tomorrow," Geoffrey said.

"I'm suffocating in this dump."

“Sandra, I’m too tired to argue and way too tired to drive.”

“What? A couple of miles? I’ll drive.”

“You’re in no condition.”

“You don’t care about my comfort. You’re just a selfish –”

“This has been a total disaster,” said Geoffrey, now wide awake but too angry to give in.

Sandra grabbed the keys to Geoffrey’s car and stormed out before he could stop her. Geoffrey ran out after her and almost got a fingernail trim from the slamming of the car door. Despite his pleas for caution and reason, Sandra screeched in reverse, nearly clipping the toe tips of one of his feet. “Stop! You’re going to”– *BANG!* She hit the bumper of the car behind in the row opposite. “That’s it! Get the hell out of my car!” Geoffrey grabbed the keys from her hand and went to find the owner of the other car. Fortunately for Sandra, the accident did not result in a police report – and a DUI charge.

“I’ve been working on *his* lousy book all day and what thanks do I get?” Sandra shouted at the motel manager. “He gets mad that I backed his car into some junk box with one of those old steel bumpers a Mack truck couldn’t scratch. I did those people a favor. Never mind just paying for the damage, the fool here will probably buy them a new car. What do I get? An ugly broach your grandmother wouldn’t wear!” She smashed her cigarette out on the reception desk counter. “Now I have to spend another night in this crapper.”

***

Once they were back in Sandra’s vacation house the next morning, Geoffrey was so rushed to finish that he tuned out Sandra’s whining and complaining. They ate every meal out, and Geoffrey used nothing more mind-altering than a glass of wine with dinner. Sandra, of course, had to make cracks about all the coffee and iced tea Geoffrey drank, and when he ordered a raspberry lime rickey at a soda shop, she suggested they try to find the nearest sock hop or bowling alley. The tension between them increased all week, yet Sandra somehow stayed focused on *ID/XX*.

Geoffrey finished the following Saturday, and Sandra sweetly volunteered to do the final proofreading. On Wednesday it was ready to be submitted to the publisher, and Geoffrey and Sandra went out to celebrate its completion. After a lobster and champagne dinner, they went for a moonlight walk along the beach. Like Andrews, Geoffrey looked at the silvery gold on the waves and thought about his own mounting regrets.

"Let's forget about Donna," Sandra said abruptly.

"What's with Donna? Give it a rest!"

"Tell me she means nothing to you! You've never once said it."

"I never said she *did* mean anything to me."

"You don't have to. You get this look on your face whenever you talk about her or just say her name."

"What look?"

"A gentle expression – wistful."

"Wistful? What century are we in?"

"The twenty-first, but you'd never know it! All you need is a top hat and spats. You've changed, and not for the better." Sandra gave the sand an angry kick. "What's she got that I don't have?"

"Come on Sandra."

"No. You come on! Tell me what she has that I don't!"

"A dozen cookbooks? Twenty-five, thirty pounds? A bigger ass? I don't know." Geoffrey said anything to get off the subject, but his insults against Donna etched more deeply the foggy glass through which he viewed her, and he could see the superficialities that kept them apart. His verbal attack against a woman, who had shown him kindness and forgiveness, burned his own ears and shamed him. He had helped Sandra drag himself right back down to the sewer.

Sandra, half satisfied that she got Geoffrey to ridicule her rival, wanted further confirmation and would not let up. "To see the contrast more clearly, tell me what *I* have that she doesn't."

"A fiancé? Silicone? Collagen? I don't know, what do they use these days as a wrinkle plumper, cadaver fat?" That crack earned him a slap across the face. Too used to Sandra's violent outbursts, Geoffrey merely pressed his hand to his stung cheek. "I thought we had an open relationship. You're sounding like a nagging wife."

"You dare insult me? You filthy cheat!"

"I'm not the one who's engaged and sneaking around every week!"

"With you – Mr. Morality!" Sandra said with a wild toss of her sea salt-misted hair. "You think Rich isn't screwing someone when he's away? What kind of fool do you think I am?" Then with more venom, she added, "He's richer and better connected than you'll ever be. All you've got is your looks and a mediocre talent that appeals to the public's lousy taste. I don't know why I waste my time."

"Neither do I. You know Sandra, you're really…"

"What? What am I but the best thing you ever had? And you know it too! You need me more than I need you, that's for sure. And you know, for sure, that the first chance *she* gets, she'll betray you."

"What?"

"You think she's going to keep quiet about your little collaboration? Just wait!" Sandra had voiced Geoffrey's deep-seated fear. "I don't know why I got so angry about that lousy pin you gave her. It's smaller than anything you ever gave me – shows what you really think."

Geoffrey winced. "You don't know what I think or want." This remark hinted at his regret and dissatisfaction. "And what do you plan to do once you marry Rich? Keep me on the side like some little boy toy?"

"Sure, why not? This relationship has been about only one thing – at least on my part. You'll take what I dish out until I get bored with you –which may happen sooner than you think."

"You know it will have to end once you're married," he said, wanting to add, "hopefully before then." Geoffrey looked away toward the ocean as if a dash into the surf might make a good escape.

"Since when did marriage, mine or anybody's, stop me? Marriage is about mutual social position and financial advancement. People who go into it for love and faithfulness are fools."

Geoffrey cursed under his breath and turned to her. "If you've got the upper hand so much, why are you jealous about Donna?"

"Jealous? Me? But you can bet one thing lover boy, I've got the upper hand all right."

"Sandra, can we just cut this out right now? I feel stressed enough. We're going home tomorrow, and we're still fighting. I'll be leaving for New York in a couple of days, and I don't want to go away angry." Geoffrey raised his hand to touch Sandra on the shoulder, but instead withdrew it to his pocket. "When is Daddy Warbucks returning?"

"In two weeks. He probably won't even call me until the end. Even if he does, he'll call my cell." Early in their relationship Sandra and Rich had established a rule to never use their home phones, lest Rich's former wife be the one to call, answer, or listen in. In Sandra's case, this cells-only agreement worked well because it also allowed her to hide her two-timing with Geoffrey. "Let me stay at your place so my commute is shorter."

"Sure. Make yourself comfortable," Geoffrey said with mild relief. By the time he'd return from his travels, Sandra would be back home and sneaking off to see him for one or two stolen hours a week, if that. Sandra's summer class (which she had passed off onto a teaching assistant for the time) was about to end. "Right now, I'm going to sleep and wake up sometime next year."

"If that's what you feel like doing, I should go out and find someone who doesn't feel like sleeping the night away. You're getting to be a bore. I worked just as hard as you, and you don't see me curling up like an old cat. Why don't you make yourself a glass of warm milk and sing yourself a lullaby, or call Donna and have her do it since she's so domestic?" Sandra's energy may have been artificially induced, but her nastiness came straight from her marrow.

***

Geoffrey said that he was leaving for New York a day earlier than planned, but instead he stayed one lonely night in a hotel by Logan airport. He was tempted to go to his uncle's house, which was not far from Logan, but he had already made a not so clean break from there. After one brief call to his brother to pick up his car from the body shop, he turned off his cell phone and cut himself off from everyone he knew.

***

Sandra felt more at home than Geoffrey did in his condo, for it was she who had decorated it with gold carpets, medium olive green (what she called "money green") walls, rough gold upholstery and black leather furniture, and a glass, shin-bruising coffee table that jutted out at weird angles like a frozen amoeba. One wall of his living room and study and the ceiling of his bedroom were painted in her signature lipstick red, which also appeared as accents throughout the apartment. Hideous paintings and oppressive sculpture proved that any piece of junk could be passed off as art if it had a high enough price tag. Heavy window treatments created a dark mausoleum atmosphere and helped hide the dirty deeds of Sandra and her friends from the outside world. Whoever had designed the uncomfortable-to-hold flatware and the strange, completely flat dishes, could not have intended them to be used for eating. The one wall clock had no numbers, and the desk had no drawers, but they too, were pieces of "art." There wasn't a comfortable seat anywhere except for the recliner and desk chair, which Geoffrey bought himself recently in his last attempt to work at home. No wonder he had difficulty writing there.

She slinked around from room to room and complimented herself on her good taste, then stood in front of a full-length mirror to admire her beauty.

CHAPTER THIRTEEN
DONNA DATES AND SANDRA SCHEMES

Donna sat thinking about the first date she had with Ginny's brother Brad. In the looks department he was no Geoffrey. The same held true for his behavior. He lacked Geoffrey's self-assurance and smoothness but possessed a genuine openness and sweetness. It was clear that he had tried to look presentable, but there was only so much that a shy, self-conscious man knew about grooming and fashion. His pant cuffs appeared to be the only tailoring that had been done to his suit, which just hung on his body like a too-large-rented tuxedo. His nondescript, average face had a pleasant expression that should have made him approachable if he only understood his appeal and the willingness of many women to just meet a nice guy.

After an initial bout of mutual shyness, they had literally broken the ice. As Donna passed him the dinner rolls, Brad knocked over a glass of water, and several ice cubes shattered on the floor. As a waiter approached the table, Donna and Brad instinctively bent down to clean the mess and bumped heads.

"I'm s..so, s..so sorry. I'm such a clumsy oaf," said Brad, his neck and face burning.

"No. No, it's just as much my fault. Grace isn't exactly my middle name," Donna giggled and grabbed his sweaty hand.

Thus, they had begun a conversation about their mutual awkwardness and shyness. At every stage of their lives, they had both been in the out crowd but, at some level, knew they were stronger people for it. Donna, who daily chatted with customers at her job, did most of the talking for the first hour of the date. Once Brad relaxed, he gushed on about everything he wanted her to know. His job as an accountant and his hobbies of bird watching, jigsaw puzzles, and computer games kept him from meeting many people face-to-face but allowed a comfortable level of human interaction.

On their next two dates they had ridden the Swan Boats at the Public Gardens before going to a concert on the Esplanade, and then ended the week with video games.

***

After dating a man who was uncomplicated and fun (and back home in Pennsylvania), Donna had the time, relaxation – and stomach to finally read *ID/XX*. She read until she reached the part where after Andrews allowed Johnson to steal his identity, he describes what it feels like to lose one's sense of self and reputation to someone else: *"Vanity and pride are different things," Andrews said. "A person may be proud without being vain. Pride relates more to our opinion of ourselves. Vanity to what we would have others think of us."*

Donna paused then reread the paragraph. She blanched. Familiar though they might be, the words were not Geoffrey's, and they certainly were not hers. Pride – and Prejudice.

"Where's that notebook?" she said out loud. She raced across the apartment from the porch to the living room. "The coffee table – not there. I must have put it where?" Donna looked on top of her desk then carefully searched through the drawers. She often read in bed, but the notebook was not in or on her night table. In a flurry she plowed through the apartment looking through every drawer, cabinet, closet, and bookshelf. How could Geoffrey have thought those notes were for the book? She clearly told him that for each book she marked the author's initials and page from which a quote came. What happened? Did he take the notebook also with everything he kept for "security"? Hadn't she explained to him exactly what she was doing? Didn't he pay attention to *anything* she said? She ran back through her memory to recollect when she had recently used the notebook. "The living room was the last place I remember," she thought as she yanked the cushions from her sofa – not there.

***

Sandra was alone in Geoffrey's condo when the phone rang. She let the answering machine pick it up. "Hello," the voice said. "Geoffrey, this is Donna. Please call me as soon as you get this message. It's urgent. Whatever you do, do not send the manuscript to the publisher. There are some serious problems with it." Donna hung up with a sinking feeling. She did not have Geoffrey's cell phone number, and Angie and Primo were still away. She could only hope that Geoffrey checked his voice mail or had a sudden urge to call her.

Sandra snickered and erased Donna's message. "Keep trying girlfriend. Good luck!"

An hour later the phone rang again. Sandra saw the name on the caller ID and decided to have some fun. "Hello, the Imperato residence," she said in a sleepy, low tone.

"Uh hello. Is Geoffrey there?"

"Who is calling?"

"Donna DiGeronamo."

"Donna who?"

"Di Geronamo. I'm a friend of his and it's important that I speak to him."

"I'm so-o-o-o sorry. He's not here and he can't be reached. He's travelling out of range of cellular service."

"I thought he was in New York."

"New York? I'm his girlfriend, and I can assure you he's certainly a lot farther away than New York – New Guinea, more like it. In fact, he's moved on by now to a more remote place than that. He finished his book and took off for a long vacation that will allow him to do some research for his next book. No, for the next three weeks he won't be anywhere with electricity or indoor plumbing. Sorry." *Click.*

Donna realized that Sandra, if in fact it was she, was probably lying. Unfortunately, Geoffrey's cell number, email address, and home address were all a mystery. By the time Primo and Angie returned, it could be too late to warn him. Sometime, someone had mentioned that Geoffrey had family nearby in Orient Heights or just over the borders in Winthrop or Beachmont. If the phone book or Information gave no result, there was no way she could go door to door. She would have to wait and hope for Sandra to pass on her message.

***

The phone rang and Sandra cursed under her breath. "Hello… Oh, you again. Tell you what bitch, you call here one more time and I'll put in a complaint with the phone company and have the number changed. I'm a very busy woman with important things to do. I don't spend my days telling frumps that the slacks they tried on don't make their asses look fat. This is the last time I'll speak to you, so make it good."

"Please, Geoffrey's future is at stake."

"Really? How come? 'Splain."

"I can't tell you. I must talk to him directly."

"Geoff trusts me more than anyone in the world. Anything you tell him you can tell me."

"I can't trust anyone else with this information. It's personal."

"Are you pregnant? Going through ice cream withdrawal? Gained another ten pounds? Tell it to someone who cares."

"It's not about me!" Donna said with greater urgency. Sandra would undoubtedly obstruct and obfuscate any effort for Donna to reach Geoffrey, but as the SLY fox was currently the only direct link to him, Donna could only appeal to her presumed sense of decency. "It's his book. He can't send it out as it is.

There are mistakes he must correct. That's all I can say. If you are in fact his girlfriend, I'm sure you'll care enough to want to help him."

"Aw, I do hope there's nothing seriously wrong with it. It's long gone," said Sandra with feigned concern.

"It can't be. How could he have finished it so fast?"

"He had help – competent help for a change. Toodle – oo." *Click.*

Donna paced the length of her apartment. If she called Tom, what are the chances he'd have Geoffrey's cell number? "It's worth a try. I've got his card. Where is it? Who else knows Geoffrey? Vinnie!" She called Mrs. Amalfitano for his number then dialed Vinnie's and got his voice mail. A look through the phone book and a call to Information in search of any possible relative produced a hit on the fourth try. Geoffrey's brother answered but refused to give out the phone number to a total stranger. "Tell you what," he said, "I'll call George myself and tell him to get in touch with you." Donna didn't tell "George's" brother the reason for her call, and it did not occur to her that the anxiety in her voice may have made her appear as an obsessed fan or stalker.

***

Sandra fixed herself a drink and, in her mind, replayed her conversation with Donna. *Geoff must have given her a copy, either the last day they were together or after we finished. I told that stupid son of a bitch not to let her read even one page. She's determined. Who knows what she'll do. Hmm. What's the best way to handle this? Should I call or what? I'd better make it fast.*

Two more days of anxious waiting passed. Donna returned home after a busy day of work, dropped off some groceries for Tina, and climbed the stairs. For the first time in five years, she heard a sound she never thought she'd welcome: screaming emanating from Primo and Angie's apartment. Donna pounded on the door as if she had just overdosed on laxatives. "Angie, Primo, open up! It's urgent!"

The door swung open mid-knock. Primo, looking at least five pounds heavier, answered. "Wha? You'd think someone's killin' ya."

"Primo, it's about Geoffrey. I've got to talk to him as soon as possible. He's in trouble."

Primo was just about to blow off Donna until he heard her last three words. "Trouble? Whatta you sayin'? Somebody after 'im?"

"No, nothing like that. Do you have his cell phone number and know where he's staying?"

"He was supposed to come home the same day as us – today. Hold on." Primo yelled, "Angie, get me Geoff's cell phone number."

Donna ran upstairs and called Geoffrey. No answer. She played her messages. One was from Vinnie and another from Tom, both with Geoffrey's cell number. Her only hope was that she could reach Geoffrey before someone read the book. "What are the chances that anyone is rushing to read it yet? Even if they do, how likely are they to recognize anything?" she asked herself with more hope than faith.

CHAPTER FOURTEEN
D FOR DISASTER

Geoffrey had just ended a heated phone call, the most recent of several attacks, and was about to enter the web of the black widow spider. For a man who usually looked well-groomed and confident, Geoffrey appeared haggard, beleaguered, and bedraggled. On the plane a child had spilled milk on him, and on the way home his cab driver drove over every pothole and made Geoffrey's soda splash on his shirt. He felt despondent but not desperate. At least until he could convince everyone that he was not the perpetrator, he would face only censure, slander, and embarrassment.

But would the truth *really* set him free, and if it didn't, what would happen to him *really*? His reputation, which he had tried so hard to protect, was damaged by a person he had trusted. The memory of Sandra's warning rang in his mind: *"Listen to me! You must be the sole author! How embarrassing for someone of your stature, especially after that last piece of shit you wrote! Pay her off or have your uncle threaten to knock her off! I'm sure she could use the money. Don't let her keep any part of it and make sure you get her original manuscript! Don't leave her alone with your laptop! Erase whatever is on her computer! Break the computer if you must and search her apartment for any disks with the story! In fact, I'll do it for you – I know you'll get cold feet. You're too honest. Ha! Yet you weren't so honest not to copy her story. Destroy anything she has as proof."*

With leaden legs Geoffrey dragged himself through the front door of his condo and snapped on the entrance light. The form of Sandra rose from the sofa.

"Why are you here?" Geoffrey asked.

"What do you mean? You knew I was staying at your place while you were away."

"I mean why are you *still* here?"

"I wanted to welcome you home and see the triumphant look on your face." Sandra stepped forward wearing black slacks and a red top.

"Sandra, why did you do it?"

"Do what?"

"Don't play games. I've been accused of plagiarism. How did sentences and whole paragraphs from other books get into mine?"

"Well why don't you ask Donna Donut instead of accusing me?"

"You and I did all the typing, and I certainly didn't do anything so stupid and self-destructive as to commit plagiarism. Donna never touched my laptop."

"What about your lap?" Sandra leaned forward, ready for the attack. "Just what exactly went on between the two of you – all those nights alone together? I know you better than that. Do you remember that Thursday, or whatever the hell day it was, before we went to the Cape? I called you several times that morning – no answer. Finally, I drove to East Boston and parked across the street. Your car was in the driveway, and I rang your uncle's doorbell. So where were you? For almost half an hour I sat in that heat until you came out with Miss Piggy. You were so absorbed and distracted that you didn't even see me. How could you have missed my car among all those junk heaps? When you got in your car, you opened the car door for her like some sixteen-year-old going to your junior prom."

"We were just going to lunch."

"Why? Didn't she have any salami in the house?"

"We ate in all the time. It was our last day working together. I felt for once I should take her out."

"To some drive-in trough? So, you 'ate in all the time' like a couple of old homebodies, then you take her out on your first date like a lovesick teenager. I tried to follow you, but the traffic in that damn place is so congested I lost you after about a mile. When I called you and you *finally* answered, I was in the parking lot of a lousy donut shop with every damn cop from Middlesex, Essex or whatever the hell sex county it was!"

"Wait, hold on. We're getting off track. You mean to say that you betrayed me because I took Donna to lunch one time and gave her a puny pin? You know damn well the only reason I *ever* got involved with her is because she caught me red-handed."

"*Plagiarizing her book!* My dear Geoffrey, you do have a problem with that, don't you? Don't try to put the blame on me! She worked with you more than I did."

"I kept her from having too much access..." Geoffrey stopped as a new reality hit him. He had been so thrown by plagiarism in his book that he didn't press to find out how it was discovered. He had asked, but he didn't get a straight answer from anyone other than they had received an anonymous tip. "Sandra," he said with a deep exhalation. "How could they have found out so soon?"

Sandra dropped the sarcasm and got serious. "I don't know," she half whispered.

Geoffrey wiped his brow with the back of his hand and headed toward the kitchen for some water.

Sandra grabbed him by the shoulders. "Geoff, I have a way out of all this. If necessary, I can claim to be the noble whistle blower, if they don't know who contacted them. We can say that you never read through the final copy, which is true. We'll say you were sick and away and trusted a deranged woman to do it, and we could blame the plagiarism on Donna. I mean this way we can say that you didn't know what happened, and then I caught it and quickly alerted them. *She really did it! It wasn't me; I swear!*"

Geoffrey shook his head. "I don't know. I think it must have happened toward the end of our working together because she used a new notebook that I had written my phone number in on the first page. I'm pretty sure the rest of the notebook was empty then."

"Why did you even need her still after I began helping you?"

"She and I only worked together about a couple of weeks longer after you started. The sneak somehow must have done it during that period because I had read the story over a few times before then and didn't notice any of the plagiarized passages that were pointed out to me. When I let you take over, I trusted that the book was in the hands of a professional."

"Well, I didn't notice anything familiar because even though I teach literature, I don't exactly remember sections of ninth grade books or uh, wherever she got the quotes." Sandra stomped out her cigarette. "If it weren't for her, none of this ever would have happened!"

"Donna wrote passages from different stories in her notebook. Her reason didn't make much sense to me. I mean, why waste time copying stuff from other books? Now I see why – all her annotations had book, author, chapter, and page number. Whoever alerted my publisher told them what to look for. Who else besides her would know?" Geoffrey pushed his hand through his hair and turned away from her. His mind swam through each sewer of a scenario and found only one way to escape the filth. "I don't know what to do. This is such a mess."

"Don't worry darling. We'll get through this. The important thing is that you're innocent. Remember, you are the victim of a vindictive woman's treachery."

"You're right. That's exactly what I am."

"I said, don't worry. Rich will be home in a few days. Let's make the most of tonight."

Geoffrey was too tense to focus on anything other than his predicament. "Sandra, I'm too keyed up right now."

"Okay, here's what we do. You call the publisher and explain that your crazy, desperate assistant did the dirty deed."

"And just why would Donna have done such a thing? We made peace the day we met and got on so well. After a while, she seemed to accept the situation, even when I made it clear to her."

Sandra scoffed. "*She seemed?* You foolishly trusted her sweet innocent act. Of course she would betray you. Anyone would!"

"But she once even indicated that she might find some of the rawer scenes embarrassing and was glad her name wasn't associated with the book. If she was fine with just getting paid for her work, why would she betray me?"

Sandra shrugged. "I don't know. Perhaps you rejected her advances, or she's just plain crazy. It would be easy to convince anyone with a brain that *she* was in love with *you*, not *you* with *her*. Remember we've got to make it clear to everyone that Donna was the one who did this to you. You can bet that when she gets to thinking about everything, she'll publicly accuse you of plagiarism."

Sandra drove back home to Rich's house with the anxious hope that Geoffrey was at least fulfilling his part of the deal. They would find some way to pin it on Donna, perhaps get her to come forward as a writing assistant. "Geoff had better use his charm on her," she told herself. He'll have to handle this. It's not my problem. Rich will be home tomorrow. I'd better pull myself together. Sandra unpacked her suitcase to hide any evidence that she had been away and then called Geoffrey. "What did they say when you told them about Donna Dimples? … What do you mean? … Waiting for what? … What's there to think about? … I'll make it airtight for you…You've been accused of something you didn't do. Are you nuts? … So, what if she claims she wrote most of the book. That's further proof she did it."

"Sandra," Geoffrey said with exasperation seeping into meltdown, "we only discussed this yesterday. Give me some time to catch my breath, will you? One day more or less won't matter."

***

After numerous futile attempts to reach Geoffrey, Donna finally got through to him. "Geoffrey! I've been calling forever to warn you that *ID/XX* has some serious problems!"

"You are telling me!" Geoffrey answered with a tone of disgust.

"While you were away, I called everyone I could think of to get your cell number. I even called your apartment on the chance that you might have been home already. I told your girlfriend that there was a problem, but I didn't get specific because I wanted to talk to you directly."

"Uh huh, and what exactly *is* the problem, Donna?"

"I don't know how it happened, but passages from other books somehow got incorporated into it."

"*Somehow got incorporated?* Really? And just what passages would those be?" Geoffrey asked in a cool, dry tone.

"Well, uh, I think there were one or two from my notebook anyway."

"You think? And just how would they have jumped from your notebook into the pages of *ID/XX*?"

"Remember the night I got upset that you found my notebook? I told you that what I had written was from other books, but I think you must have used the quotes already and forgot to delete them."

"Donna, I did no such thing. True, I found the notebook in your room, and you made a big fuss that I had 'invaded your privacy', as though it was the crime of the century. I now know the real reason you were upset."

"What do you mean?"

"You were angry that I found the evidence that you were trying to frame me! You did it because I wouldn't let you be co-author."

"Geoffrey no! I tried so hard to warn you! Why would I do such a despicable thing and then try to protect you?"

"I don't know. Guilty conscience? Or perhaps you didn't know how you'd be able to handle the backlash you would get once discovered." Geoffrey paused. "Darling Donna, you know that you always complained that I never let you read the story all the way through, so just how did you know about the plagiarism?"

Donna gulped and stammered. When Loretta, Tina, and she had hatched their scheme to get a copy of the book, Donna thought she'd know what to say if she had to confront Geoffrey about her input; when she agreed to let him have sole authorship if she got paid for her work, she let the matter drop. "Well, uh, I uh…Do, do y-you remember the last day we worked together?"

"Oh, so that's when you betrayed me!"

"*No*! I would never do that to you. I don't know how it happened!"

"Really? Well, I don't know either, but all the evidence points to you. I was warned not to trust you. What a fool I was to let someone like you into my life. I thought you were *so* nice, and sweet, and nurturing. And blah, blah, blah. That's just what you are – *blah*. Go back to your boring little existence!"

Click!

***

Tom Ambrose answered his phone. “Oh hi. How have you been? I just got back myself… What’s up? … Yes…I ran into her not long ago…Why, what happened? … She did WHAT?!? …Repeat that again…I don’t believe it! What was she thinking? … You’re kidding! … Donna Di Geronamo! I’ve known her for a while. In fact, she tried to reach me while I was away…Now what exactly happened? … Why would she do something so crazy? ... You probably know her better than I do…Any chance she’ll confess to it? … True, it’s still your responsibility because it’s your book, but today with computers, who knows what people can do? It’s not as though it was written longhand or on a typewriter… Let me know what happens…Of course I’ll do all I can to help you…You take care.”

Tom hung up and shook his head.

***

He’d go to his uncle’s before he succumbed to a chemical cure, but right now Geoffrey could not bear the risk of running into Donna. His parents’ home was out of the question. His mother, a drama queen, and his father, an overbearing boor, made Angie and Primo seem like the mom and dad from a 1950s sitcom.

***

Two days later Geoffrey called Tom Ambrose. “Tom, I’ve been lying low. Right now, I just want people to believe me. I wish I never met the bitch!”

“Don’t worry,” Tom said in his calming voice. “The truth will out. I’ve made some calls. Have you talked to her recently?”

“I’ll call her when I’m good and ready. I don’t want to deal with anyone right now, and I just want to get away. I can’t go to my parents because they make me crazy, and if I go to my uncle’s I could run into Donna. My brother’s house with the three kids is a zoo. I know this isn’t the worst thing, but I just don’t know how to handle confrontation or stress.”

"You can stay with me if you like. Just hold on."

"Thanks, I'll take you up on your offer. Tom, what if this gets out? I mean publicly. I survived my last wretched book, but this will finish me."

"Geoff, if anything gets out, we'll set it right."

***

The next afternoon as Donna was folding sweaters, snippy Sandra breezed past her straight up to Ginny Alexander. "Now *you* look like someone who can help me. I'm not used to buying off the rack, so I'd like you to show me what you have in size *four*," she said tossing the last word over her shoulder toward Donna.

Ginny, of course, had no idea who Sandra was, and she responded as she would to any customer. "Is there anything in particular you were looking for – suits, coordinates, cruise wear?"

"Let's have a look at those sweaters, shall we?" Sandra gave Donna a low-lidded sneer. "On second thought, I don't see anything *there* of quality. Why don't we start with some skirts and knit dresses in your top label. Is there a place for me to sit while you gather up some things for me?"

It may have been the second floor of Floegel's Department Store, but Sandra, with an upturned nose and a snap of her fingers, turned it into her own private boutique. "Who is your buyer? It's a wonder this place stays open. Well, I guess I can get a few things. My students may relate more to me if I dress down like them." In response to Ginny's polite smile, Sandra added, "I tend to favor black and beige for the autumn, but I certainly can handle some color. Bring me something in orange. No one will mistake *me* for a pumpkin!" She shot Donna a side glance.

Donna dug her nails into a rib-knit cardigan and wondered what was the worst they could do to her if she wrapped the sweater tightly around Sandra's neck or stuffed it in her mouth? In reality she'd be fired if she got within three feet of the couture queen. Sandra would be here only to provoke Donna in some way. She criticized every garment and looked at Donna every time she called something "ugly", "unattractive", or "tasteless." The two enemies glared like a couple of wild cats about to spring at each other.

"Ginny, I'll be back in a few minutes," Donna said without further explanation.

Loretta had just finished a sale when Donna stepped up to her counter. "I just want to warn you. Sandra is in the store, and she flung a lot of indirect insults at me. She'll probably come looking for me any second."

"Since when does the designer diva shop here?"

"She's here to cause trouble, and thanks to the lost earring incident, she now knows what both of us look like. Sorry if I involved you in any of this. Poor Ginny got stuck with her. I bet she'll monopolize an hour of her time and walk out without buying anything. I'd better get back in case there are other customers who need help."

"Hang on. Here she comes in the uckiest mustard yellow I've ever seen," Loretta whispered. "It would make a maggot gag on a hot dog."

Sandra plopped her shopping bag on the counter that was perpendicular to Donna and spoke to Loretta but with direct aim at Donna. "Ah, it's so nice to have a trim figure! You can tell exactly what looks good on you without trying anything on. You don't have to worry about bulging in all the wrong places or looking bigger than you already are. If anything, something might be too loose, especially around the hips." With half-lowered lids she scanned the products under the glass, which she annoyingly tapped with her long red nails. "Is this line any good or is it just grease and cheap cologne?" She couldn't resist pulling Donna in. "The salesgirl here will of course try to sell me the whole line, but what do you think?"

"Actually," said Donna with a sideways glance, "they have a very good cream that helps minimize scars, especially the kind from plastic surgery. And oh, their under-eye concealer really covers the dark circles and bags from too much partying and lack of sleep."

An angry scowl on Sandra's face slipped into a smirk. "Do they have anything you could use to melt off fat? Isn't there some thigh cream that supposedly does that? By the way, Miss Sitting Bull, I'm so glad we ran into each other like this. You should know you soon may be asked a few questions about some problems with a certain manuscript. Funny how your notes match up to plagiarized portions of the book!" Sandra turned on her heel and left.

Loretta grabbed Donna's shaking hand. "Don't. She's not worth getting fired over. I'll help you handle this. Just go back upstairs and put her out of your mind until we go home in a few hours."

When Donna returned to her department, she briefly told Ginny about Sandra. "Be careful! She's trouble."

Ginny replied, "That explains why when you left, she suddenly grabbed whatever I was showing her and had me ring them up. She seemed so fussy and then, in a blink, she's buying things she scarcely looked at."

"She made a beeline for Loretta's counter, but I think she already knew that Loretta worked in cosmetics." Geoffrey certainly had told Sandra that he met Donna's spy.

"For someone who spends so much on her clothes, she doesn't have very good taste. If I had that kind of money to spend, I'd look a lot better than she does," said Ginny. "That mustard top she was wearing retails for more than we charge for a suit, but you'd never guess unless you know labels."

As if Sandra's ears were burning, she suddenly appeared. "By the way," she sniffed in Ginny's direction. "When I said I wanted to see what you had in size four, I was taking into consideration the different sizing in cheaper clothing. I got a look at that blue skirt you sold me, and your chum here could fit into it. I normally wear size two or less. I'm surprised you didn't know that, seeing how you're obviously the most experienced person on this floor, not that that counts for much. Besides, I hate blue. You really should have known."

Donna couldn't hold back. "We read minds as part of our act."

"Wha- what did you say to me? You know, you're awfully flip. I think I'll head directly upstairs and complain about you."

"Sandra, what's the problem?" said a man in a striped polo shirt and khakis. Tom Ambrose had appeared so suddenly that none of the three women noticed his approach. "I heard everything that went on and she merely said, 'We don't mind if you take it back.' She wasn't being flippant. If anything, you were baiting her."

"I, wa-," Sandra cut short her reply and stalked off.

Tom followed her closely. When they were by the escalator, he said to Sandra, "Geoff told me what happened. You really should be more cautious. It's best to keep your distance from her. You've been in enough legal scrapes to know better. I know you can't resist getting satisfaction out of taunting her but think how you're complicating things."

"How so?" asked Sandra with only a slight sense that he may be right.

"You don't know how it will play out. What have you to gain? Leave her alone. It's a good thing I followed you here."

"You did what? Why? Did Geoff tell you to keep an eye on me? Doesn't he trust my judgment?"

"No, not at all," Tom answered one of her questions truthfully. "I do, however, hang around the store sometimes to see what I can find out. Since I've currently got a light schedule at the school, I have a lot of time to do…other things."

Sandra, realizing that Tom could always out-reason her, said, "Tom, can we go somewhere and talk? I'd love to know your strategy."

"And I, yours," said Tom with a grin, "but I'm already running late."

***

At 9:30 P.M. Donna lay on her bed. Several calls to Geoffrey that evening had gone unanswered. One intrusive thought, after another, shot through her brain. "What if Geoffrey offers my notes as proof that I sabotaged his book? What if he believes me but doesn't care? He might use those notes against me in case he imagines that I may yet attack him for copying my story and not letting me be the co-author. People have retaliated when merely their ideas were stolen, and here he had his mitts on most of my book! Why was Tom there at the same time as Sandra today? Did they come together? Does he believe that I did it? Should I call him and explain? Would that make matters worse? Does he even know what happened? What did he say to her when they left the store together? Are they all ganging up on me?"

She stretched out her legs and forced herself up. After one more futile attempt to contact Geoffrey, she went to her candy stash. "I can't believe I keep a whole drawer just for this junk," she thought as she ate the first of four peanut clusters and bit off the caramel end of a Sky Bar. "What am I doing to myself? Instead of making myself stronger to handle stress, I'm losing control." Before she could change her mind, she emptied the drawer of everything but the solid dark chocolate and threw it all into a plastic grocery bag, which she tied up and carried down to dump in a trashcan out back. "This will keep me from retrieving it in a weak moment." Something large, a water rat possibly, dashed in front of the bottom step and sent Donna and her sack of sweets back up to the third floor in fifteen seconds.

Just as she was about to drop the bag into her kitchen can, she pulled it back and untied it. "Walnuts and almonds are supposed to be good for you. They're covered in a little chocolate, some of it dark. I don't think that's too bad. The red licorice is fat-free, so that'll compensate for the fat in the chocolate and nuts. Lemon drops are good for when my throat gets scratchy. Hmm, Necco Wafers, barley pops, wintergreen Canada mints, jellybeans, gum drops, mint patties, orange slices, spearmint leaves, bridge mix, Swedish fish, Squirrel Nuts, chocolate kisses – childhood favorites. These imported gummy fruits are hard to find, and these caramels are hand-made in small batches." Before she knew it, the only thing left in the trash bag was an open package of hard candies that were so old the wrappers stuck to them. "I'll take care of all this some other time." She made herself some warm milk and went to bed.

A half an hour later Donna was up and at the candy. Shame and self-loathing made her choke with tears, which washed over the sweet temptations. *Have you learned nothing, you pathetic weakling? You lose a few pounds, and you sabotage your diet for what?* She plopped the bag into another grocery bag, double-tied the knot, and tossed it onto the upper shelf of the pantry.

***

"Don't worry," Loretta reassured her the next morning. "How can Geoffrey put the blame on you without having to answer some uncomfortable questions about how you had access to his writing? Besides, what's the worst that can happen to you? It's his own stupid fault for submitting it – as his – for publication. Didn't he read it?"

“I don’t know. He trusted Sandra to finish up, I think. I’m sure those creative minds will think of a way to pin it all on me, although I can’t imagine Tom would be in on it.”

“How well do you really know Tom?”

“Not well enough to know his true character. He doesn’t seem to like Sandra very much, but he’s Geoffrey’s friend,” Donna answered. “I think that if Geoffrey asked for his help, he’d give it.”

“Yeah, but you know, Geoffrey and SLY would be stupid to involve a third person, don’t you think?”

“I hope you’re right, but you know what they say about desperate times calling for desperate measures”

***

Sometimes a rough night’s sleep awakens into a compensatory gentle day – not this one. Floegel’s frosty manager, Miss Kaltbergen, called Donna into her office. “A customer complained about you this morning. She said that yesterday you insulted her, said she looked hung over, ugly, and old, and suggested she would look better with a paper bag over her head.”

“What?” Donna didn’t have to ask “who?”

“Now, Donna, this isn’t the first time this has happened, and it’s something that never should.”

“And you just believed her? You believe I would tell someone to put a bag over her head? How long have I worked here, and you think that I tell people they look ugly? Have I ever acted in any way that would indicate I would do such a thing?”

The manager leaned back in her chair and folded her hands at the edge of her desk. “Now, Donna, I realize that some people from your background see the world a little different than, may I be frank, people from a different socioeconomic level, and you might not even realize…”

Donna plowed right over her. "You mean that because I'm Italian and come from East Boston that I'm ill-bred? I'd think that even *you* should realize that speaking to *me* that way violates an employment or discrimination law."

"Now, don't put words in my mouth. That's not what I meant," said Miss Kaltbergen, her smug tone turning defensive.

Oh, that's exactly what you meant! Donna collected her last remnant of dignity and confidence. "Then you can see how easy it is for a person to *misinterpret* what you say. That's the consequence of working with the public. You get a cross-section of society, good and bad not just rich and poor." She would have added that's something that the manager wouldn't know sitting in her ivory tower. "You don't even have to tell me who it was. She's a vicious and malicious woman with a personal grudge against me."

"That tells me there *was* some unacceptable interaction between the two of you then. You cannot bring personal hostility to work. We cannot antagonize a customer of her caliber."

"Her caliber? In my neighborhood we call a woman of her caliber a *puttana*. She's not a regular or even seldom customer. She criticized the store and its merchandise and wondered how Floegel's stayed in business." Little did Donna know that for the past few years the store was on the verge of closing.

"Ah, then I'll have to call a meeting with the buyers to see who's losing their edge. And I think I'll talk to all the staff so we can reinforce proper behavior. After all, the customer is always right."

"Even when they shoplift and deliberately slip and fall? In all the years I've worked here how many people have ever complained about me – legitimately complained?" asked Donna still steaming about the class insult.

"Two since I've been here, and both in recent months. That's two too many and shows a bad trend. I didn't call you on the first one because it was a first offense, so to speak, but you might remember the woman who complained we didn't have a certain brand of panty hose."

"Because we don't and never did. As I recall she wanted the *Wasp Waist* brand only, and when someone in Lingerie told her we don't carry it and showed her what we did have, she threw a fit." Donna would have added that the woman seemed "drunk" but knew where that would lead. "I tried to help her by calling around to locate them for her, but she was irate because *we* didn't have them. She wanted one of us to go elsewhere to get them and bring them back to the store for her."

"Perhaps one of you should have."

"And leave the department unattended for at least an hour for a ten-dollar sale? How are we realistically supposed to sell something we don't stock?" asked Donna in disbelief that the store was run by such an idiot.

The manager couldn't answer the logical question, so she changed the subject. "Is something going on in your personal life that you're taking it out on our customers?"

"Two nasty, unreasonable people make bogus complaints about me, and that suggests that my life is out of control? You think only nice people shop in stores? I suppose the nasty ones buy everything online."

Miss Kaltbergen's lower jaw took on the shape of an anvil. "Donna, your attitude shows a resentment and hostility toward our customers."

"Because I'm not of their 'caliber'? I think you have a hostile attitude toward people of my 'socioeconomic background'," said Donna, putting Miss Kaltbergen back on the defensive.

"Let's not let this get out of hand," said the manager cautiously. "We've always had a good working relationship, so I see no reason to put this in your personnel file as long as we can agree to disagree and pretend this conversation never took place."

Donna managed to return to work without slamming the manager's head on her desk.

Donna called Loretta the next morning. "I'm all keyed up. What do you say we join a gym? I've got to work off some of this stress and weight."

"Picture me on an elliptical between Tiny Tina and Skinny Minnie. I don't know if I could stand it. It's so intimidating to just walk in there. Isn't there some place that has remedial classes?"

"There are women's exercise classes where we might feel more comfortable," Donna answered.

"Yeah, but if we do that, how can we meet any guys?"

"What if we first join a place for women, and then when we lose some weight, we can go to a regular gym?"

"That might work."

***

Geoffrey paced between his living room and bedroom. The phone rang. It was the motel at the Cape that Sandra and he had stayed in. A woman from the front desk said, "Mr. Imperato, your wife had reported a missing notebook from your recent stay with us. She said it was very important. We checked the second – last room you stayed in and didn't find anything, but I asked housekeeping to keep a lookout anyway. Today I believe it turned up in the first room you had stayed in earlier. I'm sorry that I didn't make the connection because your wife made it sound like an important document, like something printed in a binder."

Geoffrey gasped. "Is it a blue notebook about a third full of handwriting?"

"Yes, and on the first page it says "Geoffrey" spelled like you do, and it has your phone number, so I'm pretty sure it's it."

"I will come and get it, probably today. Whatever you do, do not release it to anyone but me. When is your next mail pickup?... Good. If I don't arrive by then, please mail it to me. I won't care if I arrive later. You have my address?... Yes. Thanks a lot." He would do nothing until he got that notebook.

***

Over the next few weeks Donna visited her parents, made some good sales, and found her medium-sized pants fitting more loosely. Loretta's hair managed to get brassier after a summer's worth of sun beating down on it. Tina's granddaughter was born and named Christina after her. Primo once put in an honest day's work, if you count eight hours at one of his three jobs honest. The Infantos were a bit friendlier to Donna but seemed ignorant of the details of their nephew's troubles. Angie, once in a sudden burst of warmth, gave Donna some baked stuffed quahogs and napoleon pastry that Primo brought home.

Loretta asked Donna, "Do you think that if Geoffrey had accused you of anything, Angie and Primo might have poisoned the pastry?"

"I'm sure they haven't a clue about what's going on with him, otherwise the whole neighborhood would hear the wailing and gnashing of teeth." Donna stared down at the quahogs. "Did we have red tide recently? Perhaps the pastry may be the safer bet," she said as she pretended to smell one for any tainted odor.

Loretta grabbed a napoleon and took a not so risky bite. "Like they say—life's short. Eat dessert first. And last and in between."

CHAPTER FIFTEEN
FRAME, BLAME, SHAME

Tom opened his recent copy of a weekly educational newspaper, which chronicled all the news of the academic world. An article that he had anticipated was one of the lead stories:

LITERARY SCANDAL TAKES A NEW TWIST

Assistant Professor of Literature May Have Framed Popular Author

A strange case of plagiarism that has threatened the reputation of a noted author has taken a bizarre turn. Sandra LeRoi Young, assistant professor at Northern University of Boston, may in fact be responsible for the plagiarism of which she first anonymously accused author Geoffrey Imperato. Later in a phone call to Imperato's publisher, LeRoi Young detailed eight paragraphs that were lifted from works by authors such as Jane Austen and Charles Dickens. Imperato claimed he was not responsible for the inclusion of the paragraphs into his book, and that LeRoi Young had assisted him in the editing and proofreading of his final manuscript, and had worked for hours alone, unsupervised.

"I believe that Sandra inserted the plagiarized sections into my manuscript out of vengeance and then, in an act of false heroics, notified my publisher of their presence. (In fact, she admitted everything in a heated argument.)" Imperato would not reveal the cause of the alleged revenge, nor would he confirm the rumor of a longstanding romantic relationship with LeRoi Young. He did say, however, "I have proof that Ms. LeRoi Young has spent many hours with me while I worked. I foolishly trusted her to review the final draft, which I submitted without

reading it carefully after her. If I am guilty of anything, it is irresponsible negligence and misplaced trust."

The case of what he said/she said is distilling down to a matter of credibility. Mr. Imperato, who met Ms. LeRoi Young at a writing seminar, is an author of five best-selling books. Little is known about Imperato's private life. One acquaintance describes him as "a pretty average guy, who lives the quiet life of a solitary man who works by himself." A handsome bachelor with boyish charm, Imperato is a fixture at local Boston restaurants and coffee shops where he is often seen writing on his laptop.

Much more is known about LeRoi Young, who was on academic probation two years ago for an undisclosed reason. Her personal life is the subject of much campus gossip. A graduate student (name withheld) related how rumors of affairs with students and faculty have circulated for years. One male student interviewed said, "You don't go to her to complain about your grade unless you want to risk being propositioned." Then he added, "As far as I know, she only does it to a few good-looking guys like me."

The wife of a colleague once interrupted a class and demanded that LeRoi Young leave her husband alone. A drug arrest, an assault charge, and lewd public behavior charges are all allegedly in her colorful past. "She can afford good lawyers. People are afraid to come up against her. She made a bundle from her first marriage, and now she's got another fish on the hook," the bitter wife said.

But does improper behavior translate into dishonesty? Two cases that had her expensive lawyers working overtime involved tax evasion and insurance fraud.

"She's a smorgasbord of dishonesty and immorality. The only reason that I think she keeps her job at the university is that she once sued for sexual discrimination and won," said an

unnamed source. "They won't touch her. She's gotten away with so much that, if she were dismissed, her lawyer would probably argue, 'Why did you tolerate her alleged worse past behavior and suddenly charge moral turpitude?' It would take an air-tight, egregious on-campus crime to get rid of her."

All these revelations, however, may be irrelevant to the Imperato case. Imperato argues, nonetheless, that he has proof that LeRoi Young helped him with his recent book. "I have her notes that match the pages in question, several people saw us together while I was writing, and some of the plagiarized sections came from books she uses in her classes. Recently we stayed at a motel on Cape Cod, and she left some notes behind, which housekeeping found."

The manager of that motel relates how one evening, after a minor accident in the parking lot, LeRoi Young blamed fatigue from working on Imperato's book.

When pressed to reveal the motive for her alleged spite, Imperato "as a gentleman" would not admit to a broken affair with LeRoi Young but did say that she had gone so far as to pass the blame onto an innocent woman to deflect suspicion from herself.

Knowing the details of the plagiarism and changing her story – first accusing Imperato, then this unnamed other woman – may be the smoking gun that implicates LeRoi Young as the culprit.

Sandra had outsmarted herself. Anxious that Geoffrey was not acting fast enough, one strung-out afternoon she had called the publisher and accused Donna of the plagiarism. The cloak of suspicion draped itself over Geoffrey, Donna, and Sandra and gave the publisher more time to unravel it.

What to do with Geoffrey and his tainted book became the issue of debate:

"Scratch the whole thing. Dump him. It's damaged goods. Besides, he's been going downhill."

"Even bad publicity is publicity. It's now forbidden fruit."

"It will sell. Clean it up. It's the best thing he's written."

"Look, he was the victim here. In all this there's a strong curiosity factor."

"What if we publish it as is, with a disclaimer, and let the reader have fun finding the plagiarism?"

In the end it came to a financial decision. All agreed that *ID/XX* was Geoffrey's best book. It would be cleaned up and probably match or outsell all his others.

***

Throughout all this controversy Donna could only imagine what was happening. For some reason, as far as she could tell, the story was not reported anywhere locally, though it might have been elsewhere. Did Primo use some clout to get it hushed up? What good would it do for the publisher to release the plagiarism story anyway? Tina thought she had heard a teaser during a commercial break, but when she watched the afternoon news, the promise of the full story had vanished. It was not until one morning at work that Thomas Ambrose showed up. He handed Donna an envelope and said, "Read this when you get a chance. You'll understand everything that went on and why it was best for you to be kept out of it. It all turned out well. The book, minus Sandra's additions, will be published. There's also a check from Geoffrey enclosed. He says it's the first you're owed for all your hard work. Another thing, can I take you to lunch so we can talk?"

"Is 12:30 okay?"

***

They went to a nearby eatery and sat in a back corner. Donna opened the envelope and found two articles and a bank check for $3,000.

Tom explained, "SLY wanted to blame you for the plagiarism, that is, after she anonymously put the blame on Geoff. Fortunately, Geoff got hold of the notes before she could offer them as proof that you were the one who inserted them in the manuscript. She made the foolish mistake of first accusing Geoff, then you, and she never offered a plausible explanation of how she detected plagiarism so fast in the first place. In his own defense, Geoff had the notebook and notes which SLY marked showing where she put everything in the manuscript. It soon became obvious that she was a flake who committed the fraud herself and then tried to frame two different people. The controversy, in a bizarre way, helped. Even people who thought he had lost his edge were on his side."

"Why did she do it?"

"Jealousy. Revenge."

"Jealous of what?"

"Geoff and you. She sensed a change in him and knew that the two of you were spending a lot of time together, so she assumed something was going on."

"But nothing was. Ever. She had no reason."

"She certainly thought she did. SLY is vindictive as hell. She once brought a sexual discrimination suit against the university when a much better qualified man was promoted over her. Then she went on a smear campaign of vicious rumors against the poor guy and the faculty on the promotion committee. I can just imagine what she's plotting against me now because I helped clear Geoff. I don't care. I've come up against more dangerous people than that harridan."

"What does Geoffrey think of all this?" Donna asked. She noticed that aside from the check, there was no note from him in the envelope.

Tom shook his head. "Sly overreacted, even if her suspicions were true. Geoff just can't believe she could be so malicious, though he had to know she was. She treated him like something you'd scrape off the sole of your shoe and let fall from the curb into the gutter. At least he had some good friends to see him through."

"You were one of them," said Donna thinking, "and I wasn't." Geoffrey didn't know how hard she had tried to warn him. Then another thought occurred to Donna. "Tom, do you think Geoffrey is angry at me for copying those pages from other books? Those notes probably gave Sandra the idea. If it weren't for me—"

"Look," said Tom, if it weren't for you, Geoff probably wouldn't have gotten past the first chapter. He was a wreck when he first went to his uncle's. His investment pals were a drain enough in their own annoying way, but Sly and her band of bloodsuckers were leaching him dry. In one month alone, she rang up a forty-thousand-dollar bill on his credit card. He figured at least a quarter of that money somehow got diverted to pay for drugs."

"Why didn't he just kick them all out? Really! I know how Loretta or I would have dealt with them."

"He wanted to fit in, I think. These were hip, artsy-fartsy, pseudo-intellectuals, who look down on anyone who isn't as cool and sophisticated as they see themselves," Tom said. "I guess Geoff saw them as superior and wanted to prove he was like them."

"Coming from our background, that would be easy enough to do," said Donna, thinking of Miss Kaltbergen's prejudice.

"Geoff knew that he had to get himself out of that situation, so he went to stay with his uncle and lay low. Too bad he let Sandra know where he was and come around. She was, after all, his main problem."

Donna said, "You know, for a while, I didn't realize that Geoffrey was staying there so much. I saw the new car in the driveway on the side of the house and assumed it was his uncle's. My first-floor neighbor complained it was noisier upstairs, and we were both aware of people coming and going. We thought they were up to no good."

"One person up to no good was Sandra. There she was, engaged to another man, and she was running around like that. She cheated on Geoff with Rich, then on Rich with Geoff, and who knows who else. Now neither man wants to have anything to do with her."

Although Donna's foolish notes had contributed to the plagiarism, if Geoffrey had been more open and allowed her to read the story through before he whisked it away, she might have at least caught some of the illegal insertions that Sandra had made before Loretta copied the disk. That discovery would have alerted him that someone had sabotaged his book. He trusted Sandra, sleaze that she was, more than he trusted her. "Geoffrey and Sandra deserve each other," Donna said. "The first time I saw her, I couldn't believe how she looked, even though she was what I expected."

"Once was on the day we had lunch together at that place on the North Shore. Donna, I didn't tell you at the time because I didn't want you to get the wrong idea, but I had followed you to that restaurant." Tom looked like a little boy who was caught sneaking a brownie before dinner.

"Really? How?"

"Some years ago, I had interviewed the leader of a crime ring that did business with terrorists, so Geoff invited me over that day – your birthday – to give him some ideas to use for a few of the characters in the book. When I got to his uncle's neighborhood, I noticed Sandra's car with its vanity license plate on the street. The likelihood that she would be anywhere else than with Geoff was too slim. I drove around the corner and parked a couple of doors down from Geoff's uncle's house.

Sandra was the last person I wanted to run into, so I sat in my car for a few minutes hoping I'd have the luck to see her leave. She'd be there for only one reason, or so I thought, so it was unlikely she'd make a day of it. Within minutes, I was surprised to see you come out the door, and that you looked very upset. Sandra had told me that she suspected Geoff was involved with an East Boston woman named Donna, and that she went to Floegel's to see what she, you that is, looked like. Imagine, she was creeping around both your apartment and the store before you ever knew she existed!"

"That's right. She already knew what I looked like when she showed up that day and tried to get me fired. I thought she must have seen me going either into or out of the house sometime," Donna said. "I can't say that I ever remember seeing her before at Floegel's, not that I necessarily would."

"How could you not remember such a unique beauty?" Tom said sarcastically. "Anyway, I knew you all were involved in a lopsided triangle. Why would the three of you be under the same roof? On impulse, I decided to follow you, and I was right behind you when Sly was at her car."

"It did seem like a strange coincidence that right after that disturbing surprise, I should run into someone who knew the two of them and could explain their relationship. You could have told me that you followed me. I would have thought that you were merely concerned I was upset."

"I didn't know what you'd think. You and I knew each other from Floegel's but not well enough for me to be frank."

"I understand. Anyway, I'm glad that you did follow me that day. You helped me a lot."

"So, let me ask you what you now think of Geoff," Tom, said, moving off the subject of himself.

"I don't know. I had thought we were friends, but he's been avoiding me. Still, now that the plagiarism mess is over, you'd think that – why should he?" Donna stopped, realizing that her "friendship" had been forced upon Geoffrey and that he probably now felt well rid of her. "Tom, none of this matters anymore. The last conversation we had was rough. He accused me and didn't even imagine for a second that Sandra might have done it somehow. I'm just a little sad about the way things ended."

"It might've been only a pause, not the end. Geoff doesn't say too much. In some ways, he's more secretive than I am, but I know he feels a lot of shame over his behavior with you. The book is only part of it, really."

"It's over – all forgiven. We all have regrets."

"Donna," said Tom as he walked her back to work, "how would you like to hang out with me sometime? Just friends. We seem to have a lot in common."

"Uh, but what about...um…" Donna wanted to add "but don't you have a significant other?" because Tom would sometimes buy women's clothes at Floegel's. She realized that it would be an awkward question and had to trust that Tom wasn't some kind of cheater, not that she could tell anyway. Besides he did say "just friends" and didn't say "just you and I." She wrestled with the question. *Too awkward. Should I say something, think of a quick excuse to say no, or let it drop?*

As if reading her mind (and eliminating any suspicion that he had any romantic interest in her), Tom said, "Like you, I'm not taken, but we single folks often waste our free time because we rely on a small number of people to be available when we want to do things we enjoy. I think it might be good for us to add each other to our circle of friends." He grinned and paused as if weighing his next words. "You know a good place to spend time as well as to do some good? The V.A. or some other organization that helps veterans. If Loretta wants to know where to meet men, that's a good way to go. Some of them are a bit broken, but they're the best."

"Tom, how do you know Loretta?" asked Donna, almost forgetting Tom's familiarity with Floegel's, "or rather that she's my friend?"

"And that she *always*, well that she often, complains about the lack of available men? I'm at Floegel's a lot, even just passing through."

"Oh, so I guess you've heard us."

"No offense, Donna, but you'd be surprised what I've heard." Tom realized that he might have offended Donna, but he could have said, "Everyone all the way up to the fifth floor has heard the lovelorn Loretta complain about not being able to find a man."

***

One Saturday, Loretta decided to go with Donna to the VA.

"I can't believe it!" Donna said as they left for home. "This was the first time you came here, and within minutes you meet someone." That someone was Fred, a career military man who lost a leg and some of his eyesight in Iraq.

"It's too soon to tell," Loretta said that afternoon, "but something tells me this is it."

***

Tom called Donna several days later and invited her to a writers' group at the home of a friend. With his encouragement, she picked out a couple of stories she had written during the past few years, but then chose to just listen with the promise that she would read them at the next meeting.

As they left the home of the host, Donna whispered to Tom, "By the way, Loretta and Fred really hit it off, as you predicted they would. She doesn't know it was a set-up. It was as though their meeting was meant to be. How did you know?"

"A great-grandmother was a Jewish matchmaker."

***

The crisp golden days, which make autumn the favorite season of many people, grew less and less frequent until they merely punctuated the usual gray drizzle. On the first Saturday in November Donna, Loretta, Fred, and Tom planned a trip to Maine to visit Fred's family.

Loretta drove and picked up Tom last. "Who'd have thought he lived so close in Winthrop all this time!"

Donna answered, "Some things are making sense now. I'll go ring the bell."

When Tom answered the door, he invited all of them in, but Loretta and Fred stayed in the car. "Have a seat, Donna. I'll be just a couple of minutes until I finish this phone call."

Donna sat on the bench in the entrance hall and was tempted to get up and go look at the photos in the living room opposite. Politeness kept her from being nosy, so she stayed seated and stared at them from across the room. One picture was of Tom and a young woman with curly hair.

"All set." Tom startled Donna.

"Oh, I was just looking at your pictures," said Donna standing.

"Those were better days in another life." Tom walked Donna into the living room for a closer look. "This is my sister Theresa," he said pointing to the photo of the young woman and himself. "She's the one I buy the clothes for. She, uh, she's disabled."

"Oh." Donna's face flushed.

"She lives next door with my parents, and often stays here for a change of scenery. I don't talk about her to many people or let them know her condition. Someday I'll explain."

Donna glanced at the wall of family photos ranging from the latter nineteenth century to the present day. Tom pointed to several of them, which included a Chinese railroad worker, a

Portuguese fisherman, a Scandinavian-English dairy farmer, a nineteenth century German Hungarian merchant, and a Cuban grandmother who came to the U.S. after the Bay of Pigs. "Wow," Donna said. "I think there might be some Greeks in my family, if that."

Tom set an alarm as they left the house, and as they got into the car, Donna introduced Fred and Tom. Fred grinned when they shook hands. "Have we met before?"

"Perhaps." Cryptic answer aside, Tom and Fred got along like close friends.

At one point the conversation briefly turned to the Iraq war, and Fred spoke as if thinking out loud. "You know, I almost gave up. The man who saved me kept telling me to hold on. Whenever I felt overwhelmed, I kept hearing him giving me encouragement. He really helped me get my life back."

Donna threw Tom a sideways glance, but she waited until they got out of the car and Fred and Loretta were out of earshot. "I had the impression that Fred was someone you knew through a mutual friend."

"We do have a mutual friend I told you about, but I don't believe I said that he introduced us."

***

Fred's family lived in the kind of big old house you'd expect to find in Maine, weathered white clapboard siding with green shutters. A veranda with a row of rocking chairs wrapped around the front and one side, and a three-season deck hugged the rear. In style and wear, the furniture looked as though every piece had grown decades ago from the pegged wood floors. A slight excess of plaid in the upholstery and the muted tones of the colors suggested a traditional, conservative taste that clashed with Loretta's idea of cheerful surroundings. Fred's family, the Greens – four brothers, one sister (the opposite of Loretta's family), and his parents were solid, upstanding, and unpretentious, the sort of people you'd imagine were raised in such a house and rugged climate. The whole place had an air of tranquility. Even their cats and dogs got along with each other.

Normally everything about Loretta – her looks, voice, and manner – was loud, yet here she seemed subdued, serene, and happy. For today, at least, the heavy eyeliner and multi-layered lash, skin, and lip glop were pared and paled down to a dewy film, giving her a relaxed, almost sleepy look. Donna had known Loretta since junior high and admired the way she meshed with the fabric of East Boston. Loretta had lived the life of an Italian American Eastie girl and could negotiate the congestion, clamor, and confusion of the city as though it were a given that life was meant to be hectic. The change in Loretta was sudden, genuine, and might not last, but it made a good impression on Fred's family.

Tom and Mr. Green chatted about the Civil War, and Donna helped Mrs. Green with lunch, which was prepared on a stove that resembled the one in Tina's kitchen.

Before they all left for home, Donna and Tom went for a walk to give Fred and Loretta some private time to spend with Fred's family.

"Nice family," Donna said. "I wish everyone had a family like that. They love each other and appreciate their lives."

Tom smiled. "Yes, I've met them before. Most people in the world are happy to just get through the day with enough food and without death. The rest of us don't always appreciate what we have. Look at how so many people run around and try to manipulate their lives all in a wasted effort to find happiness. They never learn."

"They sure don't. If you wait for circumstances to bring you happiness, you'll spend your whole life waiting."

Tom nodded. "You must choose to be happy."

CHAPTER SIXTEEN
THE PHANTOM AT THE OPERA

Just before the store opened, Donna stood in the back room with Ginny, Stacy, and a few other salespeople. "Once again, we won't have to do pre-Christmas inventory. Miss Kaltbergen is still using an outside company to do it."

"Why, doesn't she trust us?" asked Stacey.

"Who cares as long as we don't have to do it," Ginny said, "though I could use the overtime."

"I'll bet that's the reason!" said Mary from lingerie. "They'd have to pay us extra."

The women would have said what they really thought of Miss Kaltbergen – they all at different times had problems with her – but the store employees had developed a sense that Big Sister is watching. Miss K's spies were everywhere. Donna had previously grumbled to Loretta and Ginny that Miss Kaltbergen's micromanagement annoyed most of the other floor managers. "I've either got to change my attitude or change jobs."

***

One Thursday night Donna's phone rang. "Hi, Donna, it's Tom. Would you like to go to the opera? A friend I usually go with can't make it. They're doing *La Traviata.* There's just one hitch though. Both Geoff and I have season tickets so there's a chance we could run into him."

"That's no problem. I'm sure that if he shows up, he won't be with Sandra, so I don't care if we meet each other. His aunt and uncle live downstairs from me, and I don't even see him here."

***

It rained on and off during the day of the performance, so Donna chose a charcoal and pink long-sleeved dress to wear under her hooded burgundy raincoat. She headed out when Tom rang the doorbell. Angie passed her on the stairs and muttered, "The bride who wouldn't dance."

Tom was waiting downstairs, but he heard Angie's remark. "Sweetheart, isn't she? Makes you wonder what Geoff's parents are really like that he comes here to get a sense of family."

"Believe it or not, that was nice compared to the way she used to behave. She at least said it with a smile." Ever since Donna had tried to help Geoffrey, his aunt and uncle had been on the friendly side of civil.

***

After an early dinner, Donna and Tom walked in light rain to the theater. Donna pulled the sides of her hood across her cheeks to hide her face for as long as possible. Now that the chance of meeting up with Geoffrey was real, she wasn't so confident. *I'm being ridiculous. If he's here, so what? I'm not the one with anything to hide. Let him see me.* She flung her hood back once they were well inside the lobby and grabbed Tom by the arm so they wouldn't get separated.

Tom let Donna have the inner seat and he took the aisle one. "If Geoff comes tonight, he'll be one row behind us," Tom whispered, "to our left, near the middle. He's not here yet."

"Great," Donna said with a double meaning: seriously, as in "fortunate that he's not here" and sarcastically as in "why the heck didn't you tell me he'd be just one row behind us?" Once again, Donna had to remind herself that she didn't care if Geoffrey was there.

But Geoffrey was there, standing but mentally pacing, outside in the vestibule to the orchestra seats. He thought he had seen Donna (but not Tom) out in the lobby. He could feign illness or some other emergency, but the crowd behind him swept him through the door. *What are the chances that we'll run into each other anyway?*

Donna sat with her head leaning to the right toward Tom. Her hair, hung loose and curly, created a curtain that hid her profile. Well into the first act she finally dared to turn her head for a look. Geoffrey appeared something between bored and totally put out. Next to him sat a woman who was animated to the point of dramatic – a culture snob who behaved as though she appreciated the work on a profound level that no one else could.

Donna looked forward and felt a slight wave of dizziness. Slowly, she turned to get a better look at the drama queen next to Geoffrey. Yep, there she was in her brazen beauty – Sandra. Of course, *La Traviata* – Sandra in her delusions probably identified with the self-sacrificing party girl. *No wonder the bum didn't answer any of my calls!* Donna thought with disgusted anger, having only that afternoon left a message on Geoffrey's voice mail to thank him for the recent check.

She glanced at Geoffrey and met his frozen gaze. Geoffrey and she stared at each other for only a few seconds, but they exchanged a volume of information, most of it indecipherable to Donna, but patently clear to Geoffrey. Donna looked back at the stage and tried to concentrate on the music. Her heavy breathing distracted Tom, who leaned toward her and asked, "How're you doing?"

"Geoffrey is here with Sandra," she whispered in his ear.

"I don't believe it," said Tom turning in his seat. "I see Sly but not him. He told me that he wished he had never met her. He must have crawled in a hole or slid onto the floor."

During intermission, Donna and Tom went to get something to drink. Donna focused her attention entirely on Tom. Had she bothered to look several people behind her, she would have seen Geoffrey and Sandra having a heated discussion. "No, I do not want to leave. Have a glass of wine and sleep through the rest if you're tired. I'm driving anyway," Sandra whined. "Get me some. I'm going to the rest room before the line gets too long."

***

Sandra came out of the toilet stall, stopping at the mirror only to comb her hair and reapply her lipstick. So much for hygiene, but what do you expect from a woman who, at any point in the day, is only minutes from having had her hands on someone's ass? Donna, who was third in line, braced herself. They made eye contact when Sandra turned to leave.

"Tubs, if you'd lose six inches on your hips, I could squeeze past you," said Sandra, sucking in her tummy and walking sideways as though she really had a narrow passageway.

"Speaking of appearances, have you ever noticed that from your chest up, the only thing on you that moves is your tongue? Is all that plastic surgery an addiction or a hobby?" Donna shot back.

You can insult Sandra's taste, morals, or intellect even, but her looks and what she does to improve them are off limits. She raised a red nailed claw, but Donna was quick enough to grab her by the wrist and pin her to the wall.

"How would you like to go for a swim in the toilet?" Donna asked. "From what I understand, you'd actually come out cleaner."

Sandra struggled against Donna's force and strength. "The advantage of being a heavy-weight – the only one. You know, now that I see you up close, you're really very ordinary," said Sandra with a grimace.

"Seeing *you* up close, I have some advice. Tell your dentist to use something other than Chiclets next time he caps your front teeth." Donna let go of her grip and stepped back. "Do me a favor and crawl back under your rock."

"I'll do that – with Geoff." Sandra cocked her head for emphasis.

"Is this something I'm supposed to care about? The fact that he'd be in the same room with you means one thing: you two deserve each other."

"I'll make sure I tell him that."

"Go right ahead. Now if you'll excuse me, I've got something better to do," said Donna as she went into a stall and slammed the door.

***

Sandra dropped Geoffrey off at his condo. Before he shut the car door, she leaned toward him and said, "Geoff, you didn't say anything about Donna Dumpling. We had an interesting chat in the restroom where she almost broke my wrist."

"Oh?"

"I don't think she likes you very much. She did say that you and I deserve each other. How right she is. I'll see you tomorrow or the day after." Sandra slid off into the rain, which now dropped in staccato rhythm.

***

Geoffrey played Donna's message on his voice mail twice before erasing it. Dragging on with Sandra was sick enough, but having Donna see them together was embarrassing. Sandra would not say where she was spending the night. Rich had thrown her out, so Geoffrey let her stay with him while she looked for her own condo. Nothing was good enough for Sandra, and she would take her time finding that perfect place.

Now wide awake, Geoffrey looked at his watch. He called Tom Ambrose, who answered just as Geoffrey was putting his thoughts together. "Tom, it's Geoff. Believe me, I appreciate everything you do for me, but what were you thinking? Why there?"

"Are you saying why did I take Donna to the opera when you were going to be there with Sandra? How was I supposed to know? I was as surprised as Donna was. Where was your sister tonight? You got the season tickets for her."

"She's out of town, so I asked Sandra if she wanted to go."

"You couldn't come alone or with someone else, or just stay home? What were *you* thinking? I didn't tell you I was bringing Donna because it would have looked staged and expected, and I thought you weren't seeing anyone."

"I'm sorry. You're such a close friend, and you're only trying to help. Things right now are a little complicated with Sandra."

"Obviously."

***

Late as it was, Donna held the phone in her hand, itching to call someone. Why bore Loretta and keep them both up for no good reason?

Donna flossed her teeth with such force that she cut her gum. She spat out a thin ribbon of blood and watched it carry her hurt down the drain. A few sips of water rinsed away her bitter words. An eye makeup remover pad wiped away the sight of the two *faccia audacita*s sitting there, brazen and entitled. A lathering of facial cleanser washed away her expression of disappointment. A scrubbing with antibacterial soap sanitized her hands that had touched the dirty schemer. Unlike other nights in the past, she did not lie awake obsessing. She'd been played the fool, but she wouldn't play the victim.

CHAPTER SEVENTEEN
WINTER WASTELAND

Donna helped her mother cook Thanksgiving dinner. Loretta and Tina each spent the day with their families.

Now has begun the difficult time of year. The sight of a bare branch covered in snow just could not offer the same hope as one with buds about to burst open with life. Her loneliness grew as the days shortened and the temperatures decreased. The warmer seasons of the year got people out and mingling. The cold winter kept them in and eating. Just the mere threat of a snowstorm would force the cancellation of many social engagements. Every day it didn't snow was one day closer to spring. She told herself, "It's only about three or four months of this, so I can put up with it."

Her Christmas tree was decorated within a week after Thanksgiving and her holiday shopping completed by the twelfth of December.

Fred tempered Loretta's loneliness, which this time of year normally accentuated. "There's something wonderful about shopping in the men's department for someone who isn't a relative," Loretta said. "I don't think I've done that since Johnny Amoroso's eighteenth birthday party, but even he wasn't a boyfriend."

Donna said, "I got something for Tom, although he's just a friend."

***

On Christmas Eve Donna sat alone in the living room while Christmas carols played on the radio. Her small tree was decorated with ornaments she had made or collected since childhood. With the thumb and forefinger of her left hand she ate *strufoli*, from a plate carefully balanced on her lap, and with her right hand she fingered through her Christmas cards. Brad had sent her a humorous one, and Tom had enclosed snowflake confetti in his. Her friends, her parents, her brother, and her few other relatives had all sent cards this year. One person was noticeably, but not surprisingly, absent. Strangely enough, he was sitting downstairs beneath her, not tooling around Europe or swilling down wine in Napa Valley. As much as Donna could have inhaled the whole wreath of *strufoli*, she put it on the dining room table before she got carried away. The holiday season was fattening enough. Tomorrow her brother Arthur and she would visit their parents. Her friends were all busy with their families, so she would have no need to rush back home.

Arthur came by in the morning to pick up Donna and exchange presents. As they drove away a shadow appeared in a window on the second floor.

***

One of the bad things about retail is that although you get Christmas off, you pay for it the rest of the week afterward. The day after Thanksgiving and the two days before Christmas are supposed to be the biggest shopping days of the year, yet they're easier to tolerate because you make lots of sales. The day after Christmas, not only are you busy with sales, but you lose much of your commission from returns. Loretta had an easier time because the few gift sets and perfume people returned did not have to be sorted and re-hung all over the floor. Donna, on the other hand, was swamped. The after-Christmas sale would run on all week.

Donna and Loretta were invited to Ted's New Year's Eve party, but they politely declined. "What a crew! Gina had a few of them over again the other night. I accidentally on purpose spilled ice water on one who kept criticizing everything from the airplane noise to our artwork on the walls, not yours of course." said Loretta to Donna. "After Gina knocked herself out cooking, this one broad wanted to know whether everything was organic, even the tea. How can she stand being around those people? You know, they're even talking marriage!"

"Imagine Ted in your family, not that you're all a bunch of slobs or anything."

"Yeah, Vince and Ted get along famously. One's got a rope across his ass and the other a poker up his. My money's on Ted to psychoanalyze the Prince to death. Now, if Vinnie were to go to Ted's party, it might be worth going for the laughs we'd get out of it. Then again, what if Brian the turd shows up?"

"That settles it, no matter how slight the chance."

"Yeah, he might try to steal me away from Fred. Don't know if I could possibly resist such a charmer."

"Well, what do you want to do? Ginny, Stacey and a few others from work thought we might all go out together somewhere," Donna said with a shrug.

"And hang around until midnight and go home with all the drunks?"

"What about First Night?"

"What about it? We'd freeze our asses off until midnight and then go home with all the drunks."

"Yeah, but they'd be mostly drunk on wine – a more mellow group of drunks."

"Oh, there could be a lot more than wine out there. The beer alone – Besides I refuse to let a drop of zinfandel pass my lips until the Imperato Winery opens."

"What have you heard? Did he get the winery?" asked Donna, a little too interested.

"I have no idea, but I hope that, when he does, he gives it a better name than his and has the good taste to keep his mug off the label."

In the end, they sat in Tina's kitchen and ate *pasta fagiole* made with spaghetti and lentils, fried smelts, and teriyaki chicken wings. Fred called from Maine where he was visiting his family and celebrating his mother's birthday. At midnight they blew paper horns out on the back porch and shouted New Year's greetings to the other neighbors who were outside. On New Year's Day the three of them went to the movies, and for the first time in years, Donna ordered a small popcorn without butter.

"Where did last year go?" Donna asked. "From June on it's a total blur."

"Wait until you get to be my age," Tina said. "In my mind I'm still the age I was when I got married. I blinked and *poof!"*

***

Someone once said that if the United States had been settled from the inside out, rather than the outside in, New England would still be uninhabited. One of the worst physical assaults to attack the coast is the northeaster, a winter storm that sweeps in over the ocean and carries heavy wet snow to suffocate everything it covers. In mid-January a northeaster socked New England and made both the morning and evening commutes miserable. The only upside to the day was that the sales, though fewer, were bigger. Loretta was scheduled to work later than Donna but rather than brave the mess outside alone, Donna stayed so they could go home together.

A small crowd huddled and shivered, waiting for the bus which inched along the snow packed street. As they made their way to the bus door, a man apologized for stepping on Donna's toes, which were numb enough that she could barely feel anything. The bus driver was in a cheerful mood for someone who had to work for hours under such miserable conditions. "It's my job," he said to a passenger who said he felt sorry for him. "How would you all get home if I said, 'hey, I'm not going out in that?' It makes me happy to help. You're all working people like me."

As Donna and Loretta walked home from the bus stop, they leaned forward into the driving snow. Icy slivers cut their cheeks, and cold wind pounded their breath back down their throats. Every step was an effort, and they both took turns slipping and almost falling. All the fire hydrants, fences, and parked cars were covered and unidentifiable. When they reached Loretta's corner, they had to climb up over an iceberg that a snow plow had deposited, burying the curb under three feet of compacted snow. Loretta slipped and slid down toward the sidewalk where Donna broke her fall.

"Can you make it home the rest of the way?" Loretta asked Donna. "Come upstairs and stay at my place."

"It's not far, and it looks as though some of the neighbors have shoveled recently or at least some point during the day."

"Be careful."

"I will, and I'll call you to let you know I got in. If you don't hear from me in twenty minutes, come out and look for the biggest mound you see on the sidewalk."

Donna turned her back against the wind to catch her breath for a moment and then trudged home on the snow-covered sidewalk. The front stairs of the Infanto house looked as though they hadn't been shoveled for several hours, if at all. Earlier in the morning when she left for work, she had hung onto the railing and half-slid down to the sidewalk. Those footprints she had made then were long buried, though the snow over them was lower than on the rest of the stairs and therefore likely to be the easiest bet. She dug with the toe of her boot to find the first step. As she started to climb, she slipped and fell face forward into the snow.

I should just die here. They'll find me in the spring thaw. Either the need to breathe or the remembrance of the bus driver's optimism caused her to lift her head. Like a book being flung open, Donna flipped her body over to the other side of the staircase and lay face up. She looked up at the sky and thought, "If I had wings, I'd fly into the cloud that dropped that snowflake on my nose." She spread her arms and flapped them to make an angel in the snow. "Now I can fly!" she laughed inside. Her spirit soared over the rooftops into the sky and away to a place she had only seen in her dreams.

His shadow, shovel in hand, loomed in the hallway window. He should have rushed out there the moment he saw her fall, but his feet froze. He had intended to clear the stairs before she came home, but once again he had failed Donna in even the smallest of ways. When she rose to come inside, he disappeared until she was all the way upstairs.

The next morning Donna found the steps completely clean, and a path cleared all the way down to Loretta's. *Must be little elves*.

Although she never saw him, she had the sense that he was there at least throughout the rest of January. Then she no longer felt his presence. She could have asked Tina if she had seen him, or checked the driveway or garage in the back for his car, but for what purpose? Like trying to light a book of wet matches, there was nothing there to re-ignite.

CHAPTER EIGHTEEN
FLOWERS AND FROST

Loretta's Valentine's Day began with the arrival of a dozen red roses and ended with a proposal from Fred. She answered "yes" before he could say "me." The following weekend Donna took them to dinner to celebrate their engagement. They sat at a table by the window overlooking the harbor.

Donna raised her glass and said, "I wish you a long and happy life together."

"Thank you, Donna," Loretta said. "There's something I'd like to ask you. I probably should do it in private, but what the hey, would you like to be my maid of honor?"

Donna started to well up but got herself under control. "You want me, with three sisters? Of course, I'd be honored."

"That's the problem – I have three sisters, and if I choose one the others might get hurt, even though neither Connie nor Amelia picked me, and I'm sure that if Gina marries, she'd grab the first woman she met on the street before she'd ask one of us. Besides, you're my best friend and, if I had to choose to have anyone as a sister, I'd take you first."

"Even though I can't see your face too well, I know you'll make a beautiful bride," Fred said to Loretta. "I just know that you're the most beautiful woman in the world. I trust that someday science will restore most of the sight I've lost, and I'll be able to see for myself what a great beauty you are."

Loretta knew how much she fell short of that ideal. She spoke up. "Fred, I think it's a bit of an overstatement. I only wish…"

Fred smiled and reached for her hand, "No pun intended, but beauty is in the eye of the beholder. If and when I get to see you clearly, even if it's fifty years from now, you'll be the most beautiful woman I've ever seen. That's the truth of love – you see the spirit."

***

The serious scare of a church-load of people staring at a couple of stuffed sausages in satin motivated the women to get serious about diet and exercise. So far, Donna managed to keep off her small weight loss from the summer, but Loretta had gained four pounds over the winter holidays. They decided that they would support each other all the way through, even if it meant cake and cookie calls at any hour of the day. It would take months to lose weight safely and surely. A healthy, non-punishing diet retrained Donna how to eat. Whenever she got an urge, she would promise herself that she could eat whatever it was three hours later if she still had the craving. At first, she had to start with half hour increments, but when she reached the three-hour mark, she was close enough to her next meal for the desire to pass. Loretta and she found a gym for the zaftig, where they could work out without feeling conspicuous. At first the weight held on, but their increasing stamina and strength encouraged them to keep going.

***

Although by the calendar winter was two-thirds over, the only concession from Mother Nature was a lengthening of the days, something over which she had no real direct control. The air remained crisp and the snow crunchy. Even Loretta, who had acne as a teenager, and an occasional pimple still, took to slathering moisturizer over her face and body. The two times Donna felt an illness about to take hold, she'd nip it in the bud by taking to bed and not pushing herself.

One miserable night in late February a patch of black ice sent Primo's car into a back-wrenching spin, that hurt his wife and him just enough to keep them bedridden for a few days. Despite past animosity (and the certainty that if the situation were reversed, the Infantos would have shown no kindness), Donna and Tina went into their caretaker mode for Angie and Primo. They cooked meals, ran errands, and played nursemaid. One evening as Donna washed their kitchen floor the phone rang. Angie called out from the bedroom, “Donna dear, would you get that for me? Only call me if it’s someone important.”

“Sure. Hello.” *Click.* Before Donna could tell Angie that the caller had hung up, the phone rang again. Donna was quicker this time. “The Infanto residence. Who’s calling?”

“Geoff. Is Angie there?”

“Hold on. I’ll get her,” Donna answered quickly without another word between them.

Angie picked up the bedroom phone, but even with a weak attempt to soften her loud voice, her side of the conversation floated into the kitchen. “Yuh, that was her. She’s helping out while we recover…No, really. She offered…She and Tina have been a big help. They’ve cooked every meal for us, and now Donna’s cleaning the kitchen. I could get used to this…Well, you didn’t exactly come running…You didn’t know we were confined to bed from it? We were damn near killed! The car doesn’t have a scratch! Didn’t your father tell you right after it happened? ... Why, what’s going on? ... Thank God you finally got rid of her. I never liked her; neither did your uncle. She’s not for you.”

While Angie was still talking to her darling nephew, Donna went up to her apartment. The “her” Geoffrey finally got rid of was likely Sandra. *But she could’ve been talking about someone else or possibly even me.* You never know with Angie. What a family! At least Primo is a lot nicer, but he was never mean, just slimy.”

***

By the second week of March Donna was thoroughly sick of wool clothes and ready to toss her boots onto a bonfire.

The spring clothes had already decorated the store windows before there was any hope that winter was at an end, and the summer clothes would come out with the daffodils. Although each season had its beauty, to Donna, spring possessed a mystery and magic that no perfect autumn leaf, crystalline-white frosting of snow, or orange summer sun – together – could match. Minute by minute each day lengthened with the boost that Daylight Savings gave the sun an extra hour to shine. Spring, the time of rebirth, was also the season of hope, and when it arrived, Donna felt renewed.

A bud of this hope bloomed and shriveled with one phone call from Tom: "Donna, Geoff's birthday is in a couple of weeks. I was wondering, would you like to join us for dinner downtown?"

"Uh, whose idea is this?"

"Mine. I thought it might be an opportune time to get the two of you reacquainted."

"I don't think so. I haven't moved or changed my phone number, that he has any excuse not to contact me, other than the obvious. There are more suitable people in his life."

"I wouldn't say that."

"No, but I would."

***

Easter, glorious Easter, with its purple and yellow and streams of pastels blossomed. Easter candy was the best, better than even Halloween candy, which in recent years (except for candy corn) had degenerated into simply the usual stuff that was available year-round but in different wrappers. At Easter, however, you had marshmallow chicks, chocolate bunnies, jellybeans, and eggs in too many varieties to count: plain chocolate, candy-coated, caramel, coconut, marshmallow and cream filled in flavors like maple nut, strawberry, and vanilla. Fortunately, Donna's Lenten fast and controlled eating habit had numbed her sweet tooth and balanced out the pounds she would have packed on once Easter Sunday came. She bought only a bag of foil-covered chocolate eggs and put it in her candy drawer for "just in case." On Holy Saturday she made *pizza dolce* with maraschino cherries and chocolate bits instead of the usual dried citrus. This sweet, creamy ricotta pie served as breakfast, her favorite time to eat it, for almost a week.

***

When lilacs, one of Donna's favorite flowers, were in bloom, Tom brought Donna a large bouquet from his yard. Of all the things Donna did with Tom – ballroom dance lessons, drawing and painting, hiking, concerts, and baseball games, her favorite was just hanging out together. His schedule seemed a bit erratic. Some weeks they would see each other three or four times, other weeks not at all. Their friendship was just that – a platonic friendship. They had more than their share of "almost moments", which neither acted on, whether for some unknown reason or simple fear that their relationship, such as it was, would fracture. Donna, after her Geoffrey experience, would let the situation clarify itself and not jeopardize their friendship.

Tom called Donna one morning. "I'm so sorry," he said. "We had planned to go to the museum tomorrow, but my mother is having a colonoscopy, my dad is taking her, and there's no one to stay with Theresa."

"No problem." Donna thought for a moment. "Can we take her with us?"

"Oh, uh, sure. She hasn't gone too far from home since her injury and would love it."

"Okay, I'll come to you and help with the wheelchair."

***

The next day they went to Boston's Museum of Fine Arts. As they drove through the city, Theresa gazed at the brick and concrete buildings. "Boston is so beautiful. I wonder what it was like to live in these houses when they were new."

Tom said, "The people who built them and first lived in them are long gone. We are living in the land of the dead, and we ignore or disparage the wisdom they left us."

"That's if we ever knew it in the first place," Donna replied.

"What would you like to see first?" Donna asked Theresa when they arrived.

"Either the Egyptians or the Impressionists. I never thought I'd get to see another Renoir in my life."

A couple of hours later, they moved on to the Isabella Stewart Gardner Museum, also located in the Back Bay. In 1990, thirteen works of art were stolen by two thieves posing as policemen. "I'm so glad that I came here as a kid and saw Rembrandt's only seascape," Theresa said. "So sad because the case remains unsolved."

Tom said, "The paintings aren't something that can be sold on the open market. They're probably in very private collections, if they weren't destroyed in the process. The thieves cut them out of their frames, and who knows how they handled them afterwards.

Donna nodded. "When Geoffrey and I were writing *ID/XX*, the earliest draft involved an art theft until we decided that stolen art would be difficult to surreptitiously sell and too easy to trace."

Theresa gave her brother a quizzical look, and before she could ask a question, Tom whispered, "Donna and I will explain on the way home."

Donna slapped her hand to her forehead. "Sorry I let it slip. I should be more careful. Good thing I said it only in front of you and not someone else."

“Don’t worry,” Tom said. “A lot of writers and artists, for that matter, have assistants you never hear about.”

While they drove back home, Tom let Donna explain how Geoffrey and she met under awkward circumstances, then he took over from the point at which Sandra tried to frame first Geoffrey, and then Donna.

“Oh wow!” Theresa said. “To think I used to have such a crush on Geoff, that is until I met someone with more character.”

“You’re not alone in your opinion of him,” Donna said. “I could almost say the same thing about myself, although I saw through Geoffrey early enough and got to know your brother.” She turned to Tom. “I never quite understood how he and you became friends. It’s more to your credit than his. You’re both so different.”

Tom shrugged. “We met at the Marathon, and when we realized that we lived a few miles from each other, he drove me home. We liked the same books, sports, and restaurants. Our friendship took off from there.”

“From what I’ve observed, I don’t think you’d fit in with his other friends.”

“That’s an understatement and easy to see why Geoff escaped to his uncle’s. When we first met, he was almost shy. He’s always been quiet, but he seemed uncomfortable whenever people stared at him, and that was before he became a local celebrity. With each success, he got more confident and started to attract people like Sandra.”

Theresa said, “I remember when he’d call you to feel normal. He told me that you were the only person he could trust.”

“I was probably the only one of his old circle who wasn’t scared off. Once you start collecting bad friends, that’s what you end up with because they drive everyone else away.”

"Geoff probably scared off enough friends all on his own too. You and I both noticed how his personality changed. He got very materialistic, superficial, and almost arrogant."

Tom agreed. "He did become a bit full of himself, but more so in front of other people. With me, he behaved like old Geoff."

Donna said, "I've noticed that some people have sponge-like personalities that change with whatever group of people they're around. Others like you, Tom, are always the same with everyone. It is one of the definitions of integrity."

Tom smiled and checked the time. "Shall I pick up something for dinner or wait until we get home and order in?"

"I can cook," Donna replied.

"Nah, I don't want you to work after a long day."

Donna stayed until 10:00, and when she arrived home, she called Tom and said, "We should take Theresa with us as often as we can."

"She would love that. Thank you."

Long talks with Tom helped Donna to refine her attitude and approach to living. Life, Tom emphasized, held no promises and was tough for ninety percent of the people in the world. "We're not here very long so live positively," he told her, "You just have to do the best you can, if not for yourself, then for others. It gets you outside of yourself, but you already know that."

"I know my little life doesn't mean anything in the grand scheme, but I wish I had more of a purpose."

"You matter to a lot of people, and you are better than you know. Geoff's problem is that he thinks he always must be on top, and he needs material signs of success for self-validation. Yet he knows none of that has brought him peace of mind."

Donna nodded in agreement until Tom added, "The happiest I've ever seen him was the time he spent with you. He laughed and smiled more, and his needs were simpler."

"This is news to me." Donna did not want to insult Tom's judgement, but suspected that his opinion was based on optimism, not fact. "The last time I saw Geoffrey was at the opera, and since then I spoke to him only once by accident when I answered his aunt's phone."

"Some things take time. He might be too ashamed or embarrassed."

***

Brad's phone calls were now weekly instead of every other day. "Thank you, Donna for giving me the courage to approach other women," he told her. "I was always so shy and didn't think that anyone would like me, but you gave me confidence. You're still my best girl." Donna had to laugh at his honesty and sweetness. It had concerned her that Brad's sister was one of her coworkers, and that an uncomfortable parting might hurt her friendship with Ginny. It would make for an easier break if Brad found someone else first.

For months Donna had written nothing longer than a shopping list or a note on a greeting card. She had stopped attending the writers' group after four or five times, even though Tom and the others encouraged her to continue. Last summer's experience with Geoffrey overstayed its welcome in her memory, and any attempt at creative writing did not bring the relaxation that it used to, but instead brought back the mental anxiety and visceral turmoil of those hopeless, wasted days. A paintbrush had replaced a pen as a hand fixture. Everything from quick studies to paintings that took weeks to complete decked the walls of the apartment and packed the corners of the spare room.

One day instead of grabbing a paintbrush, Donna picked up a pen and began to write a letter of thanks to Tom for his friendship. She ended it: "You've always been there for me, even when I didn't know it."

Her mother had a few words to say about Donna's new hobby. "Why don't you do something that will help you get a better job?" Then her mother lowered the shrill volume and said something that showed true maternal concern: "Your future worries me. I know I sound like a nag, but I'm as anxious as any mother. You need a trade or a skill that pays a steady wage. You live on commission – feast or famine. What good is a degree in philosophy? You should've taken something useful. I can't even wish you'd get married unless you find someone wonderful and want kids."

CHAPTER NINETEEN
NOW TELL ME WHAT YOU REALLY THINK

It was not until almost a year to the day of their first encounter that Geoffrey and Donna would face each other again. Any verbal communication they had since the night before he went to Cape Cod with Sandra (the plagiarism accusation and February phone call for Angie notwithstanding), was one way with Donna's unanswered messages. By now he was out of her head, but on occasion when Donna entered the house, an aroma from Tina's, an angle of light through the stained-glass window, or even Angie's annoying voice would throw her mind back to last summer. She would enter her apartment to the fleeting presence of his spirit and a tinge of nostalgia.

During dinner at the Infantos' one night, Geoffrey's attention was distracted by the sound of Donna's footsteps upstairs in her kitchen. Donna, unaware he was in the house (for his car was tucked away in back by the garage), washed and cut up lettuce, tomatoes, red onion and cucumbers then tossed in pepperocini, artichoke hearts, slices of roasted red pepper, pitted black olives and chunks of provolone cheese. She stretched a sheet of plastic wrap over the bowl, which she then balanced on her hip and opened her back door to take the salad down to Tina. On instinct, Geoffrey jumped up from his seat and opened the door as Donna passed by. Donna gave a start and almost dropped the salad.

They stared at each other, both straining for words. Donna spoke first with a simple hello. She looked down at the salad and thought of something else to say. "I was just bringing this downstairs. Nice to see you."

"Would you like to .... Could we go for a ride sometime tonight and just talk?" Geoffrey said.

"Uh, sure. I was just about to have dinner with Tina. You're welcome to join us, or I can see you later."

"You go ahead and just knock when you're through or call me on my cell."

Donna started down the stairs. "I don't have the number," she called back, not waiting for him to give it to her.

***

"Donna, invite him down," said Tina, thirsty for some amusement.

"I already did, and he refused."

"You probably weren't forceful enough." Without waiting for Donna to give much of a reply, Tina dialed Angie's number and was on the phone with Geoffrey. "Geoffrey dear, please join us for dinner. It's been so long since the three of us sat down for a chat." Like old buddies.

Geoffrey, fresh from a barbecue steak dinner, came downstairs and tried to eat. Donna, wearing jeans in her small size, let Tina and Geoffrey do most of the talking. "What have you been up to?" Tina asked.

"Traveling and working on a new book."

"Why such a stranger?"

"I come here a lot."

"Geoffrey, I know you visit Angie and Primo, but I mean why haven't you bothered to call Donna for so long? She's right upstairs, for heaven's sake! It's been almost a year or at least eight months anyway. Donna, how long has it been?" An awkward silence answered Tina's questions.

Geoffrey was tempted to say that the phone works both ways, but he had the good sense not to. He had returned none of

Donna's calls, so she naturally stopped calling him. "I really can't say. I guess I was just busy."

"Come on, too busy to pick up the phone?"

"I guess I don't have a good reason."

"You must."

Donna spoke up to let him off the hook. "Tina, there's no reason why he should. It doesn't matter. We've both moved on."

"But last year you spent so much time together, and to just drop off the face of the earth! So, what if you're seeing other people or busy with other things? You can still be friends. What's the matter with you two?"

"Oh, what the heck," Donna thought. She looked at Tina and said, "I called Geoffrey several times, but I never got a return call." She stood up to clear the dishes before the conversation got any more strained. Tina meant well, but she was too late.

Donna washed her salad bowl, thanked Tina for dinner and left with a hesitant Geoffrey following.

"Donna," Geoffrey called after her, "can we go somewhere and talk?"

"I work tomorrow. Do you mind if we go upstairs to my apartment?"

"Do you have any ginger ale or iced tea?"

"Sure do," Donna answered with her first genuine smile of the evening.

They sat on the back porch. "I can't believe how much time has passed," Geoffrey said. "What have you been up to?"

"Still working at Floegel's, and I've got a better attitude about my job. It's what I do, so I decided to enjoy it. I took painting lessons last winter. When I really thought about what I wanted to study, I decided on dental hygiene. Arthur, my brother, is a dentist, so I can always work for him part-time and keep my job at Floegel's. I'm taking biology and chemistry in the fall."

"Did you do any of those new pictures on the wall?"

"Yes, all of them."

"They're very good."

"Thanks." She looked at him to glean some understanding of why the sudden interest. "Geoffrey, were you angry at me for my part in your problems?"

"What do you mean?" asked Geoffrey.

"If it weren't for my foolish notes, Sandra might not have had the idea to sabotage your book." This was the first time that Donna had mentioned Sandra's name to Geoffrey.

"I, uh, no, no, of course not."

"You don't sound very sure. You never called or enclosed a note with the checks you sent. What else was I to think?"

"How can you put yourself on the same level as Sandra? Do you have any idea what she put me through?"

"Oh, but you *did* blame me, and what's more, you *never* called to ask for an explanation, to hear my side!" Donna raised her voice with a sudden burst of pent-up anger. "You believed her over me because that was the most convenient and beneficial explanation. You only ever put up with "blah" me because you had to. First chance you got to incriminate me, you took it."

"But, but some of the plagiarism was from your notebook."

"Which you supposedly didn't have. How much of what I wrote in there did you even remember?"

"But when you called to supposedly 'warn' me, you didn't explain how you knew the book had been tampered with."

"I tried to explain, but you hung up on me. Worse yet, once you learned that Sandra was the culprit, you didn't bother to contact me. And even worse than all that, you kept on seeing her."

"We don't anymore."

"No, but you did after all the trouble she caused you. When was the last time you spoke to her?"

Geoffrey seemed a little startled at the question. “A while ago. There was still snow on the ground.”

“New England has snow on the ground almost the whole darn winter.”

“Uh, I think it was January or February sometime when we last spoke, but she moved –” Geoffrey stopped short of saying, “but she moved out in December” and was relieved that Donna cut him off.

“Why would you so much as cross the street to spit at her after what she did to you?”

“That whole mess didn’t clear up overnight. When she was cornered, she admitted what she did, so I owed her.”

“Owed her? What – a kick in the pants or a push off a pier? Are you kidding?” asked Donna with an expression of total incredulity.

“I couldn’t just dump her. Her engagement was broken. Rich threw her out when he learned everything that went on. She needed a place to stay for a while,” Geoffrey volunteered the information that he had nearly spilled only seconds earlier. “I know it was a long while, but I couldn’t be vindictive.”

“That was very big of you.” Not even Donna knew whether she was being sarcastic. Certainly, Sandra had enough money, if not other friends or family, to stay elsewhere. Did Geoffrey drag out their relationship to ease out gently, or did Sandra find another sucker? “What made you finally break it off?”

“In my mind it was over last summer, but I had to wait until she was ready to move on. I never loved her, and she’s incapable of the emotion, anyway. Finally, we both told each other that we were interested in seeing other people.”

“Oh,” Donna took a quick breath. So, these two clowns used each other until something better came along. “I hope you both have found what you deserve in life.” This time she was being sarcastic. She sat a moment and thought. Sandra had put him through hell, yet he took her in after *she* nearly ruined *him.* Meanwhile, good old faithful Donna didn't get so much as a returned phone call. "Enough about Sandra," she said. "Tell me about your book, I mean *ID/XX*."

"Now that all that crap is settled, word is it's at least as good as anything I've written and probably better."

"I can't wait to finally read it," Donna said sardonically. To soften the jab, she quickly added, "in its final form."

"You were a big part of it."

Donna stared straight ahead. "How much did I contribute to it? It's not as though you ever let me read it through." True, even though Donna had her own private pirated copy, Geoffrey never offered or rather allowed Donna to read the entire finished manuscript, let alone the botched version that was sent to the publisher.

"Donna?" Geoffrey paused and lost his train of thought. He had just escaped with his sanity from one woman only to have another one attack his integrity, low as it was. "Are we back on that old argument? I told you I had to finish it alone…" Geoffrey stopped with the realization that he had not, in fact, completed the book alone and that Donna knew it. "I mean I had to pull it all together and make it sound like me. Sandra merely did my editing and proofreading. Well, she did a lot more than that, as you've heard."

"With help like that, who needs amateurs?" Donna wouldn't let Geoffrey get the next word in. "You needed her? I could have proofread for you. In fact, I should have. I helped you write it – the plot, the characters, and every word that came out of their mouths and almost everything they did. None of this trouble would have happened if you didn't involve Sandra."

"But you don't know Sandra. She was so insistent and jealous. I had to do something to shut her up."

"And you didn't have the *cogliones* to stand up to her? You know, Geoffrey, I'm not such a whiner, but I don't know when I've ever felt so used."

"I'm sorry, and I'm ashamed of my behavior." Geoffrey, knowing his apology came too late to gain acceptance, struggled to bolster his argument. "But I am paying you," he offered as additional support.

"True. I worked for it, though it doesn't change what happened. Long ago, I decided the book was all yours, despite my input, but I could never understand your behavior toward me."

"Neither could I. My behavior was despicable, especially toward the end, as if the beginning wasn't bad enough." Geoffrey had no need to remind Donna of his behavior before they met, behavior that brought a cringing shame that made him shudder. He stood and moved a few steps back in an unconscious attempt to put a comfortable distance between them. "Donna, even still, there has always been this underlying tension between us. Why when we got along so well otherwise?"

"That's what I'd like to know. I suppose we just got off to a bad start that was hard to set right. It took a long time for me to trust you, and in the end, it was you who wouldn't trust me."

"It wasn't a matter of trust. You don't understand the situation I was in. As it was, we were spending too much time together."

"Who was to care? Sandra, who was engaged to another man? You came here supposedly to get away from her and her druggy friends, no? Then she followed you like a bounty hunter. Neighbors saw her skulking around their yards like some guilty adulteress, which is what she was. You two skeeves even had the nerve to use my apartment!"

"Donna!"

"Don't deny it! She should learn to clean up after herself better. Bad enough she'd leave traces of powder on my tables, but I have no idea how much she contaminated."

"She made herself at home, but—"

"That you would even be attracted to someone like her shows the kind of person you are. Didn't you recognize or care that she's despicable? And, after everything she did, you still carried on with her?"

"No, no. The relationship was over after all that trouble. I told you, I just put her up for a while. She'd disappear for days at a stretch. It was clear that she found or was looking for someone else and that I didn't want her anyway." Geoffrey wiped his hair off his forehead. "Sandra and I were involved in an unhealthy situation, which started before she even got serious with Rich. I was stuck in something I didn't know how to deal with. In a way, she was cheating on me with him." Geoffrey fortunately looked down long enough to not see Donna's expression of incredulity. "Once I met you, I began to see how peaceful a relationship could be. I never felt so connected with anyone. My whole outlook on life changed. We clicked and were happy, or so I thought."

Donna forced herself to hide her resentment. "Yes, we had some good times, for the most part."

"We still could. I missed you," said Geoffrey blushing. "I know you're going to say why didn't I call then, but my life was so complicated. At first, when Sandra put the blame on you"-

"*She*? And you had no part in it?"

"Well yes, but it came as a shock, and when I heard the section that had been lifted from Jane Austen, I recognized it as the one from *Pride and Prejudice* that made you angry at me. I figured you got upset not because I had gone into your room but because you were using it to frame me."

"So even though Sandra spent a lot of time in my apartment, where she made herself at home in every room – and had freer access to your laptop than I ever had, you assumed that I had to be the culprit."

Geoffrey groped for a response. "It was *your* notebook-"

"Which I lost, and she found. I searched my apartment and couldn't find it. There were only two people besides me that would have had any interest in it – Sandra and you. You had to know better after I explained to you what it was for, so I realized Sandra was the guilty one."

"I wish I had known. I couldn't even dedicate the book to you."

"Oh, couldn't or wouldn't," Donna said. "If you had called me for an explanation, you would have known. I called you enough times, though mostly to thank you for the payments."

"I couldn't face you with everything that was going on." Geoffrey stopped, knowing that Donna wasn't buying that baloney. "I was angry and in no mood. Then by the time everything cleared, Sandra was in a bad situation, so I took her in for a while."

Donna asked, "How smart was that? You *stunad* or masochistic?"

"I let her know that she was out as soon as she found another place to live or some other fool." Geoffrey thought of another complication. "There was also that night at the opera, which was a further setback…"

"But not even one quick return phone call? How would anyone know? If things with Sandra were as you say, you could have, no, should have called to explain."

"How much could you have known about what was going on then? Tom took care of things for me, and my lawyer advised me not to talk to anyone about it."

"Then it was completely reckless to have Sandra the framer and betrayer under your roof," Donna said. Geoffrey blanched at her insight. Donna, of course, knew more than Geoffrey could imagine, and she believed that she should have been included in his inner circle of advisers. "I foolishly thought we were friends."

"We are," answered Geoffrey. "I haven't met anyone else I cared about besides you."

"Me?!?" Donna fell back in her seat.

"Yes, you. I kept fighting my feelings, all the way from last summer. You don't know—"

"I see. I was not worthy."

"No, that's not it, not at all." Geoffrey flushed at the realization of his blunder. "I wasn't prepared."

"You needed preparation?" Donna asked and thought such a response wouldn't even sound credible if it came from Brad in his shyest moment.

"I was stuck with Sandra and had to get her clutches off me before I could start anything else. One triangle was bad enough, but to include someone like you—"

"You'd have had a square, literally and figuratively. After all, I am so *blah.*"

Geoffrey winced. "I felt like a creep the way I treated you, believe me. I was the one who wasn't worthy. For months I hid from you, even when I came here, because I thought you had to hate me."

"Did my voice messages thanking you for the checks sound angry?"

"No, but why would they if you were calling just to thank me," Geoffrey answered. Donna's shrug for a reply indicated the fatigue of surrender and an unwillingness to continue the argument. Geoffrey, however, could have chosen better words to move the conversation in a positive direction. “I’m glad we met tonight. You look great.”

So once again, it came down to looks. His last three words set back any headway he had made with his apology. “I lost twenty-three pounds and have still have at least another ten to lose, and you think that I look better?” she said with a well-concealed hurt.

“Definitely.”

“Now that I’ve lost this weight, you see me in a way you didn’t see before?” Geoffrey gave a nod that touched a sensitive nerve in Donna and caused a small tremble in her voice. “How so?” she asked.

“I’ve always liked you – a lot – and now with Sandra out of the way, I’d like us to have a more serious relationship, especially now.”

“Now that I’ll look more presentable to your friends and to the rest of the world, you mean. I see. You know, I worked hard to take off the weight, and I intend to keep it off, but there’s always a chance that I could put it back on. What then?”

“If you lost it once, you could lose it again,” Geoffrey said with a slight shrug, not realizing that “so what?” would have been a better answer.

“That’s not what I meant. In fact, I could gain even *more* weight than I lost. Then you’d have to ‘fight it’ again? Obviously, looks matter more than substance to you.”

“Come on, looks matter to everyone, and you know it. If they didn’t, you’d be with Tom.”

“Tom? What are you saying?”

Geoffrey smirked. “Well, look at him. Doesn’t exactly have them beating down the door, not that I exactly know what he does in his spare time.”

"So, you're saying that I would never consider Tom anything other than a friend?" Donna said with a slight tone of disgust. "He's kind, and I think he's quite handsome."

Geoffrey smirked. "If you need to *think* someone's handsome, then that doesn't sound like public consensus. It's just your opinion."

Donna gasped and looked away.

"That came out wrong. The point I was trying to make is that all these months, with and without Sandra, I kept thinking about you and fearing that you'd find someone else."

"You were afraid I'd meet someone, and yet you kept your distance all that time?"

"Yes, but aside from what I've already said, I just don't have a good reason for not once calling you."

"Not one that you dare to tell me. You know what? Never mind." Donna didn't care enough to fight. Guilt and shame, compounded from the first day they had met, may have taxed Geoffrey's will more than Donna could imagine.

Geoffrey just had to press his luck and follow her line of argument. "Donna. I've never felt happier with anyone else or at almost any other time in my life. You should realize I'm used to a certain lifestyle. A lot of it is crap and self-destructive, but most of it's at a speed that I don't think you understand."

She cut him off. "A level and speed that I don't understand or deserve. I'm too dull to fit in with your exciting life. You need a pill popping plastic surgery junkie to make you feel confident. You were ashamed to be seen with me. You'd have to explain to your friends and take their ridicule."

"That's not what I meant, Donna."

"Oh yes, it is. You think that just because you hang out with a bunch of high-flying degenerates that you're superior. What you are is superficial. You know Geoffrey, you and your ilk are bores and boors, despite all you have. The only exciting thing about your personal life is having sex with a slut on a staircase or some other public place where you might get caught."

Geoffrey's mouth dropped open. Donna crossed her arms. "How did I know, you're wondering? Let's see, it was on my birthday, to be exact, that I came home and thought I'd surprise you, only I was the one who got the surprise. I had to sneak back downstairs as though I was just coming home. Well, this 'little girlfriend' was on guard from that point on."

"I'm sorry," Geoffrey said in a tiny voice. "This explains a lot. I couldn't understand why you always kept me at arms' length."

"You mean why I wasn't like other women and throw myself at you? Believe it or not, some of us pathetic, desperate women have enough self-respect to know what's in our best interest. Your disregard and manipulation became so obvious, I'd have been a masochistic fool if"—

"No, you've got it wrong. I've never told anyone in my life that I care for them, let alone said it to someone I had treated like dirt. This is very hard for me."

"I've said it before – it's hard because you never had to work for anything. It all comes so easily to you. What you say and what you do are two completely different things. Your actions show what you really think."

"You don't believe me?"

"Believe what? What are you trying to say?"

"That I - I – I—"

"You can't even say it, and you expect me to believe it? Tell me what am I supposed to believe? To me, the time we spent together was just one big, fat lie."

Geoffrey needed time to recover his voice. "Donna, can we put all this aside for the moment and pretend none of this ugly stuff ever happened? I already have so much guilt and regret, and this discussion isn't helping. For just a while, let's focus on the good times we had or else we'll never get past the bad."

"Sure, let's change the subject." *Who cares anymore, anyway?*

"Not so fast. Can we at least try?"

Donna looked down. "I really, really liked you as a friend, but I have to admit, you may be what I once wanted, but you're not what I need."

Her words had a familiarity and a sting.

"I've already changed a lot because of you. I know that I took advantage of you and that I was selfish and unfair. I led you on when I had no realistic plan for ending things with Sandra."

"And you saw nothing wrong with that, did you?"

"I do now. Remember, I was involved with Sandra before I even met you. I would've been cheating on *her* if I started anything with you."

Donna's eyebrows shot up. "Sandra: the two-timer who was cheating on Daddy Warbucks with you? Once I realized who Sandra was, I had the good sense to step back and avoid any entanglement. If you were able to cheat on her with me, you would have. Geoffrey, do you understand the meaning of fidelity and trust?"

"That's not – if you help me, I can change. I'm trying to tell you, but you're not listening."

"I am listening. Please continue," she said a little cooler than necessary.

"I'd 've dropped her last August if there was any sign from you. Donna, I know I should've treated you better. I can't believe how good you were to me and how rotten I was to you."

"It's not entirely your fault. You never learned the lessons that life forces on most of us. When you always get your way, you grow up thinking that everything is yours for the taking and that no one could ever possibly dislike you." She should have stopped right there, but only paused. “You weren’t worried that I’d find someone else. You probably figured that I’d drop him for you the minute you showed your face.”

Geoffrey stared at his feet. “You make me sound like a superficial, self-centered jerk. I don’t know what else to say.”

“For sure, we both need improvement. I never hated you, but until tonight I wasn’t sure if I even still liked you.”

“I, uh, guess we’re not in a very good place, but I hope you mean that you at least don’t hate me.”

“I don’t…dislike you. Perhaps we can try to rebuild our friendship.” During the past year, Donna had slowly built an emotional wall with Geoffrey’s name chiseled on it. That wall ran concentric with all the other walls that she had built over her lifetime. “I’m tired,” she said. “I want to go to sleep. Call me sometime, if you feel like it.”

CHAPTER TWENTY
THE AMAZING MR. AMBROSE

One Saturday after Donna had lunch at Tina's, she stood to clear the dishes from the table. "So, Tina, why don't we rearrange the room."

Tina's daughter Florence and granddaughter Christina were coming to spend a few months while her son-in-law was working in Alaska, and Tina wanted to set up the spare bedroom for them. "Are you sure? We can wait until Florence comes so we can have extra help."

"Let's at least get started and do as much as we can." Donna walked across the center hall of Tina's apartment to the fleur-de-lis-wallpapered bedroom and called back, "Now do you still want to move the bookcase?"

"Yes. It'll make more room for the crib. We should probably start by taking the books off the shelves and stacking them in the living room. Then we can put the bookcase in the hall, but I think we should wait for Florence to move any furniture around. Ralph said he'd help too. How 'bout I hand you the books to take into the living room?" Some people arrange their books by subject. Tina arranged hers by color. They started with the larger reds and worked their way to the smaller ones. Tina handed Donna three or four books at a time.

"What a scream! Tina, you never told me you had this!" Donna held up a book titled *The Amazing Mr. Anselm* by George Infanto.

"Oh yeah. I forgot I had it. That was his first book before he changed his name and got good. We all bought it to help his sales, but it flopped. Florence got a copy on the Books for a Buck table six months after it came out."

"You know, I remember him saying that all but one of his books was a best seller, but I could never figure out which one it was. Every book of his that I knew did well. That's because this one is in his real name. I'll bet it's never counted."

"I can see why," Tina chuckled. "He's lucky he ever got a second chance. No wonder he changed his name! I read about half of it and gave up."

"What's it about?"

"A lonely guy who disguises himself and goes around helping people."

Donna's hand that held the book tingled. "Would you mind if I borrow it?"

"Keep it. If I ever got around to cleaning, I'd have thrown it out. Read it some night when you have insomnia."

"It can't be that bad."

"Oh, it is. Trust me."

Donna sat on the chaise and read by the afternoon light:

His remarkable features – snipped from every continent that sustained human life – made him look unlike anyone and yet like everyone on earth. It was his mind – his superior intellect – that set him apart from his schoolmates, his neighbors, and even his own family. He could have come from a lost world, so advanced was he in body and soul. His parents taught him to celebrate his unique talents and abilities and so, from an early age, Tim Anselm learned the mysticism, medicine, and martial arts of his multiethnic ancestors. He was sensitive and smart, intuitive and intelligent, tough and talented, but solitary and shy – an outsider. Rather than try to fit in, he made himself more of a misfit, a lone wolf who would rather hide behind a book than show the pain in his face. He was liked better than he knew, but his obvious decency and strong moral compass excluded his inclusion in boyish pranks and adolescent misbehavior.

It began the day he saw a picture of his Native American great- grandfather. Retrieving a worn-out tube of lipstick his mother had thrown away, he painted his face even though in the picture his great-grandfather, wearing a plaid flannel shirt, looked like a mid-western farmer and not a chieftain or brave in traditional dress. Just as he had finished his facial artwork, he heard the screech of tires followed by a loud crash. Without a thought of how he looked, he ran outside to help. The injured driver was a sixteen-year-old who had never been nice to Tim and was too stunned to recognize him behind the war paint.

Halloween was Tim's favorite holiday. A good deal of planning went into his homemade costumes, and on the next Halloween, he smeared green makeup on his face and spiked his hair. Two doors from home there was a muffled scream, and it was Frankenstein to the rescue.

Gradually a familiar pattern emerged: courageous Tim in some manner incognito, and some hapless person in need. With his compassion and combat skills, Tim was instinctively on the scene before, during, or after someone experienced a dramatic or traumatic event.

It was exhausting work and, after a few years as a semi-superhero, Tim cut back to protecting the ones he loved and only intervened when strangers were in real danger.

So much for the 'show, don't tell' rule, but that would have made this clunker about fifty pages longer. Donna flipped through the pages of the book.

Most of the book was a weak dilution of all of Geoffrey's others – an action adventure with a brave hero. Some of the scenes ranged from ridiculous to illogical, and the story had no real plot. The ending was positively beyond belief, though in a strange way satisfying. If only there were such people in the world – part guardian angels, part undercover soldiers.

"Phew, no wonder it bombed," Donna said to herself as she stared at the younger, serious face of Geoffrey on the back cover. Geoffrey was more handsome than Tom, and he was the first person to say so. Tom, however, did have a striking and distinctive face, a secret sadness about him, and a tendency to be there when you needed him.

The similarities were too obvious. How much of Tom was Tim? Wouldn't Tom have been angry to see his life used this way? Still, that Geoffrey and he had remained friends was a possible indication that Geoffrey, with his friend's permission, may have embellished most of the story.

Come to think of it, Tom had appeared in Donna's life either before, during, or after a confusing event. On her birthday he had followed her after she nearly had her heart broken. There was also that night she was almost mugged twice and had the sense that she was being followed by a familiar-looking figure that she saw in the shadows. He had helped save her from Sandra's vicious accusation. He had taken her to the opera knowing she might reconcile with Geoffrey there. "This was written long before he ever knew *me*, but it may give an insight to his behavior."

How much of the book is based in reality? This was a question that would cause insomnia tonight. "I may have to reread *The Amazing Mr. Anselm* if I can't sleep."

CHAPTER TWENTY-ONE
INDEPENDENCE DAYS

If nothing else, it was summer. On one of her days off, Donna put on her walking shoes and headed into the city. The T took on a whole different feel than whenever she had to take it to work or school. Riding the train for fun gave the sooty subway, the jostling and jerking, and the bad air a charm she had never noticed before. Her fellow passengers, many with familiar faces, possessed a humanity she hadn't recognized when her ride was mandatory and purposeful.

Today she had nothing to do until lunch, and therefore, she would do anything she wanted. The Freedom Trail, the historic walk-through Boston, was a tourist must but a Bostonian might. The red footprints led her through the spirit of the American Revolution: the meeting houses, site of the Boston Massacre, the State House, churches, and the old graveyards. Donna stood before the grave of William Dawes, a man who helped to warn the citizens of Boston and neighboring towns of the British invasion. Credit for that long night ride, thanks in part to a certain Longfellow poem, was given almost entirely to his famous partner Paul Revere, who is honored by a statue near the Old North Church and by the historical preservation of his home. "To think I made such a fuss at being denied credit for a book that will be forgotten within five years," Donna thought.

A stroll through the North End allowed Donna to test her resistance to Italian pastry, slush, and spumoni. A pair of coffee-colored pumps in a nearby shop reminded her that she was in need of a cappuccino. The café across the street looked quiet and comfortable enough for a woman alone.

"Donna?" a voice called from the far corner.

"Geoffrey?"

"What are you doing here?" they asked each other simultaneously.

Donna answered first, "It's my day off. I was roaming around and felt like having some coffee before lunch."

"Then you haven't had lunch yet? Neither have I. I can't believe we ran into each other like this! Where are you going to lunch?"

"Probably to Durgin Park to watch the waitresses yell at the customers."

"Do they really do that?"

"They're allowed to because the original owner stipulated in his will that a waitress can never be fired for insulting a customer," Donna said.

"I know it's the oldest restaurant in the country."

"The waterfront was closer back then, and the waitresses had to put up with some pretty rough characters."

"So, I guess those women had to be tough.

"Yeah, I wish they had that policy at Floegel's."

"That reminds me," Geoffrey said in a lower voice, "did Sandra really try to get you fired? Tom seems to think she might have, but she, of course, denied it."

"If you mean last year, yes, she sure did. One afternoon she came in and tried to provoke me, but I didn't take the bait, although I threw a few veiled insults at her. Hers were much more direct. The next day I was given a reprimand and told that I shouldn't offend a customer of her 'caliber'."

"Why? They don't want you to insult lowlifes?"

"I had to defend myself against her lies and exaggerations. The worst part was that I don't think the manager believed me, but of course, she's of Sandra's caliber, which is to say her name doesn't end in a vowel."

"Speaking of Sandra and her lies," Geoffrey paused to choose his next words with care. "Did she ever tell you …" Geoffrey spoke just above a whisper even though they were out of anyone's earshot. "Donna, did she ever say that I would have had you killed if you told anyone about the circumstances, uh, how we met? Please, please believe me…I never said or thought something so despicable." True. Although Sandra had pressured for Donna to receive a death threat, Geoffrey had said that he would give up writing if he ever sank so low.

Donna was a little startled even though that thought had crossed her own mind the day she caught him copying her book. "No, she never said any such thing, but I'm sure that if we ever had a longer conversation, she would have said anything to scare me off."

"Well, she said that she told you that either my uncle or I would have given you a one-way boat ride to the middle of the ocean. Then she claimed you told her I could rot in hell, that you resented me, and regretted the day we ever met and never wanted to talk to me again. This all happened months ago, but it's bothered me ever since."

Donna shook her head in disbelief. "Geoffrey, as angry as I was, I never said those things, least of all to the likes of her. The night we collided in the ladies' room, I told her that if the two of you were still together after what she did, then you deserved each other. That's all I said about you, and as I recall, she was the one to first mention your name. Besides, if you really wanted to hurt me, you'd have done something a long time ago."

"When I first came into your apartment, I only intended it to be that one time, but it wasn't. I decided then that if I ever was caught or accused of anything that I would own up or pay up and then pray for forgiveness. You let me off easy when I deserved the worst."

Donna touched his hand. “You’ve already been forgiven for that. If I don’t care, then no one else should. It’s history. Besides, if everything hadn’t happened the way it did, I wouldn’t have gotten to know Tom. I mean I already knew him, but not the way I do now.”

Geoffrey flushed and said, “He’s, uh, really um, amazing. I consider him my most trusted friend. Well, what do you say we go to lunch and be nice to the waitresses?”

“Sure. I’m meeting Tom at Faneuil Hall in a half hour.”

Geoffrey’s mouth dropped. “Oh, I’m sorry. I didn’t know. You just go ahead then. I don’t want to intrude.”

“You won’t. You just said he’s your best friend. He’ll be happy to see you.”

***

Donna and Geoffrey sat next to each other on the same side of the table, but the distance that had grown between them was apparent from the conversation among the three friends. Everything related to Tom and Geoffrey or to Tom and Donna, with no reference to anything that connected Donna and Geoffrey. *ID/XX* had been their only bond, and any mention of that, despite the brief discussion earlier, would have risked embarrassment or discomfort. Donna got to hear all about how the two men trekked across the wilderness and camped out in all kinds of weather. Geoffrey, after listening to a shopping list of everything (dancing, concerts, classes, and just plain hanging out) that Donna and Tom did together, lightly drummed his fingertips on the table. He lifted his gaze from the salt and pepper shakers and said, “Tom, I didn’t realize Donna and you had so much in common.”

“More than I ever imagined,” Tom rcplied.

After lunch they started out for the Charles River but changed direction and headed to Geoffrey’s condo because it was closer. They entered the front door to the faint smell of paint. “I’m having all the walls brought back to white," Geoffrey said. "I need a clean slate. My bedroom is finished so I won't have to look at the red ceiling anymore. This living room is next. Then I'll think about furniture." He pointed to the red wall around the fireplace. "Sandra is responsible for this mess. She had the paint matched to her lipstick to constantly remind me of her. This furniture and the rest are all her doing, hideous. She thinks that if you pay enough for something, then it's tasteful. All I got out of it was a huge bill and an ugly home."

Donna looked at the tomato red and the yucky greens and golds. "Not what you'd call serene, is it? Red and green are complimentary colors, but you must pick the right hues, otherwise you end up with something like this."

"I should have had you do it, the same way I should have had you help right to the end of the book." Geoffrey brightened his tone of regret and said, "We can sit out on the balcony and relax, or we can go someplace else, if you have no other plans for the rest of the day."

"Let's stay here a bit," Donna said. "I want to get home before rush hour. By the time we'd go anywhere else, I'd have to leave." They sat and had lime rickeys the way Donna had taught Geoffrey to make them with fresh limes, sugar syrup, carbonated water and no alcohol.

Both men offered to drive her home, but she insisted on going by herself her usual way, by public transportation. Geoffrey wanted to call a cab as a compromise, but she politely refused. They walked her to the station where she thanked them both then disappeared down the stairs.

"Well, Tom, you two are certainly close," Geoffrey said.

"Nothing you wouldn't want."

"Well, you've got it. I looked the other way for a moment…"

"Geoff my friend, you looked away a lot longer than a moment."

"I know, but why did you ask to drive her home when you have to work in the city tonight?"

"Why should you go out again when you already were home? She and I both had to leave sometime."

"That's not the point." Geoffrey could feel a tension rising in his voice. "Sure, I'm glad you two hit it off the way you do, but it's more than I expected. As long as you're not changing…changing your mind and we still have the same understanding."

"Don't worry. I keep my promises. We're friends, remember?"

"I know. I told Donna you're my most trusted friend, and here I am accusing you of something I know you're not capable of doing."

"Well, yes after all, it's not as though any woman would throw you over for someone like me," said Tom with a sly grin.

"I didn't mean it that way. I meant you're morally not capable of betraying a friend. I'm the one who's ethically challenged. I guess I'm just jealous of your relationship."

"Don't be. It's just a few months longer, then after, who knows when or if?"

"Don't talk that way. I need you. Everyone else just won't let up. Blake is pissed because I backed out of the winery. Now he feels he can't rely on me for anything, despite all I've done for him. Doug is a waste of space, who spends most of his time wasted and spaced. Hugh talks out of both sides of his mouth, and he's caused so much trouble for the rest of us, that I'm beginning to think he's either evil or insane. His wife is a whining harpy, who thinks her husband is the only one who does any work. She complains that he doesn't make enough money and insists on going back to their old slum-lord practices. To make matters worse, I haven't written in weeks." The strain these people caused Geoffrey showed in his face as he spoke.

"At least you got rid of Sandra and the souses. Imagine if you still had those losers added to the mix." Tom contemplated his next point for a few seconds and suspected that what he was about to say might be taken as an insult. "Perhaps you might ask Donna to help you with your next book. It could only help."

"Yeah, right. She'd jump at the chance, wouldn't she – just jump off a cliff, more like it."

"You know, Geoff, she and I are close for several reasons, not the least of which is that we both know that the only thing that matters in the end is the way you treated other people in your life."

Geoffrey took this remark as a reference to his own misplaced priorities. "Are you saying that I care too much about success, and that I hurt people for selfish purposes?"

"You can hurt people even when you try to do good. Donna and I recognize something you don't, that is when they close the lid, people remember how you made them feel and what you really meant to them. You'd be a lot further ahead if you understood this and did something about it."

"I'd have had a chance today —"

"If I didn't show up, you mean. Donna and I made plans to meet. Yours was an accidental encounter. If you want to keep relying on chance, then don't expect much."

"That's the problem. I don't. You haven't been very encouraging." Geoffrey asked, "How do you think it went today?"

"Fine. She seemed happy and relaxed."

"That's because you were there. I think she'd have gone straight home otherwise. She was much quieter before we met you."

"She and I are friends. You've made yourself an acquaintance."

***

Donna entered the office of Kurt Floegel and feared that he would not have summoned her unless something serious had occurred, though she could not think of any recent incident. She opened the heavy door and saw a wispy-haired, heavy-set man seated at a massive oak desk that must have been as old as the pre-Depression era building.

Mr. Floegel offered her a seat and began: "Miss Di Geronamo, may I call you Donna?" Barely waiting for her to nod yes, he got right to the matter. "Miss Kaltbergen is no longer with the company and," he paused to reconsider whether he should reveal the reason, "her departure is due to more than simple mismanagement of the store, which has not been doing well, poorly actually, in recent years."

"Mr. Floegel," Donna said, "I'm surprised to hear that. Despite competition from the internet and the other stores, Floegel's never seemed wanting for customers. People love to shop here."

"It's not for lack of sales, but as I said, from more than mismanagement – Donna you're going to hear it soon enough – there will likely be criminal charges. I cannot say more than that, and I'd like you to keep this in confidence. After all, a person is innocent until proven guilty. The worst thing we could do is to say that an accusation or even an indictment is proof of guilt. It would not be prudent, no matter what other people say publicly, for those of us in management to speak in any way that could be interpreted as slander or malicious bias."

"I understand."

"I thought you would. I've heard a lot of good things about you, and that you are very discreet and have good inter-personal skills." Apparently, Sandra's lies never reached his ears. "This brings me to the reason I asked to meet with you. With Miss Kaltbergen's sudden departure, we will need someone immediately to manage the store until we find a permanent replacement. The associate managers are extremely loyal to Miss Kaltbergen. She insisted on it. With the question of just how loyal they were, I cannot take the chance of choosing one of them. This is not to imply that they were involved, but I cannot compromise the investigation in any way."

At this point, Donna merely assumed that he was about to ask her for some recommendations, but Mr. Floegel had a different purpose. "You have been a very effective and competent manager of the second floor. I am told by reliable sources that your proficiency in math would make you a quick study for overseeing the store's accounting. We do, of course, have accountants on staff, but a manager must have an understanding of the store's finances. Your artistic ability gives you a keen eye for design, your verbal and writing skills are nothing to sneeze at, and you are well-liked and respected by the rest of the staff."

Donna wondered where Mr. Floegel got all this information. He smiled and said, "It's a small world; one hears things socially and professionally. The store naturally has detectives, but some time ago I hired a, *uh-hem*, plain-clothes private detective, a kind of security specialist or secret operative really, who usually handles all kinds of crises. You – all of you – have been observed."

Their discussion continued for another hour, and they settled all the necessary training and transition issues, with the understanding that a search for a new manager would begin immediately, but that if Donna developed the required skills and proved herself, that she could apply for the job herself.

***

Donna sat on the back porch and thought about the events of the past year. *I will never allow anyone or anything to change who I am for the worse. I'm no good to anyone if I can't respect myself. I must be my own solid person and not look for another half to make me whole.* She refused to worry about any life partner – that was for whoever he was to figure out. One of the solid bits of advice her mother gave her was that men can smell desperation the way some animals smell fear. Of course, she would always say this after badgering Donna about being single. Yet, through the bad example of others, Donna was taught what not to do and how not to be. She would sit back and let the situation unfold.

***

Brad rang the doorbell of a woman he had dated for a month. Too many times he had been told, "You're a nice person, but…" He already knew that this was the one.

***

Geoffrey unclipped the gold and ruby pin from his bedroom lampshade where he kept it as a reminder and kind of talisman. He held it a moment, recalling the day he had given her the small velvet envelope. All that brought him comfort and all that caused him shame were wrapped in Donna. She had forgiven him and agreed to be his friend, so he felt relieved.

***

Tom sat by a window and reread Donna's letter for the umpteenth time. Although his facial expression was serious, he smiled on the inside. He gently folded it and placed it back inside a metal box on his desk.

CHAPTER TWENTY-TWO
PRINCE VINCE AND THE DAMSEL IN THE RED DRESS

On the way home from the station Donna said to Loretta, "Next year I may be doing this by myself."

"Not if we get the two-story house behind you, which looks almost certain unless the inspection shows termites up to the roof and sludge coming out of the faucets."

"So, you are going through with it? It's a very nice house."

"We'd have waited until we were married to get the place, but it was too good to resist. It's below market rate, and we're getting a government loan. Because we're buying it without an agent, there's no commission, so that brought the price down further. Maura said she wanted to get the hell out of there. She's been waging a border war with Angie for years."

"Now you'll inherit the problem."

"Not for long. If she thinks her peach and apple trees are going to keep dropping rotten wormy fruit into our yard, I'll have those branches hacked and thrown onto her side. Same goes for her junk and buggy wood pile. It's all getting dumped with any other crap they try to load on us."

"You mean that woodpile behind the fence isn't Maura's?"

"Yep. Angie's parents originally owned both houses. That's why there's only a partial fence between them and the driveways connect end to end with the garages off to the side. After they sold the two-family one to Maura, they acted as though they still owned it. Maura said they used to keep a boat in her driveway, if you can believe it!"

"How did they get away with that?" asked Donna, incredulous.

"Same way they get away with everything else they do – nerve and probably some veiled threat. Well, wait until they come up against Fred and me."

"One good thing is that we'll still be neighbors, even closer," Donna said.

"Yeah, I'd even love you to have the second-floor apartment, but the tenants said they want to stay, unless they can get their kids to change schools. We'll see."

"Well, if they move. In the meantime, we can yell out our windows to each other."

"Maybe Tina and I can connect a clothesline between our back porches and send each other stuff. Angie oughta love that. She thinks she's got some kind of palace there."

"It is really a solid house. Bad vibes emanate out from the middle floor, but otherwise it's well built and has a comfortable floor plan with the center hall separating the public and private rooms." Angie, naturally, would have kept the better of the two houses – the one with the extra rental apartment and larger yard – for herself.

As Loretta climbed the front stairs to the Amalfitano house, she turned to Donna and said, "The bridal shop said our gowns should be in soon. Thanks for agreeing on the red instead of the blue."

"No problem. The red looked better on me anyway. Seeya tomorrow."

The wedding was set for September after an engagement of almost seven months.

***

Tom was asked to be the Best Man. For the past year Donna and he saw each other with increasing regularity. Tom had always treated Donna as a good, but platonic friend, but Loretta had an answer for that. "It's possible he likes you, but is afraid you'll reject him, especially since he knows all about Geoffrey and you. He doesn't seem like the type who would horn in on a friend." Still, Tom was a mystery that Donna was afraid to solve – her friendship with him was too important. Again, she told herself, she would let the situation declare itself and not jeopardize anything by forcing a change or clarification of their relationship. Besides, she wasn't ready for anyone, least of all a close friend of the person who almost convinced her that she was unworthy of anything other than spare tire status.

***

As the wedding day drew closer, Donna allowed Loretta to give her a makeover consultation. For once, Donna noticed, her makeup didn't need much touching up within hours. The day before the wedding they went for massages and manicures. Loretta said, "We should be ready to take pictures at my house around 2:00. Vinnie said he'll drive you to the church and reception, if you don't mind."

"Fine," Donna answered. *Wonder how much arm-twisting that took?* "Tina tells me that she's coming with a date, but she just giggled when I asked about him — probably one of her card playing friends."

***

At 1:45 P.M. the next day, Donna, dressed in a gown that was pretty enough to wear again for something other than tending sheep, knocked on Tina's door. "Donna, you look so beautiful," Tina said. "Have fun taking pictures – smile pretty for the camera. I won't be leaving until it's time to go to the church, so I'll see you there."

Donna smiled. "I can't wait to meet the new man in your life. You've been holding out on us, Tina."

"Oh, you mean my date? It's not what you think – just a friend."

***

The Amalfitano house was shaking from top to bottom. Vinnie, to escape the commotion, stood out on the front porch and sipped a can of soda. He gave Donna a nod as she passed him on her way into the house.

"Tell you what, Donna," Mrs. Amalfitano said, "let's get your pictures out of the way first so you can go to the church with Vinnie. He's itching to get outta here." The Prince was always on the run. If he couldn't relax in his family's house, how comfortable did he expect to be in a hard-seated church with no sofa, refrigerator, or television? As long as he didn't bolt before the wedding, Donna didn't care if he soaked his head in Chelsea Creek.

As Donna helped Loretta with her veil, years of memories flooded over both friends. Loretta looked at the loudmouths who were her family, but in a rare moment felt their love for her and hers for them. Of course, she always knew they loved each other, but it was hard on a daily basis to feel it with all the yelling and turmoil. Even now, on her wedding day, Prince Vince's comfort came first. She wished she could have Donna with her right up to the moment when they walked up the aisle. Wasn't the purpose of the maid of honor to be a constant attendant to the bride? Today Loretta would let it go as planned – anything to lower the stress level and raise the chance that Donna and Vinnie would exit the neighborhood at the right time and be out of the way.

Donna and Loretta posed for their pictures, and then Mrs. Amalfitano hustled Donna out the door. Vinnie grunted at Donna to follow him to his car. Loretta watched them drive off and thought, "Donna, I hope you forgive me for the position we're putting you in."

Vinnie, who before last night's rehearsal dinner had hardly spoken more than two sentences at a time to Donna, said, "You look really nice." *A compliment from the prince, the royal firstborn of the famiglia?* Last night's conversation must have had an impact on him. He had confided that he had recently broken up with his girlfriend and wanted Donna's advice. "I can't really talk to my sisters about this," he had told Donna as they sat next to each other in the restaurant and were drowned out by the rest of the rehearsal party's chattering. "Gina doesn't like Emily and Amelia doesn't know her. Connie and Loretta just think it must be all my fault we broke up."

Now that Vinnie and Donna were alone in his car, he had the privacy to talk. "So, Donna, did you think about what I told you last night? Was how I treated Emily wrong?"

"Well, you know the expression 'actions speak louder than words'. You can't claim to care about someone if you treat them with disregard, as though they don't matter to you."

"I treat her with respect. Emily always wants me to make a big fuss over her. If I don't tell her every day how beautiful she is, she gets grumpy."

"Why does someone who knows she's pretty need to keep hearing it? Tell me, what attracted you to Emily in the first place?"

"Her looks. She's so beautiful."

"Uh," Donna said after a pause. "And?"

"The whole package: the way she dresses, her hair, her face, her figure – nice and thin."

"What else?"

"The way she dances. Her shoes."

"Her shoes? You're serious?" asked Donna, fully understanding why she never got along very well with Vinnie.

"Yeah, she buys them in the North End. They're made in It'ly, and they're leather inside and out. Some of them are canvas or some other cloth, but the good stuff, so your toes aren't poking through the third time you wear 'em. She's got great taste. I feel proud when I'm with 'er."

"What I mean is what do you have in common? What do the two of you talk about?"

"Lots – music, movies, TV, clothes, what clubs we like." Vinnie shrugged as though he didn't get the point.

"But Vinnie, I mean, besides your fashion sense and entertainment choices – and physical attraction –what holds you together?" Heck, even Geoffrey and she had deeper discussions while they were writing *ID/XX*. Although most of their conversations had been for the book, even in their break times they talked. Geoffrey had told her about the most painful parts of his life – things he probably had never told Sandra or any other woman.

"Like I was saying," said Vinnie, continuing as though he hadn't noticed Donna drift off in thought, "we have a lot in common. How can you stay with someone if you like football and rock and they only like ballet and classical music? It's necessary to share things. And I mean, you know, we talk about other stuff, like keeping in shape and whether we'll ever have plastic surgery."

"Vinnie," said Donna with the forced patience of a stressed-out mother of four children under age four, "let's try this again. What if something happened to Emily's looks or to her ability to wear nice clothes? What would you do? Would you still love her?" The prince had to think about this one, so Donna pretended she merely had asked a rhetorical question. "Look at Loretta and Fred. They love each other for the inner person."

"Yeah, but have you seen Loretta without makeup? *Phew!* Boy is she in the right business! At least you got something to offer. I know I sometimes used to make fun of your rear end, but you know it was all in good humor. Anyway, I think most guys would rather deal with a fat ass than a *brutto* face they gotta keep lookin' at. She's got both, come to think of it."

"Man, oh man."

"Look, in this world you're either hot, or you're not. That's just the way life is." There was no need for him to explain how he viewed himself. He wasn't called the Prince for nothing *and* he hung out, however infrequently, with the Stud King.

"*Hee, hee, hee, hee, haw, haw, haw-argh!"* Donna could do nothing but laugh herself hoarse. Before her eyes could fill up with tears and possibly ruin her makeup, she composed herself. "Tell you what," she said to Vinnie. "Why don't you send Emily some flowers, tell her she's *so-o-o-o* beautiful, and that you miss her to death."

"Think that'll work?"

"What have you got to lose?"

The sight of the church assured Donna that this foolish conversation would finally end. Loretta's three sisters, all bridesmaids, arrived just after Donna and Vinnie, but Fred's brothers were already on the sidewalk outside the church with Tom. "Sorry I couldn't make the rehearsal last night," Tom said to Donna, "but I know what to do – stand at the altar and hold the rings, then escort you back down the aisle after the ceremony."

Before even greeting everyone, Vinnie said, "Not that I give a shit, but tell me again, which side of the church are we supposed to seat everyone on?"

"Vinnie, you're so vulgar and low classed," Gina snapped.

"Wha? It's not like I farted."

Two of Fred's brothers gave each other a knowing grin, and another placed a hand over his mouth and coughed a choking "ahem."

"Seriously, Vinnie," said Gina through gritted teeth, "Don't you ever stop? So inappropriate. You are a total embarrassment. The wedding hasn't even started and you're already ruining it!"

"How? There's nobody here but us. Loretta didn't hear anything to get upset about, unless she's psychic or somethin'. Besides, she's not a piss-ass like you."

Donna took control of the situation. "Why don't we all wait in the vestibule."

CHAPTER TWENTY-THREE
LORETTA IS MARRIED, DONNA IS HARRIED

Despite her brother's criticism, Loretta was indeed a beautiful bride. She floated down the aisle after a graceful Donna (whose vigorous practice in her red shoes paid off). In a joyous ceremony, Frederick Matthew Green and Loretta Madalena Amalfitano became husband and wife.

The wedding party posed for pictures in and around the church. As they made their way over to the grotto, Donna broke away from the group to say hello to Tina who was standing on the sidewalk. "It was so beautiful. I'll see you at the reception," Tina said with an imperceptible hint of nervousness. "I'm waiting for my ride to go to the reception. He went to get his car. You better go. They'll be waiting."

Donna got to spend another fun-filled ride with Vinnie behind the wedding limousine. He started right in. "You know Donna, I meant what I said about the jokes about your rear end. I hope I never hurt your feelings. You always at least had a waist, and you always had a pretty face. You look really good now. I hope you stay that way."

"I eat a healthier diet now and I go to the gym. Thanks for the compliment," said Donna. "I promise I'll try to never again have a backside like the rear end of a pick-up truck, or…"

"Buick – it was the rear end of a Buick."

"Yuh, that's right – Buick Butt. Hippo Hips, Elephant Ass, Lard Ass," Donna abruptly cut short the list of Vinnie's insults. "Vinnie, I'm sorry. You're offering a sincere apology and I'm throwing it back in your face. I seem to do that sometimes, especially with men."

"Naw, that's okay. I deserve it. You took a lot of abuse. I was a jerk, totally."

"You obviously get it now. I'm just curious about one thing, though. Why would someone do something they know is wrong to another person who never did anything to them?"

Vinnie pulled off the road and put his car in park. "Gee Donna, I'm really sorry," he said almost dolefully. "I didn't know I hurt you that bad."

"You didn't. Someone else did. I just want to know why would a man, who claims he's your friend, treat you like nothing of any value and then, at every turn, just slap you down?"

Vinnie answered, "Either he doesn't mean what he says because he just wants something from you or, I don't know, maybe he's afraid or trying to convince himself that he's independent. He might not want to change the way he sees himself. You know how some guys act like big shots in front of their friends. They want to seem powerful and smart, like they don't need anyone, so they act like jerks. It's probably more complicated than that. You know the male ego."

"I'm afraid I don't."

"You probably have the power to really hurt him, or he might just be an a-hole." As if Vinnie suddenly realized that Donna was referring to Geoffrey, he added, "If he's worth it and not full of BS, he'll come around. It's like you showed me: when someone acts like a jerk, they first have to see it, then change it. Then they must convince you that they've changed."

"And they must stay changed."

***

Weddings are a lot of fun – especially if you're not in them. While the other guests were having cocktails and hors d'oeuvres at the reception hall, the newlyweds, their parents, and the rest of the wedding party were photographed in various permutations in a small room with a pale rose brocade curtain.

After picture taking for more than an hour, the wedding party made their entrance to the flashing of more cameras. The speeches ranged from eloquent to emotional. Loretta's relatives slobbered and blubbered, but Fred's maintained misty-eyed calm. Fred raised a too-full glass and sloshed champagne on Loretta's veil, which already was snagged and torn from her own and others' clumsiness. Before the reception was over, Loretta's gown would be stepped on, spattered with tomato sauce, and splashed with red wine. No problem. She was not someone who expected her life to be tied up with a pretty pink bow, but rather a woman who would place more attention on her marriage than on her wedding.

Donna sat next to Loretta at the head table and glanced over the hall. "I see Tina sitting with some of our neighbors. She's between the Bramantes and the D'Angelos. There are the Kellys, but where's Tina's guest?"

"I didn't want to crowd the table, so I put him with some other people he knows. That's the way she wanted it, anyway. He's just a friend, and she thought they'd both prefer it this way. We also invited Tom's parents. His mother couldn't make it, so his sister Pat came instead. Mr. Ambrose and your dad seem to be getting on very well."

Donna looked at everyone seated at the table and got up to go to the restroom. Pat also rose from her seat and headed toward the rear exit of the room. As Donna entered the restroom, she held the door open for Pat, who was right behind her. On their way back to the reception hall, they continued their conversation they had started in the restroom.

Donna said, "I'm so glad Tom and I are friends. He's so understanding and kind. Although he's so knowledgeable, he never talks down to anyone. He's unlike anyone I've ever met."

"I know what you mean," said Pat. She touched Donna on the arm. "My husband and I will be staying at the house while he's away. That way we can help out. My husband can commute just as easily from there. Our parents live next door with Theresa, but there's only so much they can handle."

"Pat, what do you mean? Tom is going away?"

"Yes, supposedly for six months." At the doorway to the reception hall Pat's cell phone rang, and her conversation with Donna ended abruptly.

A tingling sadness inched up Donna's limbs and she leaned back against the wall to steady herself. In a sudden panic she rushed out of the room in search of a place that could provide an escape from the crowd. "I can't believe it!" she whispered to herself.

"Donna!" a voice called to her. Donna spun around and almost fell.

"Geoffrey? I didn't know you were here!"

"I came with Tina," answered Geoffrey.

"Where were you sitting?"

"At the same table as Tom's father and sister."

"I didn't see you."

"I know. I went over to Tina's table to say hello to some of the neighbors. When I saw you leave the room, I followed you and waited outside the restroom. Again, when you came out you were busy talking with Pat about Tom, and you didn't see me standing there." Geoffrey groped for the words to say, knowing that whatever came out of his mouth would be wrong. "Donna, I thought you knew that Tom was off-limits. This is all my stupid fault."

"What do you mean? Tom and I are friends."

"Of course you are. You mean the world to him, and he would never want to hurt you, but, but... Donna, this isn't a good place to talk. Later, I'll explain everything. Let's get back and enjoy the wedding." Geoffrey tried to lighten the mood. "Tom tells me the two of you have become good dancers. I can't wait to watch, but you'll have to save some for me."

"I told him that I liked ballroom dancing, so he came along to humor me. He's very good, although I'm not sure it's his thing."

Donna sat down as the main course was served. She poked around her plate as she was already full from pasta and anxiety. She briefly told Loretta about her encounters with Pat and Geoffrey.

"Donna, I have a confession to make. Tina and I plotted a little scheme to throw Geoffrey and you together. Even Tom knew about it. Vinnie really is having problems with his girlfriend, who was supposed to come to the wedding. Tina came with Geoffrey, but she might go home with one of the neighbors." While Loretta spoke, Donna nervously ate the rest of her meal and hoped it didn't give her *agita* for a week.

Despite Loretta's revelation, Tom was the first person to ask Donna to dance. Afterward they sat down with Tina at her now half-empty table and were joined by Pat and Geoffrey.

Fred and Loretta sliced their wedding cake and gently fed each other. A dessert buffet table had a combination of the couple's favorites: chocolate cake, *zuppa inglese*, Italian rum cake, strawberry shortcake, Boston cream pie, apple pie, and Italian cookies. Each place setting at every table had small silver toned baskets of traditional confetti almonds tied up in white nylon netting. Now that Loretta was comfortably tucked inside her gown, with no fear of pre-wedding bulging or split seams, she pigged out on everything. Donna, showing much more restraint, ate only a few slivers of dessert and realized she didn't crave certain things anymore.

Loretta kept her blue garter on her own thigh, feeling that was the only dignified use it had. She did, however, throw her bouquet into Ginny Alexander's hands. The bride's going-away outfit, which Donna had chosen, complemented the one worn by the groom. Buoyed by the blessings of the guests, Fred and Loretta Green left to live their lives together.

CHAPTER TWENTY-FOUR
THE GO-BETWEEN

Donna had assumed that Vinnie would take her home because, strange as the situation was, he had driven her to the wedding. "Oh, he went home early," Tina said, "You know the way he is. Something to do with his girlfriend. No problem though, Tom said he would take us back. Look, here he comes with Geoffrey."

The two men appeared to be having some sort of disagreement.

"No problem. It's on my way home," Tom said.

Geoffrey responded, "Yes, but I took Tina here, and I'm staying at Primo's tonight."

Donna said to Tina, "Wait here, while I go and say goodbye to the Amalfitanos and Greens for us. I'll be right back."

When Donna returned, Geoffrey was standing by himself. "Tom took Tina home. I thought you and I might go somewhere to relax. It's Saturday night, and a lot of places are still open. Let's go."

"Oh, okay," replied Donna, a little confused.

***

Tom went to his room, opened a box, and pulled out a letter – the letter from Donna, detailing all he meant to her, and how she suspected he was like a guardian angel of sorts. He read the letter one more time, put it back in the box, and went to sleep.

***

Donna and Geoffrey sat in a quiet club and ordered coffee. "Hope you enjoyed the wedding," Donna said.

"Of course. You were there," said Geoffrey quickly adding, "and Tom, and Tina, and, uh, Vinnie, some folks from the neighborhood. I knew lots of people there. Loretta and Fred make a great couple. I was surprised that Tom was the Best Man until he told me how they met."

"They've become good friends, as have Tom and I," Donna said. "Of course, Tom and you go way back."

"Yes. We met when he was starting medical school and already had a degree in computer science, which he now teaches, as you know. He hadn't fully started his most recent activities. I was in grad school at the time and had to interview someone with an interesting life. Well, Tom fascinated me so much that in eight months I churned out a novel loosely based on his life. It was total crap, but I had beginner's luck. I had no idea how the publishing business worked, and I hand-carried it to a small new publisher."

"They bought it just like that?"

"Yup. They were new and were looking for fiction writers. I was the youngest person to submit anything to them, so I think that helped. They seemed pretty impressed."

"With you or the book?" Donna would not have made such a crack if she hadn't read the stinko story about "Tim Anselm."

Geoffrey shook his head, laughing. "Ahem! No comment. Anyway, the book did poorly, so I did my homework, changed my name, and wrote my next two books, almost overlapping, before getting an agent." There was a time when Geoffrey could have fascinated Donna with every small detail of his life. Now, he could say nothing of interest, unless it involved Tom. Geoffrey droned on about himself for a while. At the first mention of Tom, Donna brought the discussion back to him.

How much reality did *The Amazing Mr. Anselm* contain? Donna debated whether to risk embarrassing Geoffrey by revealing that she had read *Anselm* and decided that it was better to be kind than honest.

"You know, it's funny," Donna continued, "Tom and I must have ridden the same train many times in the past, but I don't remember ever seeing him before we really got to know each other."

"You probably just didn't recognize him. He's often *incognito.* He told me about a few instances and that you once offered him your seat when he was disguised as an old man. There was another time he followed a pervert off the train, who had bothered Loretta. He didn't say how he handled it, and I didn't ask."

"You're kidding! I don't even remember any of that." Donna's mind drifted, and words came out of her mouth absentmindedly. "Pat said some things that implied…though, deep down I sense that he'll be all right. I'm going to miss him so much."

"I will too."

"I missed you too. It was fun to come home to you, even though … it ended the way it did, abruptly and well, the way it ended."

"I know," Geoffrey said with an emotion Donna might have taken for genuine tenderness had he not, in the past, played her so. "That was one of the happiest times in my life, but I didn't value it."

Donna turned forty-five degrees in her seat toward Geoffrey. "Can we just pretend, while we're sitting here all duded up, that we're out together having fun? It's a beautiful, clear night and it will be winter in a few months. We'll have plenty of time to redress old wounds. Right now, I just want to forget everything that brings me down."

"Me too."

"Boston can be such a miserable place to live much of the year, but on those occasions when it's good, it's great. It's sometimes magical if you hit it just right."

"If you're with the right person."

"Even if you're not," she said. "When you're out at night and see the city lights, and love and happiness is in the air, even if you're not in love, you feel the energy. Know what I mean?"

Geoffrey smiled and simply nodded. For a while they sat and pretended that there was no betrayal or deception, no Tom or Sandra, no time or tension between them.

They drove back to East Boston and, as they approached the dark house, they found that Tina had left the front porch light on for them. Tiptoeing, they climbed the stairs together. When they reached the second-floor landing, Donna said, "Goodnight Geoffrey. Thanks for everything."

Geoffrey turned the knob to the Infanto's door. "Locked," he said. "Primo was supposed to leave it open for me because he knew I would take Tina home." He fished in his pockets and overnight bag for the keys to the apartment. "Locked out." He looked at his watch and frowned. "I'll, uh"-

"Stay here," Donna interrupted. "It's very late. And you're too tired to drive home at this hour. The bed in the guest room is still"—

"Do you mind? I might take you up on your offer. I'm beat."

"No problem." Donna opened her door. "Make yourself comfortable. I'll get us something to drink," she said.

"Donna? What are all these boxes and where's your dining room table?"

"Didn't your aunt or uncle tell you? I'm moving."

"What? Where? When? Why didn't someone tell me?"

"I don't know why. I'd have told you if we had spoken."

"I know, but why at least didn't Tom let me know?" The difference between the two men reared itself again.

"Why, is Tom supposed to be your go-between?"

"Uh."

Donna could see some distress mounting in Geoffrey, so she softened her tone to keep the upbeat mood of the night elevated but could not let go of her main interest. "Speaking of Tom, tell me what you meant earlier about Tom not wanting to hurt me and how it was all your fault."

Geoffrey took a baby step forward. "Oh Donna, I'm…Look, please don't be offended, but I'm the one who set him on you."

Donna dropped back one giant step. "Please repeat that."

Geoffrey's face almost had the same panicked look it had on the day that Donna and he first met. "I asked him to look after you as a kind of chaperone and, I'm ashamed to admit, spy."

"Since when?"

"Remember that day he showed up at Floegel's and gave you the first envelope? I'd discovered that Sandra was the betrayer, and I knew you wouldn't…uh…but by then you and Tom… were getting friendly." Geoffrey shrugged. "I asked him to let me know if you were angry, how you felt about me."

"You mean if I was going to retaliate against Sandra and you for false accusation?" Donna asked without expression.

"Well, um, it had more to do with Sandra, who is unpredictable and vindictive. Also, Tom was to let me know if you did anything I'd want to know about, what was going on in your life."

"What?" Donna had to confront the reality that another relationship was just a big lie.

"In the meantime, he took you out because he really enjoyed your company. The two of you spent so much time together and really became close. It all backfired! I could see it in your face, and I heard the way you spoke about him, not just today with Pat and myself, but also that day we met in the North End."

"You're serious, aren't you? I don't understand."

"I don't understand myself either. I lost control of what was going on. That day the three of us went to lunch, you seemed cool at first, but then you perked up when we met Tom."

"That was because you and I only met by accident, and it felt strange. Tom and I had an ongoing friendship, while you and I were estranged," said Donna. She could have added that Geoffrey had never apologized for his accusation and insults.

"But Tom didn't have the audacity to come into your apartment uninvited, steal your story, and then say you couldn't be co-author of what was essentially *your* book. There was no Sandra to complicate your relationship with him and accuse you of trying to frame him. He also didn't have relatives who treated you with further disrespect. Don't say it – I love my aunt and uncle, but I know what they are. No wonder you're moving."

"They're not so bad. In fact, ever since I first tried to warn you about the plagiarism, they've been better."

"When? I didn't know that."

"It's a long story, but the last day we worked together I sneaked a copy of the story. When I read it a couple of weeks later, I called your apartment to tell you. Unfortunately, you weren't there but Sandra was."

"She never told me. What a rotten excuse for a human being! You were right when you said that my association with her showed the kind of person I was. I saw it too, but if it wasn't Sandra, it would have been just someone else, possibly no better."

"Geoffrey, you had every right to have a relationship with Sandra, well maybe not after she was engaged. It would have been nice if I had been left out of it, that's all."

"There was so much turmoil at that time, and to have you come into my life then added to the confusion. I don't mean to sound melodramatic, but it was like being stranded at sea when you think you see land. You know that you have just enough strength to make it to safety, but if it's only a mirage, you'll drown." He shook his head at his own corny emoting. "That's something I should put in my next book, if I really want to go down the tubes."

"Did you see me then as just a source of safety, or was there really anything more? Under other circumstances you wouldn't have given me a second look."

"I would look out the window to watch you come and go."

"Why? To see if the coast was clear?" Donna felt her words sting the two of them. "Geoffrey, I'm sorry for the sarcasm. It's just a defense mechanism."

"I know. You've had a lot to defend. Tom defended you from the start and kept you from being exposed-"

Donna struggled with the emotions triggered by Geoffrey's confession about his behavior the past year. "This is a lot to absorb. I finally got over everything, and now to find that even Tom…"

"I know," he said, "that Tom may have initially deceived you, but he was only trying to help. He really does like you a lot and considers you a close friend."

Donna slowly shook her head. "Confused and irrational as I might seem, if I ever felt anything for you, I gradually transferred it to Tom – he was more…"

"Worthy."

"Compatible, sincere, attentive really – we've never had one cross word. He's so kind it hurts. I just never could tell…how he felt, although he pretty much handed me over to you, so I guess I know now." Donna shut her yap and realized what she was saying. "I'm sounding cruel, aren't I? Why do I do that with you?"

"Because I deserve it." Geoffrey stared at one of Donna's paintings.

Donna looked at the time. "It's late and we're both exhausted. I know you planned to stay over with Primo anyway, and I really don't want you driving home now. The sheets in the spare bedroom are clean. There are extra toothbrushes in the linen cabinet."

Geoffrey looked at his watch. "I'll take you up on your offer. It's been years since I slept in this apartment. But where are you moving? I hope it's not far away."

"Just look out the back window. Fred and Loretta bought Maura's house, and the tenants on the second floor moved out last week. I've started painting and have taken a few things over already. Also, I wanted to give your aunt and uncle enough notice so they can find a new tenant, although I think Tina's daughter and her family want to move in now that her son-in-law is coming back from Alaska in a few months."

"Then if this place isn't rented just yet, would you be upset if I moved in here, at least for a while? I've still got to redo my condo and completely get rid of Sandra's hideous taste."

"Why should I mind? Your aunt and uncle own the place."

Geoffrey smiled. "Just leave the door unlocked a sec while I go down and get my overnight bag. I left it on the second floor." He went down the front stairs and returned in half a minute. Geoffrey took his bag into the guest bedroom and returned two minutes later. "I, um, noticed you're doing a portrait of Tom."

"Yes. It's finished even though it's on the easel. Tom doesn't know about it. I did it from some sketches I drew of him when he was distracted working on his laptop."

"Oh, I see." Geoffrey rubbed the back of his neck. "It's been a long and active day. Would you mind if I took a shower?"

"Of course not. I may take one myself. After all that dancing, I must smell like a dead hornpout."

"Does that mean you're going to join me?" Geoffrey said with a sly grin.

"No," Donna replied flatly. "Whenever I shower, I like to come out cleaner than when I went in." She shook her head and smiled. "I'll just go take off my makeup and get out of this gown."

"Would you like help with the zipper?"

"Would you like a kick where it will do you the most good?"

Geoffrey chuckled. He grew up with Eastie sarcasm, so he took Donna's remarks in good humor. Donna went to her room, changed into a robe, and wiped off her makeup. After his shower, Geoffrey carried his clothes to the spare bedroom then returned to the living room while still wearing the towel. He plunked himself down on the sofa and checked his cell phone.

After Donna finished her shower, she walked into the living room to say goodnight and ask Geoffrey if he needed anything else. Geoffrey looked up and patted on the sofa cushion next to himself. "Come, sit here," he whispered.

"You – you want me to sit right next to you while you're wearing a towel?"

"Okay then, if you like, I can take it off," Geoffrey shot back and gave the towel a slight tug at his waist as though he would follow through with the threat.

"What I'd like is to get to sleep before the birds start chirping. I just want to tell you to help yourself to whatever you want."

"Does that include you?"

"No *stunad*, I meant to anything to drink or eat."

"The question sounded intentionally vague. You should have been more specific, and said 'Geoffrey, if you're hungry or thirsty, or need a damn toothbrush, you know where everything is'."

"*Oo fa!*"

"Ever notice how Italian you get when you're angry?"

"Ever notice how slimy *you* get when you're, you're…"

"With someone I care about, have spent a lovely day with, and feel it's about time"- Geoffrey stopped and fixed his gaze on her. "Donna you are so – I can't even call it uptight – you are *so* old-fashioned! This is the twenty-first century, not the eighteenth. You are not some character in a Jane Austen novel."

"Why should I do something only you want? You and I aren't – are we even friends?"

"I should hope so! But that's not the point. It's just a physical thing. It has no meaning."

"And that's the problem exactly!" said Donna completely incredulous. "A long time ago I asked you what you thought of me. Now I know what I should have known right along." She turned to walk away.

Geoffrey got up and grabbed her by the arm. "Look, I'm sorry. What I just said was completely callous. I'm sorry." He touched her on the shoulder. "I won't try anything. I just want to give you a hug, which is something I've never done in all the time we've known each other."

They stood with their arms around each other for a full five minutes. The months Geoffrey had spent with Donna, the happiest time in his life, were over. It wasn't an exuberant kind of happiness, but it was simple and peaceful. Even with the noisy airplanes and street sounds, they enjoyed a quiet calm that allowed creativity to flow. Donna nodded off and Geoffrey had to catch her before she fell. Although Donna didn't drop, Geoffrey's towel did. They both burst out laughing. Donna choked, "I'm not laughing at you. It's the situation. S-s-sorry." Embarrassed, more because of her own behavior, Donna ran into her room and shut the door. Not wanting to check how late it was, Donna got into bed and hoped her racing mind would not keep her awake. Fatigue won the race, and she was asleep within minutes.

CHAPTER TWENTY-FIVE
DONNA'S DECISIONS

In the morning light, Donna awakened and checked her alarm clock. 10:08 A.M. For a moment she thought she might just laze in bed until she remembered that Geoffrey had stayed over, and she should get up and make breakfast. She threw on her robe and went to the spare bedroom. The door was open, so she peeked inside. The bed almost appeared unslept in, and a note was on the pillow. It read: *"Thanks Donna for everything. I went downstairs this morning. ☺♥ Geoffrey."*

Donna ate a breakfast of coffee, a hard-boiled egg and half a bagel. The sound of Angie's and Geoffrey's voices rose from the second-floor hallway. She looked out her living room window as Geoffrey's car drove away. Nostalgic thoughts washed over her, and she slowly walked around her apartment. No one to greet her when she came home. No smell of her home-cooked meals or Geoffrey's takeout food. No bottles of wine crowding her pantry shelves. No sound of fingers tapping on a keyboard. No cool breeze blowing through the porch screens while they sipped iced tea or ginger ale on a summer night. She went to her bedroom window and folded down the wallpaper she had previously peeled back to see Geoffrey's initials, GAI, and then it hit her: All those memories were long passed and replaced by ones of disappointment, rejection, accusation, and deception. For sure she had been the deceiver as well as the deceived, but her deceptions caused no one to get hurt.

Donna glanced out the window at the Green's newly purchased house where she would soon make her home. A larger apartment. A third bedroom/den. An extra bathroom. Lower rent. One less flight of stairs to climb. A fresh start.

Donna sat at her desk and stared blankly at the red shoes she had worn to the wedding. Another thought hit her. "I hope it's not too late," she said out loud. She grabbed her phone. "Hello," she said. "Are you busy? ... Last night we didn't get to say goodbye.... Can we get together? ... Great. I'll come to you. I'll pick up lunch on the way…Okay, we could do that instead…See you soon."

On her way out, Donna checked in on Tina and told her she would call her later. She got in her car, took a deep breath, and said a quick prayer to her Guardian Angel for guidance.

***

When he opened his door, the first words out of her mouth were, "I hope it's not too late! Last night I didn't get a chance to tell you because you left. Please tell me you haven't made any commitments yet! Please don't go!"

"Come inside," Tom said and escorted her to the sofa. "Donna, what's wrong?"

"Please don't go back to Iraq! Six months is too long. Theresa needs you. Your friends and family need you, and I…I… don't want anything to happen to you!"

"Donna, I'm going on sabbatical for six months, to New York for part of the time only. Where did you get the idea that I was going to Iraq?"

"Pat told me that you were going away for six months, and I just assumed because you had been there before."

"No, I don't intend to leave the northeast anytime soon. Although I was a medic, I gave it up and committed myself to other things."

"Sorry for over-reacting. I was worried and wanted to see you."

"I'm both touched and flattered that you were worried about me." Tom sat on the sofa next to Donna, and she giggled in response.

"What's so funny?" he asked.

"I was thinking that at least you're wearing pants. Oh, shoot!" Donna's face flushed. "It's just – never mind."

"Why do I get the sense that you're talking about Geoffrey?" Tom looked as though he was holding back a grin. "I've traveled with the guy, I know."

"Well last night was a little weird. I can't say any more. He is your friend, and I don't want you to get the wrong impression. Nothing bad happened. It was in fact kind of funny. Suffice it to say, I wished I had gone home with Tina and you." Donna looked at Tom's angular face with its bony nose, greenish brown eyes, and prominent cheekbones. A monk from the Middle Ages would have had such a face. True, he wasn't classically handsome like Geoffrey, but Tom's was a face she much preferred.

It was handsome in its own unique way, a more lovable and kinder face which matched the inner man.

Tom's cell phone rang, so he excused himself and went into the dining room.

"Hi, Geoff, what's up?" Tom said, barely out of earshot but within Donna's sight. Tom's face first clouded over, but he chuckled a few times. At one point he glanced up at Donna and quickly looked down with a frown.

They're talking about me! Donna stood and tried to suppress the impulse to just leave – dash out the door without saying goodbye. Before she could act, Tom ended his conversation with Geoffrey and reentered the living room.

"We need to talk," he said, as he motioned to Donna to sit back down on the sofa.

"Okay," Donna said softly. "What's wrong?"

"I need to explain some things that I couldn't before because of certain circumstances." Tom paused to collect his thoughts. "Donna, do you remember when we first met? I recognized you from the train and had seen you at Floegel's, but never spoke to you until I started shopping in your department for my sister. I thought that you were someone I would like to know better, but you never picked up on any conversation or showed any sign."

"It might have helped if you weren't buying women's clothing. I assumed you were taken. When you bought me lunch on my birthday, I thought you were just a nice man trying to cheer me up."

Tom nodded. "When you told me why you were upset, I realized that you had feelings for Geoff, who was my friend, so I backed off. Then when Geoff asked me to do him a favor, I agreed because I thought you would both benefit in some way."

"You mean when he asked you to befriend me and report back to him? Last night he told me about your agreement."

"Oh, so you know," Tom half whispered. "Donna, I couldn't tell you…"

"It wasn't your place to. Geoffrey made you promise. I'm not sure of his motives, but none of that matters now, at least as far as he's concerned. After my birthday, the cobwebs cleared." Donna looked away. "A lot of things now make sense. I know you hung out with me as a favor – out of friendship to him, but I'd like to know, are you and I really friends?"

"At the very least – and more, I hope. Donna, you don't know how hard it was to keep my promise to Geoff and not act on my feelings. I couldn't betray my friend, and I didn't know how you really felt until this morning."

Donna looked at Tom, and he could read the confusion in her face. "Donna, we all – Loretta, Tina, and to some extent even Geoff thought that Geoff had hurt you."

"Yes, but not in the way you all apparently thought. I was hurt because he deceived and falsely accused me. Of course, it was fun being creative together, but the negatives outweighed the positives. You, on the other hand…" Donna stopped as another thought occurred to her. "What do you mean you learned this morning how I really felt?"

"That was Geoff who called. He told me about last night – I wish I had been a fly on the wall," Tom chuckled. "Anyway, your behavior confirmed his long-held suspicions. After a few choice expletives, the first words out of his mouth were, 'I'm done. She's all yours. You can have her'."

They smiled at each other and kissed until they had to catch their breath. It was to be the kind of day they should have had before – before the deceit, interference, and misunderstandings that kept them apart.

"Excuse me," Tom said as he got up and went upstairs. When he returned, he got down on one knee and said the words he had wanted to say for many months. Unlike Loretta, Donna at least waited for Tom to utter the final word "me."

Tom slipped the ring on Donna's finger and said, "Perfect fit."

Donna lost her voice for a full thirty seconds. "It's so beautiful!" she said. "How did you know my size?"

"From your ruby ring. One time you had left it on the kitchen counter, and I made an impression on a slice of provolone cheese, and another time I traced the ring on a piece of paper for comparison. I had to act quickly but was able to estimate the size."

Donna laughed. "Sounds like something you would do." She thought a moment. "But when did you get it? How did you know this day would ever happen?"

"I didn't know. I hoped."

***

They both had the week off, and Tom helped Donna paint her new apartment so she could move in the rest of her furniture and put up shades and curtains the following weekend.

Tom grinned, “We got a surprising amount done despite being so distracted.” He checked the time. “Don’t cook. I’ll order something for delivery.”

After dinner, they played some music and started dancing.

***

Across the yard, Geoffrey sat in the dark and poured himself yet another drink. “Oh puh-lease,” he said out loud.

Primo stepped onto the deck. “Geoff, did you say somethin’?”

“I think I’m going to be sick!”

“Then you should stop drinking. Do you need something to puke in?”

“Nah. It’s just the sight of those two goofs dancing around.” Geoffrey shook his head in disgust. “You wouldn’t believe that guy has seen more blood and guts than a butcher in a slaughterhouse, and now look at him!”

Primo shrugged. “Well, maybe he needs a break. It had to be rough.”

“He’s taken more than a break. Now he’s playing Sherlock Holmes and Dr. Watson rolled into one.”

“Well, at least he’s got a nice girl. I’m going to miss having her around. Now we’re going to get Tina’s grandkid screamin’ and cryin’ all day.”

Geoffrey’s head snapped toward the direction of his uncle. “Since when did you think she was a nice girl?”

“Aw, come on! She’s not a slut like that other one who used to come here. Donna was never any trouble, and she took good care of us when we had that accident last winter. That lasagna she made for us, I still dream about it. She made me another one and promised to make it again for me. Did you ever have her lasagna?"

"No, I never had her damn lasagna. And, and why this sudden epiphany about Donna? Auntie was always so mean to her."

"You know how Angie is. She thinks you're supposed to marry some princess. You could have done a lot worse, in fact, you have done much worse."

"Unbelievable!" Geoffrey paused. "Look, I think he's coming over here." Geoffrey took another gulp of scotch and rushed to the rear door of his uncle's apartment. "Tom!" he shouted as Tom climbed the stairs. "What brings you here?"

"Hi, Geoff. I just came over to get something. Donna and I were working on the apartment. We had dinner and she realized that she didn't have any dishwasher detergent." Tom reached the second-floor landing, and the two men stood facing each other.

"Oh, I see, you were *working*. It's so nice to see how domesticated you're becoming. Didn't take you long to move in and take over."

"Didn't we settle this yesterday? You might as well know;" Tom paused and rethought what he was about to say. "This isn't the time or place to tell you. I thought we could get together for lunch and—"

"And what? Act like nothing happened?"

"If you're talking about Donna. Why should you care? You had your chance. You were only afraid that she would retaliate. Once you knew she wouldn't, you left her and me hanging."

"This isn't about Donna. It's about you!" Geoffrey shouted and gave Tom a shove.

Tom was quick and maintained his balance. He shouted back, "Someone almost killed my sister by pulling a stunt like that! Don't make me—"

"What? Beat me senseless? Go to hell!"

“Sorry pal, I’ve already been there and don’t feel like going back any time soon.”

The door opened and Primo yelled, “What the hell is going on out here? Geoff, you okay?”

“Get back inside, Primo,” Tom said in a low voice. “Your nephew and I can handle this without any violence.” He turned his attention back to Geoffrey. “You know I saw her first, but I had to play the good soldier while you just wasted our time.”

“I didn’t know how you felt about her, and I wasn’t sure.”

“Why, because she was decent and not high maintenance? Have you ever noticed that all the women you date are either eccentric, histrionic, or just plain crazy?”

“I have my reasons.” Geoffrey sighed and ran his fingers through his hair. “Look, Tom, I’m sorry. I’ve been drinking and a certain reality hit me. You both mean a lot to me, and I wish you well.”

“Does that mean we have your blessing?” asked Tom trying to be conciliatory.

“Don’t tell me you already proposed?”

“Your Church requires a six-month engagement and pre-marriage classes, so there was no more time to waste.”

“Yah, well, congratulations.”

Tom returned to the new apartment and said to Donna, “I don’t think you should stay by yourself at either apartment tonight, especially with Fred and Loretta still away.”

“Okay.” Donna gave Tom a hug. “Now that our families know, would you mind if I called Tina?”

Tina answered her phone, and when she heard the good news, she slapped her hand to her chest and said, “Thank goodness! He’s so much better for you. Deep down I was afraid you’d end up with that narcissist!” She lowered her voice and continued, “I hope no one heard me. Good thing the windows are closed.”

***

The following Saturday, Geoffrey pulled into the Infantos' driveway and walked across to the Greens' house, where Tom's car was parked. He climbed the front stairs and rang the doorbell to the first-floor apartment. Loretta answered, "Oh, hi Geoffrey, come in. We got home a little while ago from our honeymoon. Tom picked us up at the airport. He's with Donna in her old apartment. They're cleaning up after the move."

"Oh," Geoffrey said. "I just want to give you this housewarming gift. It's a gift card – I didn't know what you needed."

"Thank you," said Loretta, giving Geoffrey a hug. "Come in the kitchen and have some tea with Fred."

Fred stood up when Geoffrey entered and gave him a friendly slap on the back. "Good to see you," he said. "We came home today so Loretta would have a day off before she goes back to work on Monday."

Obviously from Loretta's and Fred's behavior, Tom hadn't told them about their fight. They chatted a while, and Geoffrey left to go to his uncle's house. As he walked back across the yards, he debated whether to use the back or front entrance. He walked around to the front of the house for the extra seconds it gave him, a stalling tactic to help delay the inevitable meeting. He shuddered at the recollection of his last encounters with Donna and Tom – the former a clumsy, failed seduction, and the latter a near blowout. Again, in the front hallway, he dithered. Should he ring the bell or climb the stairs to knock on the door? The bell would give them all a little extra time to compose themselves.

Tom opened the door, and Geoffrey spoke first. "Tom, I want to apologize to both of you. I'm so sorry and ashamed of myself. The two of you are my most trusted friends, and I let you both down with my selfish and thoughtless behavior."

“Come in,” Tom responded. “There’s no need for you to apologize to me. We’re old friends, and I understand you, more than you do yourself. Everything worked out as it should for Donna and me. She and I became friends first, so there is no doubt that we are meant to be together.”

“I’m glad that you see it that way.”

“Of course. Come inside and talk to Donna yourself. She’s cleaning in her old bedroom.” Tom stayed in the kitchen to give them enough privacy to talk but not enough for Geoffrey to upset Donna.

When Geoffrey entered the bedroom, Donna was washing one of the two windows. She turned as Geoffrey approached, and before he spoke, he flicked down the corner of the wallpaper under which he had long ago written GAI. They both stared a moment at his initials. Geoffrey asked, “What made you look?”

“Curiosity.”

“But I told you about this the last night we worked together.”

“I know… but for some reason I just looked.” She shrugged. “Who knows why we do some of the things we do without thinking – or caring – when we do them.”

Geoffrey took a deep breath. “Donna, I want you to know how much you – your friendship – means to me. You deserve the best, and you have it in Tom. I’m so sorry for what I put you through. You forgave me for all of it, and in the end, I didn’t have the decency to treat you right. I apologize for everything from day one, through the accusation, and beyond. Last week after the wedding, I was a total jerk. When I saw the portrait you did of Tom, I guess I got jealous. I don’t know how to express how truly sorry I am.”

Donna smiled. “Geoffrey, you’ve already made it clear. All is forgiven.”

“Yes, but we had some rough times that were all my doing.”

Donna shrugged. "Tom and I care about you. You have to know that. We might have found each other without you, but you did help bring us together. I will always value the time you and I spent together. We had a lot of fun, didn't we?"

"We did," Geoffrey whispered.

***

On his way out, Geoffrey stopped to talk to Tina. She, of course, invited him in for coffee and homemade biscotti.

"Tina," he said, "I want to apologize for all the noise earlier in the week."

"What noise?" answered Tina, being somewhat disingenuous, although noise from the second floor wasn't exactly a novelty. She looked at Geoffrey with true empathy now that Donna was in a situation where he could no longer hurt her.

Geoffrey smiled, knowing that Tina was being polite. "Tom and I had a heated exchange and almost came to blows. He's my best friend, and I never want to lose him."

"You won't, I'm sure. I suppose you've heard the good news."

"Yes. It was a bit of a shock, to say the least, and I'm not quite sure how to deal with it yet. I've never been hurt before." He paused and weighed his next words. "I suppose if you have to lose the only person you ever loved, it should be to someone you also love."

Afterword

Some readers might wonder if DiGeronamo, Amalfitano, Imperato, and Zingarella are actual Italian names. I don't know. They popped into my head, so I either heard them somewhere before or made them up.

A person might argue that although East Boston has many three family houses, there aren't any that share a driveway with a two-family house behind them, and that there is no bile green three decker on the corner of the same street.

Of course, Boston has no Floegel's Department Store (I stole the name from a friend) and as far as I know, no Lily Floret cosmetic line exists.

In my entire life, I can recall only one person who admitted, or rather implied that they vandalized someone's car, and they were NOT from East Boston, so please don't assume that such behavior is typical for East Bostonians.

Also, I don't know which Catholic churches in Eastie, if any, have a grotto. The parish could be almost anywhere.

Notice also that nowhere in the book do I indicate the ages of any of the characters or give detailed descriptions of their appearance. I want the reader to imagine them as they like.

In short, none of the people, places, behavior, or events in *Donna's Deceptions* are based on fact, and the story is a pure work of fiction.

Made in United States
North Haven, CT
12 December 2024

61481042R00186